# CROCODILES
## AND ALLIGATORS

Dieter and Mary Plage/Bruce Coleman Ltd.

# CROCODILES
# AND ALLIGATORS

CONSULTING EDITOR
Charles A. Ross

EDITORIAL ADVISOR
Dr. Stephen Garnett

ILLUSTRATIONS BY
Tony Pyrzakowski

**Facts On File**
New York • Oxford

Published in the United States of America by
Facts On File, Inc.
460 Park Avenue South
New York, New York 10016

Produced by Weldon Owen Pty Limited
43 Victoria Street, McMahons Point NSW 2060, Australia
Telex 23038; Fax (02) 929 8352
A member of the Weldon International
Group of Companies
Sydney • Hong Kong • London
Chicago • San Francisco

President: John Owen
Publishing Manager: Stuart Laurence
Project Coordinator: Jane Fraser
Editors: Lesley Dow, Claire Craig
Editorial Assistant: Helen Cooney
Picture Research: Annette Crueger
Illustrations Research: Kathy Gerrard

Captions: Carson Creagh, Stephen Garnett,
Lesley Dow
Index: Diane Regtop
Maps and Diagrams: Greg Campbell
Series Design: Sue Burk
Designer: Andi Cole, Andi Cole Design
Production Manager: Mick Bagnato

© 1989 Weldon Owen Pty Limited

Library of Congress Cataloging-in-Publication Data

Crocodiles and alligators/consulting editor, Charles A. Ross;
Illustrations by Tony Pyrzakowski.
p. cm.

Bibliography: p.
Includes index.
ISBN 0-8160-2174-0

1. Crocodiles. 2. Alligators. I. Ross, Charles A.

QL666.C9C76 1989
597.98–dc19

89-30416

Facts On File books are available at special discounts when purchased in bulk
quantities for businesses, associations, institutions, or sales promotion. Please
contact the Special Sales Department at 212/683-2244. (Dial 1-800-322-8755,
except in NY, AK, HI)

Typeset by Keyset Phototype
Printed by Kyodo-Shing Loong Printing Industries Pty Ltd
Printed in Singapore

10 9 8 7 6 5 4 3 2 1

A Weldon Owen Production

Cover:
Well adapted to its role as an aquatic predator, this Indopacific Crocodile survives in one of the world's
dwindling wild places.
Photo by Reg Morrison/Auscape International

Endpapers:
Although once feared, the Johnston's Crocodile of tropical Australia is harmless to humans.
Photo by Vincent Serventy/Transglobe Agency/Planet Earth Pictures

Page 1:
Aggressive and intelligent hunters, this Mugger and other adult crocodilians can, however, survive without
food for long periods.

Page 2:
Crocodilians have a complex and sophisticated social life that involves elaborate mating rituals, subtle
gradations of status, and a high degree of care for the young.

Page 3:
An Indian Mugger basks open-mouthed on a river sandbank. Evaporative cooling allows the brain to
remain cool while the rest of the body heats up.

Pages 4–5:
This American Alligator hatchling will face a multitude of dangers from predatory birds, reptiles, and
mammals to survive to adulthood.

Page 7:
Only in recent years has the subtlety and complexity of crocodilian behavior been appreciated as
researchers seek ways to protect these magnificent creatures.

Pages 8–9:
Survivors from the age of dinosaurs, crocodilians are highly evolved reptiles that have much in common
with birds in their physiology, egg structure, and some aspects of behavior.

Pages 10–11:
Submerged so that little more than its eyes and nostrils show above the surface, this Common Caiman,
coated in mud, relies on patience, speed, and stealth to secure much of its prey.

Francois Gohier/Auscape International

Australian Picture Library

C O N T E N T S

Crocodilia are the last remnants of the great age of reptiles and were contemporaneous with, and sometimes predators on, the dinosaurs. The living Crocodilia, which include today's alligators, crocodiles, caimans, and gharials are but a minute reminder of the vast evolution of crocodilians ranging from duck-billed swamp dwellers to the narrow-snouted Gharial with its multitude of uniformly sized teeth.

Throughout the evolutionary history of the Crocodilia, lasting some 200 million years or so, these reptiles have occupied diverse habitats—from the terrestrial dog-like protosuchians to the ocean-going metriorhynchids with paddle-like limbs. They varied in size from less than one meter to larger than most dinosaurs.

Living species of crocodilians are found throughout the tropical and subtropical areas of the world in aquatic habitats and vary in size from the infamous "man-eating" species of the Pacific and Africa to the innocuous Dwarf Crocodile of the forests of central Africa.

References to crocodilians are found in prehistoric artwork, earliest writings, and the works of Pliny and Aristotle, yet even today we know little of the remarkable life history of these fascinating reptiles. Alligators and crocodiles figure prominently in early accounts of exploration and adventure. There is no doubt they played an important role in the lives of tribal peoples, explorers, and settlers living along the banks of rivers and lakes in the tropics.

In this book, the third in the series "Mighty Creatures of the World," we present in fifteen chapters written by leading authorities, a glimpse at the wonder of these little-known, maligned reptiles. The prehistory, evolution, natural history, and mythology surrounding crocodilians will be explored. The fear and loathing expressed by humans for these denizens of our waterways, marshes, swamps, and sometimes golf courses and swimming pools, will hopefully be dispelled and replaced by a respect and appreciation for these animals, truly the last remnants of a past age and our looking-glass into the ancient world of ruling reptiles.

Charles A. Ross

CONSULTING EDITOR

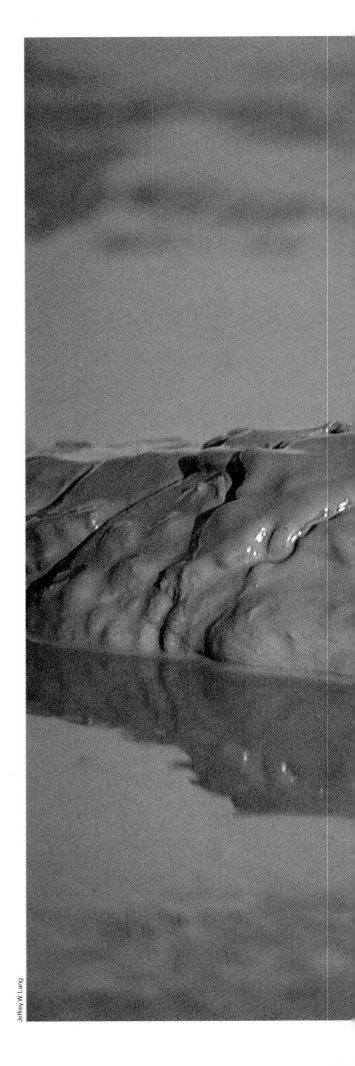

Jeffrey W. Lang

Crocodilian evolution since the Late Triassic has involved a number of important transformations in crocodilian anatomy although living species retain some of the features of their ancestors.

# EVOLUTION

# AND BIOLOGY

# THE PLACE OF CROCODILIANS IN THE LIVING WORLD

HANS-DIETER SUES

Crocodilians are the only living representatives of one of the most successful groups of land-dwelling vertebrates ever known — the Archosauria or ruling reptiles. These reptiles dominated animal communities on the continents during the Mesozoic era (245–65 million years ago). In addition to the crocodilians, the Archosauria included the dinosaurs, the pterosaurs or flying reptiles, and an assortment of early Mesozoic forms often referred to as thecodontians, which included a variety of primitive archosaurs, some of which may have been the precursors of later groups such as crocodilians.

Despite their antiquity it is quite inappropriate to treat crocodilians as "living fossils" whose "inferiority" forced them into a marginal ecological role as amphibious predators in a world now dominated by mammals. In fact, they are highly specialized for their particular mode of life and have undergone considerable changes during their long evolutionary history, which spans more than 200 million years.

► Despite its "primitive" appearance, the Nile Crocodile is a highly specialized crocodilian, a member of a group whose 200 million year history spans a number of major evolutionary developments.

## LIVING RELATIVES

Among living vertebrates, crocodilians are most closely related to birds rather than to lizards (despite the largely superficial resemblance). Crocodilians and birds both have an elongate outer-ear canal, a muscular gizzard, and complete separation of the ventricles in the heart, to name but a few readily apparent anatomical similarities. Both crocodilians and birds build nests out of plant material and both show some degree of parental care. These features reflect a more recent common ancestry shared by birds and crocodilians even though the two groups are now adapted to strikingly different modes of life. British paleontologist Alick D. Walker even suggested in 1972 that birds arose from a stock of lightly built crocodilian precursors, some of which took to climbing around in trees while others adopted an amphibious mode of life and continued to develop into true crocodilians. After a thorough review of the anatomy of all major groups of archosaurs, however, most experts today agree that birds probably descended from small carnivorous dinosaurs. The special anatomical resemblances between birds and crocodilians are thus likely to have been acquired at an earlier stage of the evolutionary history of the ruling reptiles.

The next closest relatives of crocodilians among living vertebrates are the lepidosaurs or scaly lizards, named for the nature of their skin, which is usually covered by overlapping horny scales composed of keratin (a substance similar to that of human fingernails). This group includes the tuatara of New Zealand, lizards, and snakes. Crocodilians (along with other archosaurs) and lepidosaurs share a peculiar configuration of the

skull frame. Behind each eye socket or orbit, the cheek region of the skull is perforated by two large openings (temporal fenestrae), which are delimited by horizontal bony arches. One opening is high up on the skull roof, the other down on the side of the cheek.

Two hypotheses have been proposed to account for the origin of these openings at the rear of the skull. The more traditional explanation relates the presence of these openings to the contraction of the jaw-closing muscles, which extend between the braincase and the superficial bones of the cheek. When the jaws close, the jaw-closing muscles contract. As the muscles shorten they do not, of course, decrease in bulk and thus have to expand in diameter. The acquisition of openings in the cheek region would permit the contracting jaw muscles to bulge into these openings during jaw closure. American anatomist Thomas H. Frazzetta has provided an intriguing alternative explanation for the origin of the temporal openings. According to his scenario, the openings developed in order to lighten the skull and to provide additional areas for better attachment of the jaw muscles around the edges of these bony "windows." The skull frame around the braincase would be reduced to a mechanically efficient system of bony struts and thus, strangely enough, become stronger and more able to resist the stresses generated by the bite forces.

The presence of two such openings behind the eye socket on each side of the skull is the distinguishing feature of the diapsid or "two-arched" reptiles. In lizards, the lower bony arch is always incomplete. In snakes, both the lower and upper arches are absent, leaving the entire cheek

14

TOP VIEW

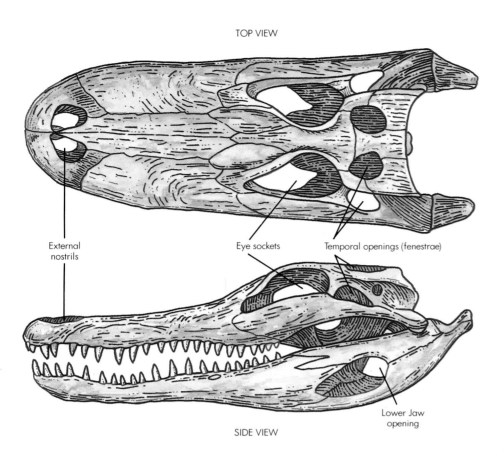

External nostrils

Eye sockets

Temporal openings (fenestrae)

Lower Jaw opening

SIDE VIEW

▲ Paradoxically, the dual openings behind the eye socket may serve to strengthen the crocodilian's skull, providing muscle attachment areas to aid the jaws' tremendous crushing power.

open. Crocodilians retain the typical diapsid configuration with two relatively small yet well-defined openings on each side. In birds, the large eye and the considerably expanded braincase have encroached on the cheek region and consequently the bony bars between the eye socket and the two openings have largely disappeared. By comparison mammals, including humans, have only one opening for the jaw muscles behind the eye socket (synapsid condition) whereas turtles have a solidly roofed cheek region without any openings (anapsid condition).

## PRINCIPLES OF SCIENTIFIC ANIMAL CLASSIFICATION

In order to discuss the evolutionary history and other aspects of crocodilian biology, it is necessary

to understand the ways in which biologists classify and name all forms of life. Even though formal classification can hardly be considered an exciting intellectual pursuit, it is of vital importance because it provides an important means of scientific communication.

Terms such as crocodilians, birds, and insects are used to talk about individual animals or assemblages of animals. Each of these terms is based on a scheme according to which we compare and sort living organisms into groups, and each name concisely summarizes sets of traits that characterize such groups. The word "bird" denotes a feather-clad, warm-blooded vertebrate that, typically, is capable of powered flight and displays a host of distinctive structural and physiological properties.

The branch of biology devoted to the theory and practice of classifying organisms is called taxonomy. Humans have always sought to distinguish and name objects in the complex world that surrounds them. The basic purpose of any classification is simplification of description. We assemble objects into categories according to criteria of utility. The most ancient people, for example, would perhaps have simply distinguished between edible and inedible or useful and dangerous animals and plants. This approach would have served their particular needs. Biologists today, on the other hand, are interested in developing classifications that express similarities and differences in the structures of organisms as well as evolutionary relationships. Consequently, their criteria for and their systems of classification have become increasingly more refined. Several such systems are currently in use, and each has a substantial number of practitioners.

The three approaches most widely used today — phenetic, cladistic, and eclectic systematics — differ in the emphasis that they place on the various criteria for classification.

Phenetic systematics compares degrees of structural similarity between organisms. As many characters as possible are counted and measured, and all traits are regarded as equally important.

▶ Protected by a skin flap (here held open by forceps), the elongate ear canal of a Johnston's Crocodile leads to a relatively small opening in the skull behind the lower temporal opening.

C. Pollitt/Australasian Nature Transparencies

A taxonomic category or taxon (plural: taxa) in a phenetic classification simply expresses the degree of overall structural similarity between two organisms but does not necessarily reflect common ancestry. Dolphins and sharks, for example, share a number of similarities in body shape, presumably related to swimming, yet dolphins descended from land-dwelling mammals and have no close evolutionary ties to sharks.

Cladistic systematics is based exclusively on how long ago two organisms shared a common ancestry. The recency of common ancestry is inferred by the possession of advanced characters shared only by the organisms in question, features not found in other forms. A mouse and a lizard, even though quite different in appearance, are more closely related than either is to, for example, a perch. Both mouse and lizard share the possession of four bony limbs, a five-fingered hand, lungs, and a clear separation of head and trunk — advanced traits that are absent in the perch but are characteristic of a clade, namely all four-footed vertebrates (tetrapods). A cladistic classification expresses the evolutionary history of organisms but it provides no information concerning the degree of overall structural similarity between them. Closely related organisms may, in fact, look very different.

As its name implies, the third system, eclectic or evolutionary systematics, draws selectively on information from both the cladistic and phenetic approaches. It involves inferences concerning the degree of evolutionary change after taxa have diverged from a common ancestor and attempts to account for the relative length of time elapsed since the date of separation of the organisms in question. As both of these criteria are difficult to quantify, evolutionary systematics is, of necessity, the most subjective of the three approaches.

Applied to crocodilians, phenetic systematics would classify them with lizards and their relatives, in order to express a superficial resemblance in body form. Cladistic systematics would group crocodilians and birds together because these two taxa are thought to share a more recent common ancestry than either does with lizards and their relatives. Although mindful of this evolutionary history, an eclectic system would emphasize the distinctiveness of birds and, by default, would place the crocodilians with the lizards and their scaly kin. The latter classification is still used.

In 1758, the great Swedish naturalist Carolus Linnaeus (1707–78) published a work entitled *Systema naturae,* in which he first developed a formal nomenclature for classifying all living beings. His system is now universally employed by biologists. The nomenclature introduced by Linnaeus uses names that are, in most cases, derived from Greek or Latin words (and hence are commonly italicized or underlined in print), thus providing a common language among scientists regardless of their respective native tongues.

The basic unit of classification is the species. The so-called biological species concept defines a species as a population or group of populations whose individuals can freely interbreed with each other *and* produce fertile progeny but cannot successfully interbreed with members of other species. (This definition assumes the existence of sexual reproduction; certain asexually reproducing organisms, such as yeasts, still have to be classified on the basis of overall appearance.) As the descriptions of most species are based on preserved specimens in museum collections, the

▲ The tuatara (*Sphenodon punctatus*), a species of lizard now restricted to islands off New Zealand, grows to a maximum of 80 centimeters (30 inches) in length and is a predominantly nocturnal predator. Phenetic systematics would classify crocodilians with the tuatara and other lizards because of the superficial resemblance in body form and despite the lack of recent common ancestry.

◄▼ Although the ancestors of birds and crocodilians diverged some 300 million years ago, it is possible to draw inferences about the way they lived by examining modern predators such as the Secretary Bird (left), which, like the extinct coelurosaur (below), is a fast-moving predator that hunts insects, reptiles, and small mammals on land.

reproductive isolation of these organisms in their natural environment cannot be established and has to be inferred from the existence of differences such as body size and shape. The distinguishing features of each species are enumerated by its first describer in a diagnosis. An individual specimen of a new species is designated as the type-specimen and comes to serve as the ultimate standard of reference for all future comparisons with other species.

In the scheme proposed by Linnaeus, species that closely resemble each other are grouped together into a higher category, the genus (plural: genera). (It is important to remember that genera and other higher categories are constructs of the human mind designed strictly for ease of scientific communication; only species are real entities that can be discovered in nature.) Thus each species bears two names, one identifying the species itself and the other the genus to which the species belongs. This is not unlike our use of first and last names. The species name would correspond to the given name, whereas the generic name would represent the surname. The scientific name or binomen of the Nile Crocodile is *Crocodylus niloticus*. *Crocodylus* identifies the genus to which the species belongs, and *niloticus* is the name of the species itself. Some scientists occasionally distinguish certain populations of a species as subspecies if they appear to deviate from other

populations of that species in aspects of their biology. In such cases, a third name — the name of the subspecies — would be appended to the scientific name.

Linnaeus grouped genera into a hierarchy of higher taxonomic categories. Closely related genera are united into families. The names of such families are derived from the name of a constituent genus and have the common ending -idae. The genus *Crocodylus* lends its name to the family Crocodylidae, which includes all living genera of Crocodilians as well as many now extinct genera. Families are grouped into orders; orders into classes; classes into phyla; and phyla into kingdoms — all describing different levels of relationships among organisms. The sequence of common Linnean categories for the Nile Crocodile is as follows:

Kingdom: Animalia (animals)
Phylum: Chordata (chordates)
Subphylum: Vertebrata (vertebrates)
Class: Reptilia (reptiles)
Order: Crocodylia (crocodilians)
Suborder: Eusuchia (modern crocodilians)
Family: Crocodylidae (alligators, crocodiles, and relatives)
Subfamily: Crocodylinae (crocodylines)
Genus: *Crocodylus* (true crocodile)
Species: *Crocodylus niloticus* (Nile Crocodile)

▼ Superficially similar in appearance to the living Gharial of the Indian subcontinent, this fossil mesosuchian represents one of the major evolutionary radiations among crocodilians. Mesosuchians appeared in the Early Jurassic, about 190 million years ago and are assumed to have been fish eaters.

Philip Quirk/Wildlight Photo Agency

Fossils, the petrified remains of long-extinct organisms, pose special problems for taxonomists. They display only a small percentage of the potentially useful characters for biological classification since usually only the hard parts (such as bones and teeth) are preserved and these have been subjected to the vagaries of geological processes. Biologists attempt to accommodate them in the scheme of classification based on living organisms because fossils provide the only direct evidence concerning patterns of evolutionary change through geological time. Studies on the biology of living organisms are, in turn, needed for biological inferences regarding extinct organisms; discussions concerning dinosaurian behavior, for example, can draw on a rich body of observations on living species of crocodilians and birds.

## GEOLOGICAL TIME

Geologists have developed special systems to name units of rocks and the various intervals of the geological time scale recorded by these rocks.

The many bodies of rock that make up the earth's crust provide a record of geological time. In undisturbed sequences of rock, the oldest strata lie at the bottom and progressively younger strata are placed successively higher. Thus the early part of any interval of time is represented by the lower layers of a rock sequence.

The oldest known rocks, which are at least 3.7 – 3.8 billion years old, contain no identifiable traces of life. Traces of simple life forms may date back to about 3.5 billion years ago. Beginning with these very ancient rocks and looking at increasingly younger ones in many regions of the globe, geologists noted that fossils "suddenly" become very abundant at a certain level, about 590 million years ago. This transition was used to divide all of geological time into two major intervals, one of which, the Phanerozoic eon, is characterized by the appearance of most multicellular life forms. The Phanerozoic (meaning visible life) is divided into three eras, each of which is characterized by major events in the history of life. The earliest is the Paleozoic (old life) era (590 – 245 million years ago). The first reptiles appeared during this era (about 300 million years ago). The Paleozoic is followed by the Mesozoic (middle life) era (245 – 65 million years ago), which is frequently called the Age of Reptiles or the Age of Dinosaurs and which marks the first appearance of crocodilians in the fossil record.

The Mesozoic era marks the first appearance of the majority of groups of organisms that populate existing environments, including birds and mammals, advanced bony fishes, most living insects, and angiosperms or flowering plants. It also marks the arrival and reign of dinosaurs and the rise to dominance of both major lineages of diapsid reptiles and is therefore aptly referred to as "The Age of Reptiles."

▲ All crocodilians share features in common but vary in length from the 1.5-meter (5-foot) Cuvier's Dwarf Caiman to the larger *Crocodylus* species of 6 meters (20 feet) or more. Further anatomical differences enable the order to be divided into eight genera and 22 species, found mainly in tropical and subtropical habitats throughout the world.

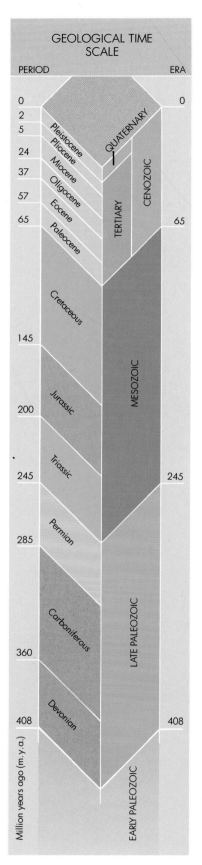

## GEOLOGICAL TIME SCALE

The Mesozoic era is subdivided into three periods: from oldest to youngest these are the Triassic (245–200 million years ago), the Jurassic (200–145 million years ago), and the Cretaceous (145–65 million years ago). The end of the Mesozoic era was marked by global upheaval in the animal and plant communities on land and in the seas, most notably the extinction of dinosaurs and many other large reptiles. It is still not fully resolved whether this crisis was due to the impact of an extraterrestrial object or some earthly cause such as a decrease in temperatures or even a combination of extraterrestrial and terrestrial factors.

In the subsequent era — the Cenozoic (meaning new life) from 65 million years ago to the present — mammals, birds, insects, and flowering plants quickly rose to dominance, and, some 5 million years ago, the first human beings appeared in East Africa.

Crocodilians that could be assigned to the present crocodiles and alligators are first definitely known from the Campanian stage of the Upper Cretaceous, some 80 million years ago.

### FOSSIL "RELATIVES"

Crocodilians share a number of anatomical features in common with other archosaurs such as dinosaurs, most notably the pronounced difference in length between the forelimbs and hindlimbs. The key feature that distinguishes all archosaurs from other diapsid reptiles is the presence of an extra opening (the antorbital fenestra) in front of the eye socket on each side of the snout. Modern crocodilians (like most birds) lack this feature but more ancient representatives of this lineage retain a small opening. The functional significance of this feature is still unresolved; it may be related to a forward extension of certain portions of the jaw-closing muscle system. In most archosaurs, another opening developed near the back or posterior end of each lower jaw.

The evolutionary history of crocodilians is a very ancient one, reaching back to the Triassic period. The earliest known crocodilian-like reptiles have been found in sedimentary rocks of the early Late Triassic (about 230 million years ago) in Europe, South America, and South Africa, and the oldest known true (but now extinct) crocodilians are little more than 200 million years old. The earliest crocodilians and their immediate precursors were probably terrestrial predators that, judging from their long, slender limbs, were capable of fast running. It would appear then that crocodilians adopted an amphibious mode of life at a slightly later stage of their evolutionary history.

▶ A simplified "family tree" of land vertebrates demonstrates the common, if distant, ancestry of living crocodiles and birds, both of which — like the dinosaurs — stemmed from thecodontians. The early stage at which crocodilians began to pursue a separate evolutionary path can easily be seen.

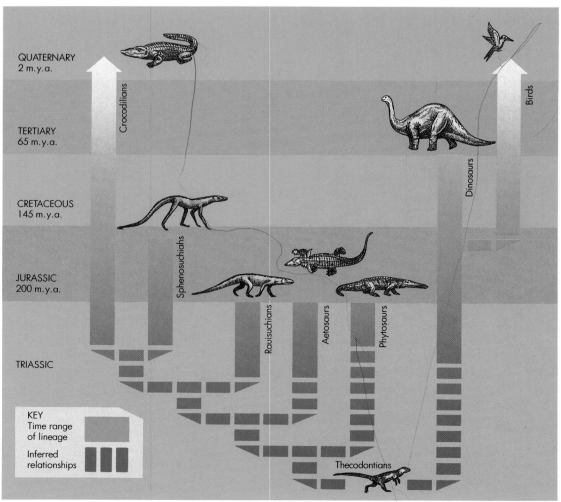

D. Parer and E. Parer-Cook/Auscape International

Crocodilians may have descended from some group of thecodontians, the stem group of all archosaurian reptiles and birds. In 1963 Swiss paleontologist Bernard Krebs first pointed out that crocodilians shared a peculiar form of ankle joint with certain species of thecodontians. In most reptiles, the joint passes between the upper (proximal) and lower (distal) rows of bones comprising the ankle region of the foot. In the feet of crocodilians and certain thecodontians, the ankle joint passes between the two large bones that make up the upper row. One of these bones — the astragalus — moves with the two bones (tibia and fibula) comprising the shank. The other one — the calcaneum, equivalent to the heel bone in the human foot — is functionally part of the foot itself and bears a socket into which a peg from the astragalus fits. This type of ankle joint appears to be functionally related to the way in which

crocodilians walk. Crocodilians are unusual among vertebrates in that they employ two completely different main methods of moving on land. Like lizards, they can carry the belly rather close to the ground, with the limbs splayed out so that the upper arm and thigh appear to move in a horizontal plane. This sprawling gait is usually employed when the animal moves only a short distance. The second mode of walking, the high walk, resembles the mammalian pattern of limb motion. The belly is carried very high off the ground, and the hindlimbs are drawn in until they are very nearly underneath the body. In the high walk, which is employed for fast walking on land, stride length is increased. The sharp twist in the ankle joint produced by the peg-and-socket configuration allows the foot to swivel and permits the powerful twisting movements that occur at the ankle during the high walk.

▲ ▼ Crocodilians, like this Indopacific Crocodile (above), can move sedately over some distance in a "high walk," which resembles mammalian locomotion. The crocodilian ankle joint (below) allows for the twisting and swiveling movements required for this walk.

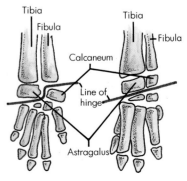

CROCODILIAN ANKLE STRUCTURE

TYPICAL REPTILIAN ANKLE STRUCTURE

Tibia

Fibula

Calcaneum

Line of hinge

Astragalus

Tibia

Fibula

▲ *Terrestrisuchus,* a 0.5-meter (1.6-foot) long sphenosuchian from the Late Triassic of England, was a long-legged, fast-moving land predator. Its short claws indicate that its limbs had become so well adapted to running that it probably relied on its teeth and jaws to capture prey.

▲ *Desmatosuchus* was a 3-meter (10-foot) aetosaur from the Triassic of the southern United States. Its vital organs were protected by wickedly sharp, backward-curving spines but, despite its fearsome appearance, its simple teeth indicate that *Desmatosuchus* browsed on plants.

▲ Although some Triassic rauisuchians reached 6 meters (20 feet) in length, *Ticinosuchus* was a more modest 2.5 meters (8 feet) long. Notable for the twin rows of bony scutes protecting the back, rauisuchians also had large heads and blade-like, serrated teeth for grasping and shearing their terrestrial prey.

▲ Triassic crocodilians were contemporary with long-jawed thecodontians called phytosaurs. Despite its resemblance to a modern fish-eating crocodilian, however, *Rutiodon,* a distant relative, had its nostrils far back on the long snout, just forward of the eyes.

The closest relatives of crocodilians among the archosaurs are the sphenosuchians, of Late Triassic and Early Jurassic age. Specialists distinguish between crocodilians and sphenosuchians on the basis of relatively small differences in the structure of the skull and the latter may, in fact, represent a "mixed bag" of crocodilian precursors and forms more distantly related to crocodilians. One well-known sphenosuchian, *Terrestrisuchus* from the Upper Triassic of England, has an extremely slender skeleton with very slender and elongate limb bones, which would indicate running habits.

A distinctive thecodontian group, the aetosaurs of the Triassic, had the crocodilian type of ankle joint and are known from Europe, and North and South America. Aetosaurs were reptilian "armadillos" whose bodies were almost completely encased in a bony armor. Large quadrangular plates extended along the back and down the sides, surrounded the tail, and protected the belly. The simple, leaf-shaped crowns on the teeth may indicate plant-eating habits. The tips of the snout and lower jaw are devoid of teeth and were perhaps covered by a small beak.

Another group with the crocodilian type of ankle joint, the rauisuchians, were the dominant carnivores on land during much of the Triassic period until they were replaced by the dinosaurs. Best known from skeletal remains found in Argentina and southern Brazil, rauisuchians reached up to 6 meters (20 feet) in length and had proportionately very large skulls. Fossilized tracks and limb proportions indicate that they walked on all fours. The large, blade-like teeth had serrated edges not unlike those on the blade of a steak knife. Two rows of small bony plates extended along the back of the trunk; adjacent elements were linked by a small peg at the front end of each plate that fitted into a groove on the preceding plate.

A more primitive group of thecodontians with a somewhat crocodile-like ankle is represented by the phytosaurs. Even though they were only distantly related to crocodilians, phytosaurs closely resembled them in overall body form and inferred habits, and hence are often referred to as parasuchians (literally "near-crocodiles"). They restricted to the Late Triassic and were very common and widely distributed throughout Europe and North America. Phytosaurs differed from crocodilians mainly in the placement of the nostrils far back on the long snout, almost at the level of the eye sockets, and in the lack of an extensive bony palate.

In order to express the evolutionary connection between crocodilians and the various thecodontians with the crocodilian type of ankle joint, Bernard Krebs assigned both, in 1974, to a new group called Suchia. (Suchia and *-suchus,* a frequent ending of scientific names for various living and extinct crocodilians, are derived from the Greek word *souchos,* which in turn is an adaptation of the Egyptian name of a crocodile-headed god who was worshipped in some regions of ancient Egypt.)

Other thecodontians had a different type of ankle joint, which superficially resembled the crocodilian type except that the structural relationship between the two principal bones of the ankle was "crocodile-reversed" — the astragalus bore the socket and the calcaneum the peg. A number of recent discoveries, mainly from the Middle and Late Triassic of Argentina, indicate that these "crocodile-reversed" archosaurian reptiles may have been part of the lineage leading to dinosaurs and perhaps also to the pterosaurs. Many of these forms were, at least occasionally, capable of running on their hindlegs, as shown by the more elongate hindlimbs and modified hip girdles. Dinosaurs developed a joint between the two rows of ankle bones similar to that in, for example, lizards and this may be related to the adoption of a fully erect gait by these animals. The hindlimbs were drawn underneath the body and the ankle joint became a simple but very strong hinge mechanism, much as in birds.

◄ The common term "crocodile" comes from the Greek *krokodeilos,* meaning lizard. The more technical Suchia and the stem-*suchus* from the Greek *souchos* or *soknopaios,* are themselves corruptions of Sebek or Sobek, the Egyptian crocodile deity worshipped as a god.

# *DEINOSUCHUS,* A GIGANTIC CROCODILE FROM THE LATE CRETACEOUS OF NORTH AMERICA

The genus *Deinosuchus* (terror crocodile), sometimes referred to under the technically invalid name *Phobosuchus* (fright crocodile), included some of the largest crocodiles of all time. This gigantic predator is known mainly from a number of skull fragments, teeth, vertebrae, girdle bones, and scutes from the Late Cretaceous of both eastern and western North America (some of which were initially misidentified as belonging to dinosaurs on the basis of their immense size). More recently, a partial skeleton with an almost complete skull has been found in Texas but this specimen has yet to be described.

Bones of *Deinosuchus* are always found in association with the remains of dinosaurs, especially those of the plant-eating duck-billed dinosaurs or hadrosaurs. Based on the latter association, American paleontologists Donald Baird and Jack Horner have inferred that *Deinosuchus,* rather than the large meat-eating tyrannosaurid dinosaurs, may have been the principal predator upon the hadrosaurs in some places.

*Deinosuchus* far exceeds the largest living crocodile in size. A recent conservative estimate, based on comparisons with living crocodiles, would place its maximum overall length at 11 meters (36 feet), with a weight of about 6 tonnes. The reconstructed lower jaw of a specimen from the Upper Cretaceous of Texas is about 1.8 meters (6 feet) long. The bones and scutes of *Deinosuchus* are extremely robust. The snout is deep and bears huge, stout teeth.

The currently available evidence suggests placement of *Deinosuchus* in the family Crocodylidae.

▼ Although its snout is now known to have been incorrectly reconstructed, the awesome size of this skull of *Deinosuchus* is testament to the accuracy of its scientific name — literally "terror crocodile." Note the difference in size between the skull of *Deinosuchus* and that of a large modern crocodilian.

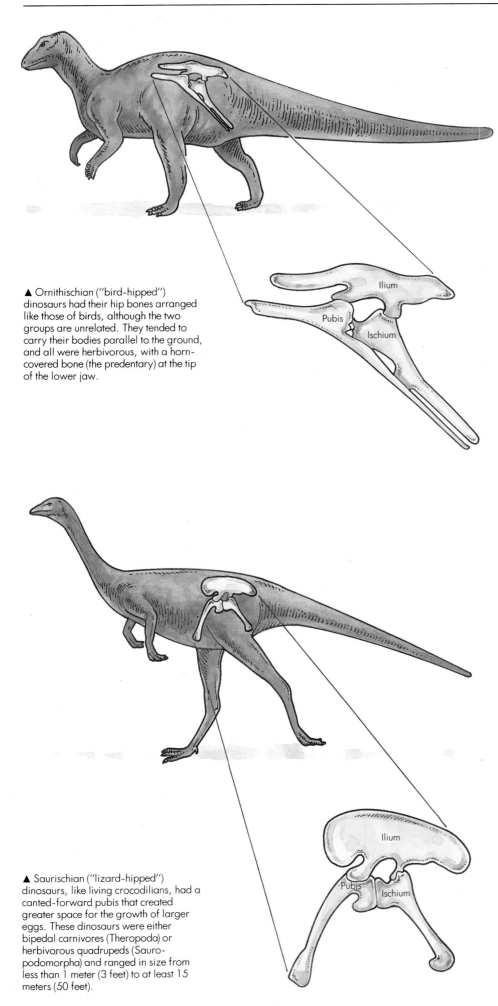

▲ Ornithischian ("bird-hipped") dinosaurs had their hip bones arranged like those of birds, although the two groups are unrelated. They tended to carry their bodies parallel to the ground, and all were herbivorous, with a horn-covered bone (the predentary) at the tip of the lower jaw.

▲ Saurischian ("lizard-hipped") dinosaurs, like living crocodilians, had a canted-forward pubis that created greater space for the growth of larger eggs. These dinosaurs were either bipedal carnivores (Theropoda) or herbivorous quadrupeds (Sauropodomorpha) and ranged in size from less than 1 meter (3 feet) to at least 15 meters (50 feet).

The dinosaurs were the dominant land animals for most of their 145 million year history. The name Dinosauria, meaning "terrible lizards," was coined in 1842 by the brilliant British anatomist Sir Richard Owen who, even with the sparse bony remains available at that time, first clearly recognized the distinctive nature of these forms.

Based on the structure of the hip girdle, two major lineages have been distinguished. One lineage — the saurischians or lizard-hipped dinosaurs — had an arrangement of the hip girdle similar to that found in lizards. The front bone of the hip girdle or pelvis (the pubis) projected forward as in lizards and crocodilians. The saurischians included two major groups, the Theropoda and the Sauropodomorpha. The Theropoda were bipedal meat-eaters, ranging in size from the less than 1-meter (3-foot) long *Compsognathus* to the 15-meter (50-foot) long *Tyrannosaurus*. The Sauropodomorpha were generally quadrupedal plant-eaters, mostly of very large size, and included the largest land-living animals ever known. In the second lineage — the ornithischians or bird-hipped dinosaurs — the pubis pointed backward and extended parallel to the rear bone of the hip girdle (the ischium) much as it does in birds. In many ornithischians the pubis developed a new projection at the front end of the bone. In addition, all ornithischian dinosaurs had an unpaired, scoop-shaped bone at the tip of the lower jaw (the predentary), which was probably covered by horn. They also had a lattice of ossified tendons extending along either side of the backbone, which presumably helped to stiffen the back, hip region, and tail. The ornithischian dinosaurs were all plant-eaters.

It was long thought that the two principal lineages of dinosaurs arose independently from different groups of thecodontian archosaurs, but more recent studies favor recognition of the Dinosauria as a natural grouping derived from a single ancestral stock.

## CROCODILIAN DISTRIBUTION AND PAST CLIMATES

Living crocodilians are poikilothermic, that is, their body temperature (like that of lizards, snakes, and turtles) largely depends on the temperature of the surrounding environment. Unlike mammals, crocodilians lack insulation (such as hair or feathers) and have no internal means (such as shivering) to raise their body temperature above that of the environment. Consequently, crocodilians are today restricted to those parts of the world where the average temperature of the coldest month of the year does not drop below 10°–15° C (50°–59° F). The alligators do not fit into this pattern of geographic distribution. Experimental studies indicate that the American Alligator (*Alligator mississippiensis*) can survive temperatures as low as 4° C (39.2° F). Field studies suggest that the optimal temperature for the American Alligator ranges from about 32°–35° C (89.6°–95° F). Below that optimum, however, alligators are still capable of sustained activity down to temperatures ranging from about 12°–15° C (53°–59° F). Based on this data, crocodilians cannot be used as very precise "geological thermometers" but they do indicate that their ancient environment was not subjected to harsh cold spells. If we also take into consideration other geological evidence, such as the presence of coals and plants whose living relatives are now restricted to subtropical or tropical regions, it would appear that fossil crocodilians did indeed prefer warm climates.

During the Early Tertiary, some 65–35 million years ago, numerous crocodilians related either to present alligators or crocodiles flourished in many parts of North America and Europe that are now devoid of large reptiles. Unlike their distant relatives, the dinosaurs and flying reptiles, crocodilians appear to have been unaffected by the global mass extinction on land and in the seas at the end of the Cretaceous period, about 65 million years ago. During the Late Tertiary, just prior to the beginning of the Pleistocene Ice Age, crocodilians rapidly retreated toward the equator; this coincides with a well-documented substantial decrease in annual mean temperatures. Crocodilians are no longer found in Europe. The American Alligator now has a rather restricted range of distribution in the southern United States although fossils indicate that, prior to the Ice Age, alligators ranged well into the northern regions of that country.

▼ Living crocodilians have evolved a sophisticated array of behavioral techniques to help control their internal temperature and most living species are now confined to regions where temperature variations are kept to a minimum. The American Alligator (shown here) and the Chinese Alligator are the exceptions, being the only crocodilian species able to withstand the colder temperatures of the temperate zone.

# EVOLUTION

ERIC BUFFETAUT

Crocodilian evolution spans more than 200 million years. It began in the Late Triassic, at the time when dinosaurs were beginning to dominate continental ecosystems and the first mammals were diversifying. Although many details remain obscure, the long history of crocodilians is relatively well documented because the fossil record is good, largely because the aquatic habits of most crocodilians are favorable to fossilization. Fossil crocodilians were among the first extinct vertebrates to be scientifically studied by the pioneers of paleontology at the beginning of the nineteenth century, and soon came to be considered as good evidence of biological evolution.

▼ The evolutionary history of crocodilians is one of variations on a few well-established themes. Adaptations to a fish-eating lifestyle in the fossil *Steneosaurus* from the Early Jurassic and in the living Gharial are suggested by their narrow snouts and numerous teeth.

Mike Price/Bruce Coleman Ltd

## SPECIALIZATION AND PARALLEL EVOLUTION

The evolutionary history of the crocodilians has been marked by repeated variations on a fairly constant theme, the general crocodilian body form, which has proved remarkably successful despite the considerable environmental changes that have taken place since the Triassic. Although the first crocodilians were apparently mainly terrestrial, relatively long-limbed, and short-snouted, the principal adaptations to an amphibious way of life found in the living crocodiles and alligators seem to have become established quite quickly (geologically speaking). From the groups of freshwater crocodilians that succeeded each other through the Mesozoic and Cenozoic eras, more specialized forms have repeatedly arisen, in a pattern typical of parallel evolution. Two main types of specialization have occurred again and again in crocodilian evolution. In many groups, a trend toward elongation of the snout is clearly perceptible and is usually interpreted as an adaptation to a fish-eating diet associated with a more strictly aquatic habitat; a living example of such a specialized crocodilian is the Gharial (*Gavialis gangeticus*) of the Indian subcontinent. In several extinct groups, however, this trend was pushed further than in the Gharial and long-snouted crocodilians invaded the seas, the trend culminating in the Jurassic metriorhynchids with their paddle-like limbs and tail fin. On the other hand, groups of terrestrial crocodilians have also frequently arisen from presumably amphibious ancestors. These animals had deep, narrow snouts containing laterally compressed and serrated teeth that were strikingly similar to those of carnivorous dinosaurs. Although these terrestrial crocodilians have no living representatives, they seem to have played a fairly important part in terrestrial ecosystems during the Tertiary in some parts of the world.

The frequent occurrence of parallel evolution in the course of crocodilian history has been a source of difficulty and dispute among paleontologists but there seems to be a measure of consensus about the main lines of crocodilian evolution. Crocodilian evolution has traditionally been divided into three main stages, which were first considered as natural suborders, but may in fact be mere evolutionary grades through which various crocodilian lineages have passed during their history. Whatever the real significance of these suborders, they do represent important transformations of crocodilian anatomy and will be used here to describe crocodilian evolution. Those evolutionary steps are distinguished mainly on the basis of the structure of the secondary bony palate. In living crocodilians this efficiently separates the mouth from the respiratory passage and is of considerable importance for aquatic forms, enabling the animal to breathe from the surface even when the mouth is open underwater. (A second advantage of a bony palate is that it braces the long snout against the heavy stresses engendered by the capture of large prey.) As the bony palate became longer in the course of crocodilian evolution, the internal nostrils (choanae) at the back of the palate were, in effect, "pushed" backward until they reached the position they occupy in living crocodiles, alligators and gavials, within the pterygoid bones. Another, unrelated, character that has been used to distinguish the main stages of crocodilian evolution is the shape of the vertebrae. Primitive crocodilians had spool-shaped biconcave (amphicoelous) vertebrae, whereas living species have (procoelous) vertebrae with a concave surface at the front and a convex surface at the back. The ball-and-socket articulation that results from procoelous vertebrae seems to provide better flexibility of the spinal column.

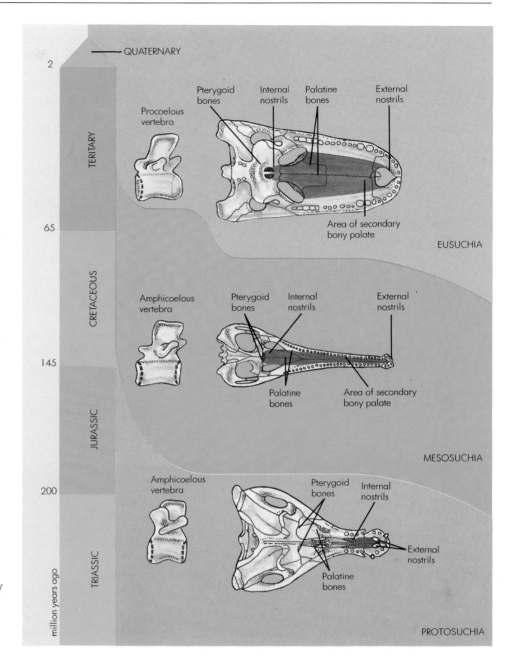

**QUATERNARY**

TERITARY — 2 — 65

Procoelous vertebra — Pterygoid bones — Internal nostrils — Palatine bones — External nostrils — Area of secondary bony palate — EUSUCHIA

CRETACEOUS — 65 — 145

Amphicoelous vertebra — Pterygoid bones — Internal nostrils — External nostrils — Palatine bones — Area of secondary bony palate — MESOSUCHIA

JURASSIC — 145 — 200

Amphicoelous vertebra — Pterygoid bones — Internal nostrils — External nostrils — Palatine bones

TRIASSIC — 200 — PROTOSUCHIA

million years ago

▲▼ Two main features can be traced throughout crocodilian evolution — increased spinal flexibility and strength as a result of the development of procoelous (ball-and-socket) vertebrae from primitive amphicoelous (spindle-shaped) vertebrae and the gradual enclosure of the secondary bony palate to allow the mouth to be opened underwater while still permitting breathing.

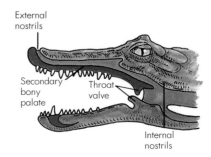

External nostrils — Secondary bony palate — Throat valve — Internal nostrils

▶ *Steneosaurus bollensis*, a long-snouted mesosuchian, shows many adaptations to its marine habitat, most notably a flexible body and a powerfully muscled tail that provided efficient propulsion in pursuit of fast-moving prey. The hindlimbs, which were probably strongly webbed, may have aided in propulsion as well as steering.

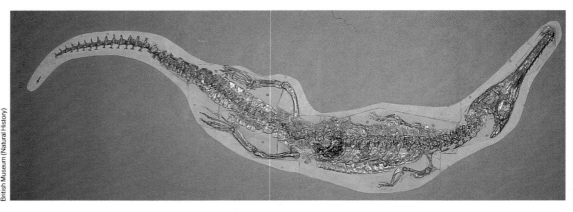

British Museum (Natural History)

▼ The placement of the nares, or external nostrils, at the front of the snout allows this hunting Indopacific Crocodile to expose no more than its eyes, ears, and nostrils. The closure of the secondary bony palate in the Eusuchia means the internal nostrils open toward the back of the skull, and air inhaled through the nasal passages passes through chambers in which "smells" are sensed. These nasal chambers lie near the olfactory lobe of the brain.

## EVOLUTIONARY STAGES

The earliest and most primitive stage of crocodilian evolution was represented by the Protosuchia, which flourished in the Late Triassic and Early Jurassic. In the protosuchians, the secondary palate was still at the initial stages of its development, being formed only by the maxillary bones (the internal nostrils thus opened between the maxillae and the palatines). The vertebrae were amphicoelous.

The next stage was represented by the Mesosuchia, which enjoyed considerable evolutionary radiation from the Jurassic to the Tertiary. In them, the palatines had become part of the palate and the internal nostrils were located much farther back than in the Protosuchia, between the palatines and the pterygoids. The vertebrae were still amphicoelous.

Finally, in the Eusuchia, which include all the living crocodilians, most of the Tertiary, and some Cretaceous forms, the pterygoids have been included in the palate and the internal nostrils opened within these bones, close to the back end of the skull. The vertebrae are procoelous.

Jean-Paul Ferrero/Auscape International

This is a very simplified sketch of the history of the crocodilians. Some fossils show that reality was not so clear-cut, which is hardly surprising: there is no reason why the evolution of the palate and that of the vertebrae should be linked or should have proceeded at the same pace. The result is that we would expect to find some crocodilians with a mesosuchian type of palate and procoelous vertebrae or, conversely, forms with a euchian palate and amphicoelous vertebrae. The fossil record shows that at least the first combination did occur in some extinct forms.

## PROTOSUCHIANS

The origins of the crocodilians are to be found among a group of Triassic archosaurs loosely called the thecodontians. The thecodontians are not a natural systematic group; they in fact included the ancestors of other archosaur groups, such as the dinosaurs and the flying pterosaurs, as well as a variety of forms specialized along different lines. The ancestry of the crocodilians among the thecodontians has proved difficult to trace although most paleontologists agree that it should be sought among the pseudosuchians, a group of terrestrial predatory thecodontians that enjoyed some evolutionary success in the Triassic.

Deciding what should still be considered as a pseudosuchian and what should be regarded as a true protosuchian crocodilian has proved an arduous task because, as often occurs in paleontology, it is difficult to draw a precise line between the stem group and its immediate descendants. Despite this, we now have a fairly good general idea of what the earliest crocodilians looked like some 215 million years ago. They were small, being hardly more than 1 meter (3 feet) long, and rather lizard-like in general appearance. The snout was short and the limbs proportionately longer than in modern forms. Such body proportions do not suggest aquatic or semi-aquatic animals, and protosuchians have usually been considered as mainly terrestrial predators although some of them, such as *Orthosuchus* from Lesotho, may have been partially aquatic. The bony armor was well developed in protosuchians, with two rows of plates along the back and tail, and a belly shield as well. This armor was to be retained, in a more or less modified form, by most later crocodilians.

Protosuchians were widely distributed in the Late Triassic and earliest Jurassic, their remains having been found in North and South America, southern Africa, Europe, and eastern Asia. This wide distribution was made possible by the geographical conditions at the end of the Triassic — all the major continental masses were still united into a single supercontinent (known as Pangaea) and dispersal of terrestrial animals was easy. The breakup of Pangaea through continental drift, from the Jurassic onward, was to play an important part in crocodilian evolution.

## MESOSUCHIANS

The transition from the Protosuchia to the Mesosuchia is still poorly known. The earliest well-known mesosuchians were already highly specialized in some respects although still primitive in others. They have been found in large numbers in Early Jurassic rocks about 190 million

▼ Looking more like a lizard than a living crocodilian this reconstructed *Orthosuchus* from Lesotho, like all protosuchians, was a long-legged, short-snouted, and probably terrestrial animal less than 1 meter (3 feet) in length. Not only was the spine protected by two rows of plates, but the belly scales were more or less fused into a protective shield.

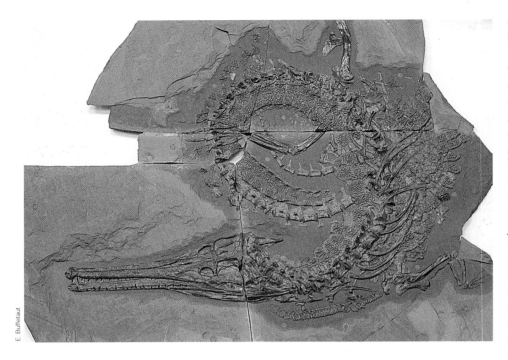

E. Buffetaut

▲ The exaggerated curvature of this mesosuchian is the result of the contraction of tendons after death; however, its flexibility — developed to enable it to pursue marine prey — is obvious.

▼ Until they became extinct in the early Cretaceous, metriorhynchids occupied a similar marine predator's niche to living dolphins. This group had lost their ancestors' body armor, and well-preserved fossils from Germany show that they propelled themselves with a shark-like dorsal fin near the tail.

years old, mainly in Europe. The rocks in which these mesosuchians occur were deposited in marine environments, and the anatomical features of these crocodilians do indicate adaptation to life in the sea. The members of one mesosuchian family, the Teleosauridae, were rather gharial-like appearance, with very long and narrow snouts provided with numerous piercing teeth, which suggests that they fed on marine invertebrates and fishes. Although the forelimbs were reduced, teleosaurids were still able to walk on land (where they presumably came, at least to lay their eggs) and they retained their outer armor until the end

of their evolutionary history, at the beginning of the Cretaceous.

A more pronounced adaptation to marine life was shown by the Metriorhynchidae, which were closely related to the Teleosauridae. Although the earliest known metriorhynchids, such as *Pelagosaurus,* were still teleosaurid-like, with armor and little modification of the limbs, they soon lost their armor and acquired revealing locomotor adaptations. The limbs were transformed into paddles and there was a small fleshy dorsal fin near the tip of the tail, as shown by remarkably preserved specimens from the Upper Jurassic of Germany. Propulsion in the water was effected mainly by lateral movements of the tip of the tail; the limbs being used for steering and balance. Whether metriorhynchids still had to come onto land (where they must have been extremely clumsy) to lay their eggs or had become viviparous, like other Mesozoic marine reptiles, remains unknown. They disappeared, for unknown reasons, in the Early Cretaceous after producing very large forms in the Late Jurassic.

Because relatively few continental vertebrate faunas are known from the Middle Jurassic, little is known about the freshwater and terrestrial crocodilians of that period. The Late Jurassic fossil record is much better, however, and reveals that some diversification had taken place. A number of groups of relatively advanced mesosuchians are known from that time, about 150 million years ago. Most of them persisted into the Cretaceous. The adaptive type, represented today by such species as the Nile Crocodile (*Crocodylus niloticus*)or the Indian Mugger (*Crocodylus*

# CROCODILIANS AND CONTINENTAL DRIFT

Crocodilians appeared at the end of the Triassic, when the continental masses of the world were united into the supercontinent Pangaea. Their subsequent evolution was therefore much influenced by the breakup of that supercontinent, which began in the Jurassic and led to the present geographical distribution of land and sea. As oceans opened they separated land areas that had hitherto been joined; populations of continental vertebrates, including crocodilians, became isolated from each other and evolved independently along divergent lines.

The biogeographical history of crocodilians provides several examples of the influence of continental drift on evolution. The case of the Cretaceous crocodilians of Africa and South America is especially well documented. Fossils found in several localities in Niger and Brazil show that in the Early Cretaceous, some 115 million years ago, several genera of freshwater and terrestrial crocodilians were represented on both continents by closely related, if not identical, species. The enormous pholidosaurid *Sarcosuchus* and the small short-snouted *Araripesuchus* are the best known of these African–South American crocodilians, which were part of a vertebrate fauna common to both areas. Fossil crocodilians thus confirm that at that time the South Atlantic was still in the early stages of its opening and Africa was not yet completely separated from South America by a seaway. It was not until the very end of the Early Cretaceous, some 100 million years ago, that such a seaway became established, preventing easy faunal interchange between the two continents.

The crocodilian faunas of Africa and South America then evolved independently of each other, which led to an increasing divergence between them. The Late Cretaceous crocodilian faunas of the two continents still showed some resemblances inherited from the Early Cretaceous but the effects of divergent evolution were already obvious and became more so in the Tertiary. Some forms such as the dyrosaurids and some gavialines, however, adapted to a marine habitat and were still able to cross the proto-Atlantic up until the end of the Cretaceous and into the Early Tertiary.

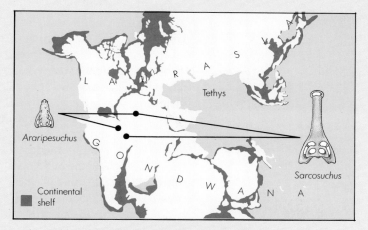

▲ The world as it was 200 million years ago, when the first crocodilians were beginning to disperse throughout the original supercontinent of Pangaea. As Pangaea separated into Laurasia and Gondwana, various groups became isolated from each other and were thus presented with opportunities to move into new ecological niches.

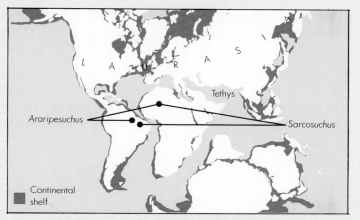

▲ The fossil crocodilians of Africa and South America were once identical or closely related species. However, as their homelands drifted apart 100 million years ago they diverged — an example of vicariant speciation. The crocodilian fauna of South America is now more diverse than that of Africa, which lacks alligatorines.

*palustris*), was represented in the Late Jurassic and Early Cretaceous by the Goniopholididae, fairly large mesosuchians with a (usually) moderately elongated snout. The goniopholidids were widely distributed over the northern (Laurasian) continental masses, from Thailand to western North America via western Europe, but they do not seem to have been present on the southern (Gondwanan) continents. The Pholidosauridae, closely related to the Goniopholididae, had more gharial-like skulls and can be considered as essentially long-snouted goniopholidids. They were not restricted to Laurasia, as shown by the occurrence of the huge pholidosaurid *Sarcosuchus* in the Lower Cretaceous of both Africa and South America; this was one of the largest known crocodilians, with a skull reaching a length of

2 meters (more than 6 feet) and a total length of perhaps 11 meters (36 feet). Both the goniopholidids and the pholidosaurids persisted into the Late Cretaceous, a time when some particularly long-snouted pholidosaurids took to the sea, with the genus *Teleorhinus,* which has been found in both Germany and the United States.

Another group of advanced mesosuchians, the Atoposauridae, seem to have been mainly terrestrial in their mode of life. The atoposaurids were small crocodilians with short snouts and relatively long legs. Their remains have been found in the Upper Jurassic and Lower Cretaceous of Europe and possibly Asia. Like the goniopholidids, they do not seem to have inhabited the southern continents, where other groups of small terrestrial crocodilians played a similar ecological role.

▲ Ziphodont or "dinosaur-toothed" trematochampsids had very robust jaws, similar to this one from the Eocene of Algeria. These terrestrial crocodilians were found in South America, Africa, and Europe.

This geographical differentation between the crocodilian faunas of Laurasia and Gondwana at the beginning of the Cretaceous resulted from the breakup of the supercontinents. The vast east–west seaway known as the Tethys apparently formed a relatively efficient biogeographical barrier between the northern and the southern land masses (although separation was not total, as shown by the distribution of the pholidosaurids). The Atlantic Ocean, however, was still in the first stages of its opening and Africa was not effectively separated from South America by a continuous seaway until about the middle of the Cretaceous, some 100 million years ago. This explains the very close resemblance between the Early Cretaceous non-marine crocodilians of the African and South American continents.

The forms common to South America and to Africa in the Early Cretaceous included small terrestrial mesosuchians of the genus *Araripesuchus*, a member of the family Uruguaysuchidae. The uruguaysuchids were fairly primitive mesosuchians with short snouts. They seem to have been widespread in the Cretaceous of South America. On this continent they may have given rise to another, more specialized, family of terrestrial crocodilians, the Notosuchidae, which are Late Cretaceous in age. The African uruguaysuchids may have been ancestral to the Libycosuchidae, another very short-snouted family that occurs in the Upper Cretaceous of Africa. The notosuchids and the libycosuchids could thus be considered as the result of divergent evolution on both sides of the proto-Atlantic, from a common uruguaysuchid ancestral stock.

The Trematochampsidae, another group of African–South American mesosuchians, appeared before the separation of these continents and evolved along distinct lines during the Late Cretaceous, after the opening of the South Atlantic. Early trematochampsids were rather crocodile-like in appearance, with moderately elongated but very robust jaws. They are known from Africa, Madagascar, and South America, and seem to have played the same ecological role on the southern continents as the goniopholidids in Laurasia. Later trematochampsids seem to have become more terrestrial in their habits and to have given rise to "dinosaur-toothed" (ziphodont) crocodilians in South America, Africa, and Europe.

## THE FATE OF THE LAST MESOSUCHIANS

The Early Cretaceous seems to have witnessed the appearance of the Eusuchia, the modern suborder of crocodilians. As early as the Late Jurassic, *Theriosuchus pusillus*, a species from England related to the atoposaurids, possessed vertebrae that were intermediate in shape between the amphicoelous and procoelous types; its palate, though still mesosuchian, was of an advanced type. By the Early Cretaceous species of *Theriosuchus* apparently had fully procoelous vertebrae. "Semi-procoelous" vertebrae also occurred in another very advanced mesosuchian from the Lower Cretaceous of Europe, *Bernissartia*, which also had a progressive palate and a "modern" kind of dorsal armor, consisting of several longitudinal rows of plates, as in eusuchians, instead of the two rows usually found in mesosuchians. It thus seems that in the Early Cretaceous several groups of mesosuchians approached the eusuchian

▼ An advanced mesosuchian from the Lower Cretaceous of Europe, *Bernissartia* showed some eusuchian features and, despite being discovered among dinosaur skeletons, had blunt teeth that suggest a diet of shellfish.

condition in the structure of the vertebrae or in the construction of the palate, or in both. One form of mesosuchian from the Lower Cretaceous of England, *Hylaeochampsa,* actually had its internal nostrils in the same position as living crocodilians although it also exhibited some aberrant features.

The fossil record of crocodilians from the middle part of the Cretaceous is rather poor. Procoelous vertebrae from various parts of the world, from Australia to Africa and Europe, suggest that eusuchians, which presumably appeared in Laurasia, were becoming widespread but little is known of these early forms. That some fairly rapid and widespread diversification had taken place is suggested by the occurrence of *Stomatosuchus* in the basal Upper Cretaceous of Egypt. It was a strange creature with a huge flat skull shaped somewhat like the bill of a duck and it had procoelous vertebrae.

Several groups of ziphodont mesosuchians with deep snouts and dinosaur-like teeth evolved during the Late Cretaceous. The South American Baurusuchidae were one such group; they exhibit very unusual specializations but their affinities are obscure. The trematochampsids seem to have produced other ziphodont forms in the Early Tertiary of both Africa, and Europe.

Trematochampsids apparently crossed the Tethys Sea from Africa to Europe sometime in the Late Cretaceous. In the Early Tertiary, ziphodont mesosuchians also played a fairly important role in the South American faunas, with the family Sebecidae. The sebecids were apparently powerful terrestrial carnivores with efficient jaws and teeth. They may have been derived from South American trematochampsids and persisted until the Late Tertiary, some of them reaching a very large size. A ziphodont mesosuchian may also have survived until the Late Tertiary in Australia but it is known only from very scanty remains.

Apparently, ziphodont crocodilians enjoyed their greatest ecological success as terrestrial predators after the carnivorous dinosaurs became extinct at the end of the Cretaceous and before efficient large mammalian carnivores entered the scene. Such carnivores became widespread in Europe much earlier (in the Eocene) than they did in South America (at the end of the Tertiary) and this may explain why ziphodont crocodilians became extinct much earlier in Europe than in South America.

Another late group of mesosuchians, the Dyrosauridae, specialized in a completely different direction from that followed by ziphodont crocodilians. The dyrosaurids were large long-snouted forms that lived in the latest Cretaceous and the Early Tertiary along the shores of the Tethys Sea, from the Indian subcontinent all the way to North and West Africa, the east coast of North America, Brazil, and the region of the present Andes. The origin of the dyrosaurids is

MESOSUCHIAN
SEBECID

EUSUCHIAN
PRISTICHAMPSINE

▲ Convergent evolution, where organisms from different lineages develop similarities in response to similar pressures or opportunities, is seen in the flattened and serrated teeth found in both the mesosuchian sebecids of South America and the eusuchian pristichampsines of the Northern Hemisphere.

obscure although they may have been distantly related to the trematochampsids. They seem to have been fairly successful and to have diversified substantially at the beginning of the Tertiary; some forms had a very slender snout whereas others had much more robust jaws and teeth and may have fed on marine turtles. Although they were not as thoroughly adapted to marine life as the Jurassic teleosaurids and metriorhynchids, the dyrosaurids apparently spent much of their time in coastal waters and were able to cross the Atlantic, which was narrower than it is today. Like most other crocodilians, the dyrosaurids survived the events of the end of the Cretaceous; they diversified afterwards, which may have been made easier by the disappearance of the other groups of predatory marine reptiles. This last radiation of marine mesosuchians came to an end during the Eocene, some 45 million years ago. One can only speculate about the causes of the extinction of the dyrosaurids but their demise may have been linked with the evolution of marine gavialines and/or early whales during the Eocene.

# THE CRETACEOUS-TERTIARY BIOLOGICAL CRISIS

Most crocodilians were unaffected by the biological crisis of the Cretaceous-Tertiary boundary, which wiped out the dinosaurs and so many other groups of organisms some 65 million years ago. Why the crocodilians were able to survive while other reptiles became extinct is not perfectly clear but their very survival has some implications for the current speculations about the nature of the events at that time.

Living crocodilians are known to be sensitive to temperature changes and cannot survive in a cold climate. This means that all theories that postulate a major climatic deterioration with severe temperature drops at the Cretaceous-Tertiary boundary are unsatisfying since crocodilians are known to have survived the crisis, even at high latitudes.

One explanation for the survival of crocodilians is that they belonged to a community of living beings that was little affected by whatever happened 65 million years ago: freshwater vertebrates (including fishes, amphibians, turtles, and crocodilians) are known to have survived the crisis much better than either terrestrial or marine communities. A possible explanation for this differential survival is that the freshwater food web was based on neither marine plankton nor flowering plants, both of which were severely affected at the Cretaceous-Tertiary boundary. This may have been a consequence of a meteorite or comet impact, or, perhaps, intense volcanic activity. The disruption of food chains in the sea and on land may have led to the extinctions in these domains, whereas the freshwater communities were little affected. Whatever the exact reason may be, the survival of the crocodilians at the end of the Cretaceous is certainly a measure of their ecological and evolutionary success.

Mark Hallett

## RISE OF THE EUSUCHIANS

Crocodilians that can safely be assigned to the modern (eusuchian) families appeared and became dominant in the Late Cretaceous, some 80 million years ago, with indisputable alligatorines and crocodylines from western North America. The separation of these two subfamilies must therefore have taken place earlier but virtually nothing is known of the ancestral stock common to the Alligatorinae and the Crocodylinae. A very late representative of this stock may, however, have survived until historical times in New Caledonia, where abundant bones of a very primitive eusuchian with characters of both alligatorines and crocodylines have been found in recent cave deposits and described as *Mekosuchus inexpectatus.*

The alligatorines had already developed their short and broad snouts, with the lower teeth fitting within the upper tooth rows when the jaws are closed. In the crocodylines, the jaws are usually more slender, with a well-marked notch on the snout where a large tooth of the lower jaw is

lodged when the jaws are closed. The largest tooth of the maxilla is the fourth in alligatorines, the fifth in crocodylines. In the latter, a bone on the side of the skull bears a spine that is absent in alligatorines. Such skull characters allow paleontologists to distinguish fossil remains of crocodiles and alligators, which are often found together in Late Cretaceous and Early Tertiary localities on the Laurasian continents, where both subfamilies seem to have originated and diversified. The Middle Eocene fauna of Europe, for example, included at least three species of crocodylines and two or three species of alligatorines, in addition to the ziphodont mesosuchians such as trematochampsids.

In addition to forms such as *Diplocynodon,* a rather caiman-like animal widespread in Europe during almost the whole Tertiary, there were small short-snouted alligatorines with crushing teeth at the back of the jaws. Such alligatorines were widespread in the Early Tertiary, being known from Thailand to the Canadian Arctic; it seems likely that they fed largely on hard-shelled invertebrates.

The most unusual Early Tertiary representatives of the crocodylines were the
pristichampsines, ziphodont forms with hoof-like
toes. They seem to have been terrestrial predators
or scavengers descended from "normal"
crocodiles. They were widespread on the
northern continents and seem somehow to have
reached Australia, where a ziphodont eusuchian,
*Quinkana fortirostrum,* was found. The North
American, European, and Asian pristichampsines
disappeared during the Late Eocene (perhaps
because of the competition from carnivorous
mammals); *Quinkana,* however, has been found in
Pleistocene deposits and is the most recent
ziphodont crocodilian hitherto known. Its late
survival in Australia may be linked to the absence
there of placental (non-marsupial) carnivores.

The origin of the remaining subfamily of living
crocodilians, the extremely long-snouted
Gavialinae, has been (and still is) the subject of
some controversy. Several characters of the living
Gharial have been considered by some as
indicating that gavialines are very different
from crocodylines and alligatorines, and are
possibly related to some group of long-snouted

▲ Gaps in the fossil record mean that the
first "modern" crocodilians appear
rather suddenly, around 80 million years
ago. They were already recognizable as
modern forms, with both crocodile-like
and alligator-like (as seen here) forms.

E. Buffetaut

◄ Pristichampsines were an aberrant
group of "hoofed" crocodilians that may
have been terrestrial predators. Although
they disappeared in the Northern
Hemisphere during the Late Eocene, a
late survivor was found in Pleistocene
deposits in Australia.

# NEW CALEDONIAN CROCODILE
## *(Mekosuchus inexpectatus)*

JEAN CHRISTOPHE BALOUET

New Caledonia's vertebrate fauna, drastically diminished by the impact of humans, included more than 30 species of terrestrial vertebrates that are now extinct. An endemic land crocodile, *Mekosuchus inexpectatus,* the only representative of the extinct family Mekosuchidae, was discovered in 1980.

The fossilized specimens were trapped in deep caves of karstic formation (limestone with underground drainage or sinkholes) and were collected from two paleontological sites — one on the Isle of Pines, dating back to 3,500–3,900 years ago, and the other on New Caledonia itself, dating from 1,670–1,810 years ago. The discovery of a fragment of a jawbone in an archeological midden at Nessadiou, on the west coast of New Caledonia 200 kilometers (124 miles) north of Nouméa, provides evidence of human involvement in its extinction.

Fossil remains of *Mekosuchus* have only been found in lowland areas, close to the beaches, where it was probably first hunted. Its extinction occurred within less than 2,000 years and overhunting appears to be the best explanation for such a rapid disappearance. It was probably extinct before the arrival of European colonists and no oral tradition can be assigned to that species. (Some legends on the west coast can be attributed to the Indopacific Crocodile.)

Terrestrial crocodiles are very rare (although *Quinkana,* an extinct Australian crocodile was also terrestrial), and *Mekosuchus* is the only terrestrial insular form known at present. Its terrestrial adaptations are particularly evident in the anterolateral openings of the nasal passages (nares) and the developed musculature of the limb bones.

*Mekosuchus* fed on mollusks, as indicated by its posterior rounded teeth. Its length is estimated at 2 meters (6.5 feet) and it was the largest reptile of the island. Its populations were also the most numerous among the large, extinct reptilian fauna but, like other large species, it could not survive the hunting pressure.

*Mekosuchus* shows a number of derived characters in the skull, such as its height, the maxillary bone forming part of the orbit (a unique feature in crocodiles), very large pterygoids, and narrow palatines. Some primitive characters of the cheekbone (jugal) area are reminiscent of the Mesosuchia. Other characters enable it to be placed in a related group to all Eusuchia (Crocodylinae, Alligatorinae, and Gavialinae).

The original evolution of this primitive crocodile probably took place at the end of the Mesozoic era, when New Caledonia was still connected to Australia. Its survival until such recent times poses a number of questions, especially how it survived the covering of New Caledonia's land by sea in the Late Eocene.

Why do we not know of other insular terrestrial forms? Such a possibility was not even considered before 1980. Perhaps other forms will be discovered on other large Pacific islands, where paleontological research has not yet been undertaken. *Mekosuchus* does at least provide evidence of crocodiles' colonization and survival in insular, terrestrial environments for millions of years before extinction.

Jean Christophe Balouet

*Mekosuchus inexpectatus*

Image removed.

mesosuchians. In fact, both biochemical and paleontological data suggests that the gavialines are closely related to the crocodylines and may be considered as long-snouted offshoots of the latter. A number of long-snouted eusuchians from the Eocene and Oligocene of North Africa appear to be primitive gavialines. In contrast to the living Gharial, which is a freshwater form, these early gavialines seem to have frequented coastal waters and this probably accounts for their wide geographical distribution along Tertiary seaways. From a possible North African center of origin, the gavialines may have reached the Indian subcontinent in the east, Europe in the north, and even America in the west. In South America, the primitive gavialines even enjoyed a minor evolutionary radiation in freshwater habitats during the Tertiary before becoming extinct for unknown reasons. Climatic deterioration probably caused their disappearance from Europe and North America but it is not clear why they also became extinct in Africa. Only in Asia could the gavialines survive until the present day. Fairly abundant remains of various species, more or less closely related to the living Gharial, have been found in freshwater Tertiary sediments in India and Pakistan.

Although crocodilians survived in Europe until less than 5 million years ago, climatic deterioration at the end of the Eocene, some 38 million years ago, had already led to a sharp decline of their diversity there and there is little doubt that the increasingly cool climate during the Late Tertiary was the main cause of their disappearance from Europe. Similarly, in North America and in China, crocodilian faunas never regained their former variety after the end of the Eocene although alligators have survived in both regions to the present day. The Late Tertiary and Pleistocene history of the crocodilians took place largely in the tropical regions where the great majority of the living crocodylines, alligatorines, and gavialines are still found.

## ORIGIN OF LIVING SPECIES

Tracing the fossil history of the living species of crocodilians is not always an easy task. The Late Tertiary history of gharials in the Indian subcontinent is relatively well documented by fossils. Although a number of Late Tertiary and Pleistocene fossils from eastern Asia have been linked to the genus *Tomistoma*, little is known about the exact origin of the living False Gharial (*Tomistoma schlegelii*). The genus *Crocodylus* is first known with certainty from the Early Tertiary (Eocene or Oligocene). The ancestry of the Nile Crocodile (*Crocodylus niloticus*) and, to some extent, of the African Slender-snouted Crocodile (*Crocodylus cataphractus*) is known with some precision because of abundant crocodile fossils

▼ The American Alligator (shown here) and the Chinese Alligator can tolerate a wider range of temperatures than other crocodilians and survived the deterioration of climate at the end of the Eocene.

Ian Beames/Ardea London

from the Tertiary and Pleistocene of northern and eastern Africa. *Crocodylus lloidi,* a species known from the Tertiary and Early Pleistocene of Africa, is supposed to have been ancestral to the Nile Crocodile and possibly also to the Mugger (*Crocodylus palustris*) of India; the extinct *Crocodylus sivalensis* from India and Pakistan being presumably intermediate between these species. Very little, however, is known of the evolution of the Southeast Asian and Australasian species of *Crocodylus,* although Pleistocene remains of the Indopacific Crocodile (*Crocodylus porosus*) have been reported from Australia. Similarly, the evolutionary history of the American Crocodile (*Crocodylus acutus*), Orinoco Crocodile, (*C. intermedius*), Cuban Crocodile (*C. rhombifer*), and Morelet's Crocodile (*C. moreletii*) remains obscure; a fossil crocodile from Cuba may correspond to the ancestral stock of both the Cuban Crocodile and Morelet's Crocodile. Much therefore remains to be done to unravel the evolutionary history of the genus *Crocodylus.* As to the African Dwarf Crocodile (*Osteolaemus tetraspis*), except for subfossil specimens from Angola, nothing is known of its paleontological history.

There are also many gaps in our knowledge of the evolutionary history of the living alligators and caimans although a fairly large amount of fossil material is now available from North and South America. The ancestry of the American Alligator (*Alligator mississippiensis*) may be traced back to *Alligator olseni,* from the Miocene of Florida. The Chinese Alligator (*Alligator sinensis*) is reported from the Pleistocene of China but its evolutionary history and its exact relationships with the American Alligator are unclear.

In South America, alligatorines were known as early as the Paleocene. *Eocaiman cavernensis,* from the Eocene of Patagonia, already exhibited many characters of the living caimans and may well have been ancestral to both *Caiman* and *Melanosuchus.* The evolutionary history of *Paleosuchus,* however, is not known. A fairly important evolutionary radiation of the South American caimans took place during the Tertiary and gave rise to the living species as well as to extinct ones, including giant forms such as *Caiman neivensis* from the Miocene of Colombia.

This brief survey of crocodilian evolution since its beginnings in the Late Triassic shows how successful the basic crocodilian body plan has been through the vicissitudes of geological and biological history. From the succeeding groups of "generalized" crocodilians that have occupied freshwater environments during the past 200 million years, specialized offshoots have repeatedly separated to adapt to a fully marine or essentially terrestrial mode of life. In this respect, the extinct mesosuchians were more diversified than the eusuchians that replaced them. After

E. & P. Bauer / ZEFA Düsseldorf

► American Alligators have survived in Florida since the Eocene although hunting for skins severely reduced their numbers. The greatest sources of pressure on this species today, however, are environmental pollution and habitat destruction.

some success, however, the specialized offshoots have died out but crocodilians of a more "usual" kind have persisted. Crocodilians have been able to spread to all parts of the world (although no fossil remains of crocodilians have yet been found in Antarctica there is no reason why they should not have lived there before the onset of glaciation) and, as a group, they are apparently subjected to little competition in the niches they occupy as amphibious predators.

Until recently, the main reason for their decline in some parts of the world has been long-term climatic change. With the ascent of human beings, however, a quicker and more lethal agent of crocodilian extinction has appeared. Some species are in immediate danger of extinction and the group as a whole is undoubtedly threatened. Whether more than 200 million years of crocodilian success will soon come to an abrupt end now depends on us.

Leonard Lee Rue III/Bruce Coleman Ltd.

◄ Crocodilians may have been restricted to the role of aquatic predators because of the dominance of mammalian predators on land; conversely, large mammalian predators may never have been able to establish themselves as aquatic predators simply because crocodilians are so superbly adapted to that niche. Only recognition of the unique role these magnificant animals play can prevent their 200 million years of success coming to a tragic end.

# WORLD DISTRIBUTION OF CROCODILIANS

## MAP 1: NORTH AND SOUTH AMERICA

- American Alligator
- Common Caiman
- Broad-snouted Caiman
- Black Caiman
- Cuvier's Dwarf Caiman
- Schneider's Dwarf Caiman
- American Crocodile
- Orinoco Crocodile
- Morelet's Crocodile
- Cuban Crocodile

## MAP 2: AFRICA

- African Slender-snouted Crocodile
- Nile Crocodile
- Dwarf Crocodile
- Mugger

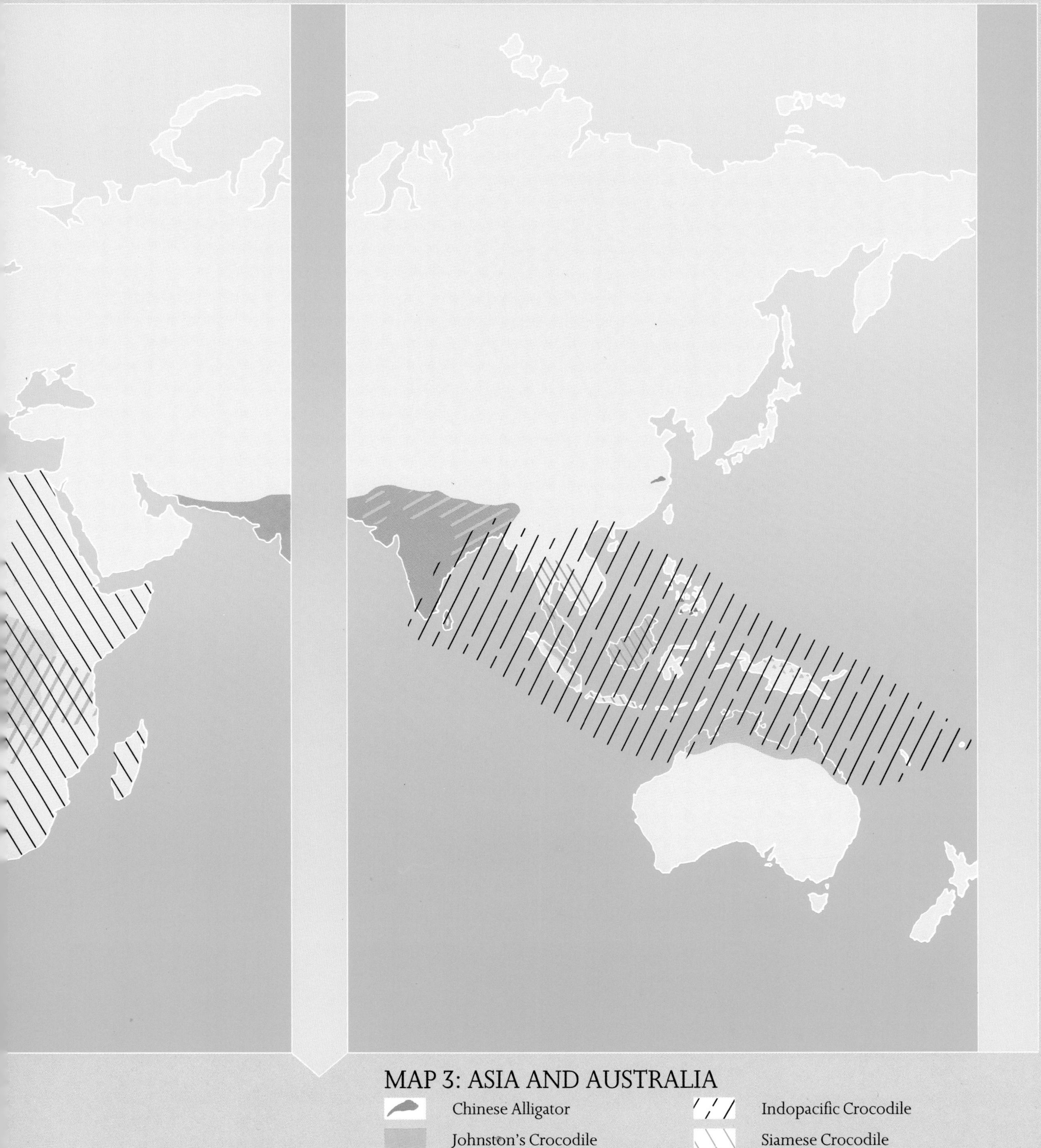

# MAP 3: ASIA AND AUSTRALIA

| | | | |
|---|---|---|---|
| | Chinese Alligator | | Indopacific Crocodile |
| | Johnston's Crocodile | | Siamese Crocodile |
| | Philippine Crocodile | | False Gharial |
| | New Guinea Crocodile | | Gharial |
| | Mugger | | |

41

# STRUCTURE AND FUNCTION

FRANK J. MAZZOTTI

Crocodilians are the most advanced of all reptiles. Most of these "advancements," such as their four-chambered heart, diaphragm, and cerebral cortex are internal, while their primitive external morphology reflects their primarily aquatic habits. Crocodilians are elongated, armored, and lizard-like, with a muscular, laterally shaped tail used in swimming. The snout is also elongated, with the nostrils set at the end to allow breathing while most of the body remains submerged under water. Their skin is formed from a thick dermal layer covered with non-overlapping epidermal scales or scutes. The surface layer of each scute sloughs off individually rather than shedding in large patches. Bony buttons or plates called osteoderms are embedded in the skin, forming a dorsal armor. The teeth are thecodont, that is, they are set in sockets in the jaw rather than fused to the top (acrodont) or side (pleurodont) of the jaw as in other reptiles. The crocodilian skull is diapsid with two openings in the temporal area that allow expansion of the jaw muscles. The snouts of crocodilians range from broad (in alligators) to very narrow (in Gharials) and, to some extent, are related to the major components of their diets — narrower snouts usually indicating fish-eating species. Crocodilians do not have lips and their mouths leak when closed. Crocodilians have two pairs of short legs with five toes on the front feet and four toes on the hind feet; the toes on all feet being partially webbed. The success of this body design is evidenced by the relatively few changes that have occurred since crocodilians first appeared in the Late Triassic, about 200 million years ago.

► The upper jaw of crocodilians is almost solid bone and has little flexibility. However, between the toothsome rims of the lower jaw the skin is loose and elastic.

Wendy Shattil and Robert Rozinski/Tom Stack & Associates

► The webbing on the hind feet of crocodilians helps them to balance and maneuver in the water (the main thrust for swimming is provided by the tail). Only four toes are ever developed, the fifth digit being a small internal bone.

Ralph and Daphne Keller/Australasian Nature Transparencies

J.M. La-Roque/Auscape International

◄ "Tail walking" is an apt description of this Indopacific Crocodile attempting to catch a proffered fish although this type of behavior is not common among crocodilians.

## LOCOMOTION

How crocodilians move is very much a consequence of their body form. Although crocodilians spend a great deal of time on land, they are usually basking there with little movement. However, crocodilians do move on land to satisfy thermal or reproductive requirements, to move from one body of water to another, to escape from disturbance, or to feed. Although not equal to their grace and ease of movement in water, terrestrial locomotion can be surprisingly coordinated and rapid. There are three distinct styles of movement on land — the high walk, the gallop, and the scuttling belly run.

In contrast to their rather limited ability to move on land crocodilians are excellent swimmers. Swimming (both at the surface and underwater) is effected by lateral S-shaped undulations of the tail. The limbs are held closely against the body, streamlining the profile and reducing drag. Crocodilians generally cruise slowly with a gentle sweeping motion of the tail.

▼ ► Encountered in the open sea off the Northern Territory, Australia, this Indopacific Crocodile (below) displays the sinuous, energy-efficient swimming motion in which power is provided by slow sweeps of the long, muscular tail. The buoyancy effect of water enables this hatchling (right) to keep its nasal disc close to the surface of the water while the rest of its body "floats" almost vertically.

However, when being chased or chasing prey a crocodile can move quite rapidly, even leaping out of the water in a "tail walk" reminiscent of dolphins. When stationary the limbs are held away from the body, apparently to aid in maintaining or adjusting position.

Despite their excellent swimming abilities crocodilians, for the most part, avoid areas with strong wind and wave action. In calm water a crocodile needs to keep only its nasal disc above the surface of the water to breathe. In rough water the snout has to be raised at a steep angle above the surface during inspiration. This apparently makes swimming more difficult. Crocodilians therefore seek protected water and frequently come ashore when calm water is not available.

# WALKING, RUNNING, AND CRAWLING

GEORGE R. ZUG

Crocodilians, individually and collectively, have a diversity of locomotor patterns. When moving unhurried on land, a crocodile or alligator proceeds with a stately high walk but, if frightened, it will plunge down an embankment in an inelegant belly crawl. A few species can even gallop across a beach with hare-like bounds. No crocodilian, however, shows any skills as a climber and certainly none has developed skills as an aerialist.

The high walk of crocodilians is unique among the living reptiles. Turtles and lizards walk with a sprawled posture; the limbs project outward from the body, rather than downward, so that the body is hardly raised above the ground. In contrast, the limbs of a bird or mammal extend directly beneath the body and elevate it high off the ground. The high walk of crocodilians is much more similar to the mammalian walking posture than to the typical sprawled reptilian one. Crocodilians hold their limbs nearly, although not completely, vertical beneath the body, resulting in an elevated posture that is high enough to raise much of the tail off the ground.

The walking gait of crocodilians shows the same sequence of limb movements as in all four-limbed animals — right fore, left hind, left fore, right hind, and so on in sequence. This diagonal sequence produces a well-balanced tripod of support as the animal moves forward. With an increase in speed, the diagonally opposite limbs begin to move forward almost simultaneously and faster in a trot-like gait. The resulting bipodal support is less stable but the quick back and forth shift between diagonal support pairs establishes a dynamic equilibrium.

However, if the limbs move too fast this equilibrium is lost and the crocodilian, especially if it is an adult, appears to stumble into a new mode of locomotion, crashing onto its chest and belly with the limbs splayed to the sides. With side-to-side twists of the body and rowing-like swings of the limbs, the crocodilian thrashes and slides on its belly into the water. This belly crawl is most effective on steep shorelines for fast escape but can also be used to slip quietly into the water.

In smaller crocodiles the running gait can change into a bounding gallop — the hindlimbs push the crocodile forward in a leap; the body straightens; the forelimbs extend and catch the body at the end of the leap; the hindlimbs swing forward as the back bends; and then the hindlimbs leap the animal forward again. This bounding gallop produces speeds of 3–17 kilometers (2–10 miles) an hour, not the 15–30 kilometers (9–19 miles) an hour of some mammals but considerably faster than the 0.3–4.5 kilometers (0.2–3 miles) an hour of the crocodilian high walk.

▶ One of the characteristic tracks on the banks of tropical rivers is the splayed mud created by crocodilians sliding into the water. Large animals, in particular, have little hope of heaving their bellies up above the mud (top). Crocodilians look more like their dinosaur ancestors when walking on land. A stately motion, never performed at great speed, the high walk is nevertheless a more efficient means of transporting this Mugger's great bulk across hard ground than a belly crawl would be (middle). The fastest crocodilian motion on land, however, is the rarely seen gallop, performed by only a few species, such as the Johnston's Crocodile, usually when startled (right).

Bill Green

Gunter Ziesler/Bruce Coleman Ltd

Gunther Deichmann/Auscape International

Robert C. Simpson/Tom Stack & Associates

◄ Effectively the inside of this American Alligator's mouth is outside its body and as much in touch with its surroundings as the skin. Only when food passes the flap at the back of the mouth does it enter the alligator's "internal environment."

## RESPIRATION AND CIRCULATION

Crocodilians are adapted to breathing in an aquatic environment. The nostrils are located on the tip of an elongated snout and close reflexively against incoming water during dives. Like mammals crocodilians have a well-developed secondary palate made up of maxillary, palatine, and pterygoid bones meeting in the roof of the mouth. The nasal passages extend above the secondary palate, opening directly into the throat behind a valve formed by a fleshy fold at the back of the palate meeting with a similar fold on the tongue. This separates water from inspired air, allowing the crocodile to breathe while submerged (except for the nares) or while holding prey.

Crocodilian lungs have numerous large chambers, each filled with many smaller individual chambers, giving these advanced reptilian lungs a spongy appearance due to pockets of trapped air. The lungs are filled by suction as the trunk muscles raise the ribs, expanding the body cavity. As the air pressure in the cavity around the lung decreases, atmospheric pressure inflates the lungs. Crocodilians have a counterpart to the mammalian diaphragm — a muscular septum separating the lung cavity from the peritoneal cavity. This system provides for more efficient lung ventilation.

Unlike other living reptiles the crocodilian has four chambers in the heart, as in mammals. A septum completely divides the ventricle, separating the flow of oxygenated from deoxygenated blood within the heart. Some mixing of blood occurs when the arteries carrying oxygenated blood from the left ventricle "communicate" with arteries from the right

ventricle via the foramen of Panizza.

Crocodilians can adjust their peripheral circulation in response to temperature, movement, diving, or fear. Obviously an increase in peripheral blood flow would be an advantage to an animal heating up for it would maximize heat transfer from the exterior to the body core; a decrease in peripheral blood flow would reduce heat loss in cool periods. Crocodiles may decrease peripheral circulation during diving, which would reduce blood flow to muscles while maintaining

▼ Unique among reptiles, the crocodilian four-chambered heart enhances the efficiency of blood circulation by separating oxygenated blood from deoxygenated blood, though the foramen of Panizza permits some mixing. During a dive, blood flow to the pulmonary arteries is reduced and the foramen of Panizza closes. Thus the brain and heart continue to receive oxygenated blood while deoxygenated blood goes to less vital organs such as the stomach, liver and intestines.

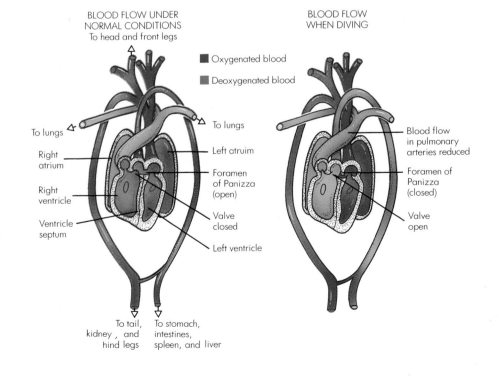

BLOOD FLOW UNDER NORMAL CONDITIONS
To head and front legs

■ Oxygenated blood
■ Deoxygenated blood

BLOOD FLOW WHEN DIVING

To lungs

To lungs

Right atrium

Right ventricle

Ventricle septum

Left atruim

Foramen of Panizza (open)

Valve closed

Left ventricle

Blood flow in pulmonary arteries reduced

Foramen of Panizza (closed)

Valve open

To tail, kidney, and hind legs

To stomach, intestines, spleen, and liver

an oxygenated blood supply for the heart and brain. (Unfortunately, human disturbance can cause some of the same symptoms so interpretation of observations can be difficult if controls for investigators' activities are not incorporated.)

Crocodilians have two main physiological responses for adjusting peripheral blood flow. They can speed up (tachycardia) or slow down (bradycardia) their heart rate, and/or they can widen (vasodilate) or narrow (vasoconstrict) their blood vessels. By using these responses in combination crocodilians can effectively control the flow of blood and, consequently, oxygen and heat to different portions of the body.

### THERMOREGULATION

Crocodilians are poikilothermic, that is, they rely on external sources of heat to raise their body temperatures. Body temperature depends upon heat exchange between an animal and its environment, and is strongly influenced by solar radiation and conduction in water. Water can be used both as a source of heat during periods of low temperature and as a heat sink when the animal is too warm. Large crocodilians are influenced only slightly by ambient air temperatures. However, as body size decreases body temperature is more dependent on the convective environment.

Thermoregulation (the raising and lowering of body temperature) of crocodilians is determined primarily by behavior. Thermal selection (choosing temperature regimes to regulate temperatures) is a complex behavioral process that varies among

different species of crocodilians, especially those with temperate and tropical ranges, and is also a function of a number of influences on individual animals. Size, sex, feeding activity, health, and social behavior all influence thermal behavior. In addition to behavior, physiological mechanisms can influence body temperature by altering heat production and heat flow within the body, as well as heat exchange between an animal and its environment. The effect of metabolic heat production on body temperature is negligible for small animals but may be significant in large ones. Heat flow within a body can be influenced by shunting blood between different areas of the body. Various organs have different heating rates and cardiovascular changes can affect heating and cooling rates on a regional basis. The osteoderms of at least some species of crocodilians have many blood vessels, which may influence the gain or loss of heat. Mouth gaping may also serve to alter the rate of heat exchange in the head versus the body by exposing moist membranes in the mouth and cheek area to increased evaporative cooling.

Specific heat-seeking and heat-avoiding behaviors on land and in water are the primary methods of regulating body temperatures in crocodilians. The significant differences in the thermal behavior of different species result in correspondingly different body temperatures. Perhaps the most striking difference is in the thermal selection of temperate alligators compared with species occurring in tropical areas.

▼ The cool waters of a shallow stream help carry excess heat away from this Nile Crocodile. Behavior is the main means by which crocodilians regulate their body temperature.

Heather Angel/Biofotos

For example, alligators seek heat in the morning by moving onto land to bask and in the afternoon by exposing portions of their backs while in the water. They maintain a more or less constant body temperature during the day and move into the water at night. Since water cools more slowly than land areas the body temperature of alligators drops slowly during the night until basking is again initiated in the morning. During winter months they extend the amount of basking time during sunny days, remaining in the water on cloudy days when solar radiation is reduced. The behavior of tropical species is characterized more by thermal avoidance than heat seeking. Indopacific Crocodiles (*Crocodylus porosus*) surface in the water in the early morning for a brief period then submerge and remain submerged for most of the day. To aid in cooling they move onto land at night. In winter Indopacific Crocodiles and Common Caimans (*Caiman crocodilus*) spend

more time basking during the day. Common Caimans and American Crocodiles (*Crocodylus acutus*) will continue to bask in winter even when air temperatures are lower than water temperatures. A consequence of these different thermal behaviors is that tropical species have lower and more variable body temperatures than temperate species.

Contrary to many published reports, crocodilians do not survive cold winter temperatures by hibernating. Most species remain active during the warmer periods of winter and only alligators are regularly exposed to freezing temperatures. Many investigators from Louisiana, and North and South Carolina have observed a unique behavioral adaptation for surviving freezing conditions. When severe cold fronts approach, alligators take up a submerged breathing posture in shallow water with only their nostrils above the surface.

▲ Although crocodilians are poikilothermic — their blood temperature varies with their surroundings — they maintain their body temperatures within a narrow range by behavioral means, moving from warm to cool environments (or vice versa) without losing opportunities for rest, hunting, or social interaction.

# OUT IN THE COLD

I. LEHR BRISBIN, JR.

Alligators in the ice and snow? The idea sounds preposterous and yet the ranges of both the American and Chinese alligators extend northward into parts of the temperate zone where several hard freezes may occur each year, along with the formation of temporary ice cover and even an occasional snowfall. Studies of the ways in which alligators have adapted to these brief but challenging cold-weather conditions are of particular interest with regard to the possible role of prehistoric climatic change and lowered environmental temperatures as a factor in the demise of other large archosaurian reptiles.

Laboratory studies of seasonal changes in alligator physiology have shown that, while these animals tend to show reduced blood-glucose levels and little or no appetite during the winter months, they will become active during this period whenever temperatures are high enough, and there is no seasonal change in metabolic rate. Alligators are therefore not true hibernators even though, like all poikilothermic reptiles they will become inactive and enter a dormant state whenever their body temperatures drop below levels required to sustain normal activity.

Radiotelemetric studies of free-ranging adult alligators faced with brief periods of cold winter weather, with air temperatures sometimes falling as low as − 3.1° C (26.5° F), have found, surprisingly, that in no case did any of these animals ever seek shelter in either underwater or subterranean dens as had been previously assumed. Rather, with the approach of the cold spell, these alligators consistently sought out shallow backwaters where they could position their nostrils in such a way as to keep a small round breathing hole open in the ice that was forming above them. Often the tail and rear body parts of the larger adults extended into deeper and warmer waters further from shore but in all cases it seemed essential for them to maintain the tip of the snout beneath the breathing hole in the ice, which in some cases was up to 1.5 centimeters (0.6 inches) thick. Since these alligators, unlike many turtles, frogs, and other amphibians, are apparently unable to drop their metabolic rates low enough to exist on anaerobic respiration alone, maintaining constant contact with an open breathing hole would seem to be essential. Indeed, in one case where the breathing hole did eventually freeze over, the alligator was later found to have died. Some wild and captive alligators have even been found with their snouts frozen into the ice; the animal being unable to pull itself loose! However, as long as the nostrils remained above the surface and open, the alligators survived with no ill effects when the ice subsequently thawed. Temperature-sensing probes implanted in radio-collared wild animals have recorded core body temperatures as low as 5° C (41° F) during cold spells, with full recovery later.

Although smaller juvenile alligators apparently need the shelter of their mother's den to protect them from the cold, at least during their first winter, larger adults can apparently survive the brief periods of relatively intense cold encountered in the northern portions of their range. They survive by capitalizing on the thermal inertia inherent in their large body masses combined with microhabitat selection and the use of very specific and effective means of behavioral thermoregulation.

Ice layer

Mud substrate

Deeper, warmer water

Bill Green

◀ Mud is as good a buffer against extremes in environmental temperatures as water. Being in mud probably prevents the crocodilian from overheating, while also keeping parasites and insects at bay.

External and internal factors modify crocodilian thermoregulation. Circadian rhythms, climatic conditions, social interactions, and reproductive state all influence thermal behavior. Selected body temperatures are affected by nutritional status, age, health, social context, and the temperature of incubation for a particular animal. Crocodilians move between land and water in response to light-dark cycles as well as to seasonal differences in temperatures. Larger animals exert social dominance over smaller animals and may keep them from areas with preferred temperature regimes. A variety of behaviors associated with reproduction, especially courtship and nesting, may also take precedence over thermal behaviors.

Thermophily (heat seeking) following feeding occurs in all species of crocodilians tested but occurs less often in tropical genera such as *Crocodylus* and *Caiman* than in the more temperate *Alligator*. Elevated body temperatures following feeding increase the rate of digestion (passage of food through the digestive system) and the rate of protein breakdown and absorption. However, in other reptiles, and possibly in crocodilians too, digestive efficiency (the amount of energy extracted from food) does not change over a wide range of temperatures. The main benefit of thermophily appears to be reduced time required for digestion. This results in increased feeding (if food is available) and more time for other activities such as predator avoidance and social behaviors. The selection of lower temperatures when not feeding reduces the energy required for basic maintenance and therefore maximizes net energy gain.

Studies of crocodilians in natural settings indicate that the body temperatures of juveniles and adults do not differ, in spite of size-related differences in heat exchange with the environment and heat transport within the body. This underscores the importance that behavioral thermal selection plays in thermoregulation. However, an initial period of thermophily may be characteristic of hatchling crocodilians. Here thermophily may facilitate digestion of residual yolk stores, promoting growth and enhancing survival.

Birds and mammals, when infected by pathogens, frequently develop fevers that are fueled by internal metabolic heat production. Recent research has shown that poikilotherms are also capable of developing "behavioral" fevers in response to infections, and that these fevers enhance survival. Jeff Lang of the University of North Dakota has demonstrated experimentally that American Alligators (*Alligator mississippiensis*) respond to infection by developing a behavioral fever. Alligators free to thermoregulate in land-water temperature gradients were more able to resist infection. As this is similar to responses of other reptiles, most crocodilians probably respond in a similar manner.

Incubation temperatures of reptilian eggs affect embryonic growth and development and, in some cases (especially crocodilians and turtles), actually determine the sex of the individual. In addition, thermal imprinting during development may affect physiology and behavior of hatchlings — hatchling alligators incubated at higher temperatures apparently select higher body temperatures, although how this occurs and whether alligators are unique in this aspect is unknown.

Jean-Paul Ferrero/Auscape International

▲ The Indopacific Crocodile is adapted to life in a marine environment by having, like all crocodilians, thick skin that prevents loss of fluids and kidneys that concentrate nitrogenous wastes into uric acid. It also has special salt glands in the tongue (as do some freshwater species) that excrete excess salt.

## OSMOREGULATION

The most important feature of crocodilian osmoregulation (maintenance of salt and water balance) is the semi-aquatic nature of living species. Crocodilians dwell primarily in freshwater habitats, with even the most aquatic species spending considerable time on land basking. Two species — Indopacific and American crocodiles — can be considered estuarine specialists but no species can be considered truly marine.

Crocodilians osmoregulate in a manner similar to other aquatic reptiles and maintain salt concentrations in the body fluid at a level typical of other vertebrates (about one-third that of sea water). However, the divergence of habitat use (from fresh water to estuarine) results in different strategies being employed to maintain salt and water balance. Another, probably equally important aspect of crocodilian osmoregulation, is the exposure of some species to periodic droughts. The physiological consequences of dehydrating conditions are little known but must be considerable.

The osmoregulatory problems posed by life in fresh or saline waters are related to the amounts of water and salts exchanged across various body surfaces. In crocodilians, potential routes of intake of water and salts are drinking without feeding,

drinking incidental to feeding, feeding, and through the skin and mouth lining. Loss of salts and water occurs in feces and urine, through respiration, excretion from salt glands in the tongue, and through the skin. The relative importance of each route varies with external salinity, permeability of different membranes, and differences in behavior among species. For example, estuarine-adapted Indopacific and American crocodiles will not drink sea water, even when dehydrated, while the more freshwater-adapted American Alligator and Morelet's Crocodile (*Crocodylus moreletii*) will. This greatly increases the amount of sodium influx and has led to death in some laboratory animals.

Although crocodilians are primarily found in freshwater environments, relatively little is known about how salt and water balance is obtained by crocodilians while submerged in fresh water. The alligator is by far the best-studied species and some information is available on Indopacific and American crocodiles. Plasma concentration of ions in crocodilians in fresh water resembles that of other freshwater reptiles. These animals face the classic problem of hyper-osmoregulation (maintenance of a body-fluid composition far above that of the surrounding environment) and to overcome this they would be expected to

# VARIATIONS IN DORSAL ARMOR

FRANKLIN D. ROSS

Many of the early archosaurian ancestors of crocodilians possessed mid-dorsal bony armor in the skin immediately overlying the vertebral column. Fossils of the earliest crocodilian group, the Protosuchia, dating from the Late Triassic or Early Jurassic, have paired rectangular bony plates straddling the vertebrae and joined on the midline. Each pair has downturned and slightly rounded lateral edges and, from small elements immediately behind the head, the scute pairs broaden to a parallel-sided series extending for most of the neck, all of the body, and much of the tail before narrowing to very small pairs posteriorly. The function of this narrow dorsal armor is not known for certain but it may have been supportive, strengthening the relatively weak protosuchian vertebral column for walking on dry land.

In the Mesosuchia, a largely aquatic group of crocodilians preceding the Eusuchia or "modern" crocodilians, the first few rows of dorsal armor immediately behind the skull were reduced or deleted to allow the flexibility required to toss the head back and get the mouth up out of the water when swallowing. Mesosuchians kept the protosuchian one-to-one ratio between transverse osteoderm rows and underlying vertebrae but often possessed wider midbody armor, sometimes with big bony points at the lateral ends with interlocking pin-and-socket articulations and rows extending laterally with more than two scutes. This broad, studded, and sturdy armor was defensive but was also probably an aid in thermoregulation, acting as a solar collector enabling many blood capillaries to get close to the surface safely in order to absorb energy.

In modern crocodilians there are species with extensive and heavily ossified armor and other species that have reduced scute size or number (or both) to make them less bony and buoyant, less protectively armored but also more flexible. Some species combine pairs of transverse rows on the neck into special elements of a cervical shield and sometimes a space of bare skin, due to the deletion of transverse scale rows, occurs at the base of the neck and over the shoulders, making the dorsal armor discontinuous. Occasionally, minor left-right asymmetries occur in the dorsal armor, probably caused by embryonic curvature inside the egg. Crocodilians with moderate to broad snouts and differentiation in tooth size tend to be more lightly armored and more defensively flexible than narrow-snouted species like the Gharial (*Gavialis gangeticus*) and the False Gharial (*Tomistoma schlegelii*), which primarily eat fish and tend to have all their mature teeth more or less the same size.

The Gharial has unusual dorsal armor for a modern crocodilian because it has the same number of scales across in the two pelvic rows as it does at midbody, over the shoulders, and on the posterior part of the neck — six in very young Gharials and four in adults. This loss of two scale rows, the lateral one on each side, is unique among living crocodilians. Most living species retain the same number of scales during their lives — typically four scutes across in the two pelvic rows, from six to eight across at midbody, from none to four in a narrowed shoulder and base of neck juncture, together with compounding of scale rows in the nape and neck regions.

The most reduced nape and neck armor occurs in American and Indopacific crocodiles, the two salt-water tolerant species with oceanic distributions. The most extensive dorsal armor occurs in the Common Caiman and the Black Caiman (*Melanosuchus niger*), where as many as 12 scutes may occur in a transverse row at midbody, and to a slightly lesser degree in the dwarf caimans (genus *Paleosuchus*), the Dwarf Crocodile (*Osteolaemus tetraspis*), and the Chinese Alligator (*Alligator sinensis*) where heavy ossification and extensive contact and overlap of plates create a rigid and formidable armor on the back and neck. In the dwarf caimans and the Dwarf Crocodile there are as few as 11 double-crested transverse tail rows before the single-crested caudals (of the tail) commence. Most species have 14 or 17–19 double-crested caudal rows.

▼ The Black Caiman (left) has body armor almost unparalleled among living crocodilians with each of the dark scales on its back and neck being as thick and as tough as the heel of a boot. The Indopacific Crocodile (right), normally lacks the series of ossified scales, immediately behind the head, found in other crocodilians.

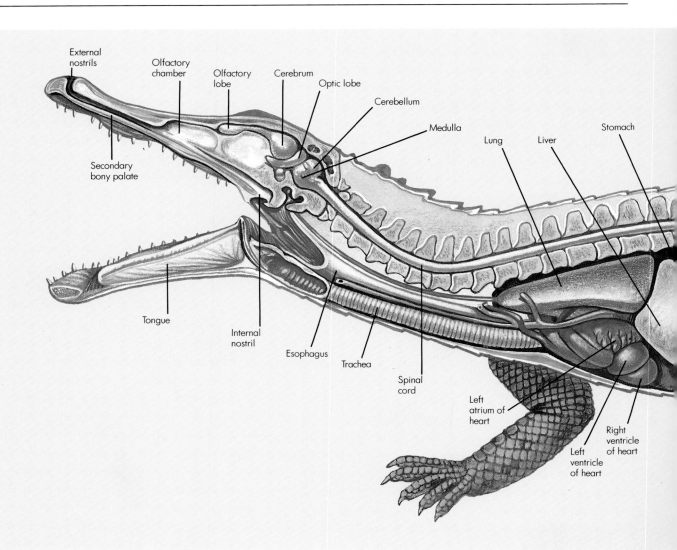

External
nostrils

Olfactory
chamber

Olfactory
lobe

Cerebrum

Optic lobe

Cerebellum

Medulla

Lung

Liver

Stomach

Secondary
bony palate

Tongue

Internal
nostril

Esophagus

Trachea

Spinal
cord

Left
atrium of
heart

Left
ventricle
of heart

Right
ventricle
of heart

▲ Crocodilian anatomy is an intriguing combination of reptilian and mammalian or avian characteristics. Crocodilians have an advanced hard palate, a complex, bird-like brain, a four-chambered heart and an efficient respiratory system but they have no bladder and a relatively unmodified reptilian digestive system. Crocodilian teeth are designed for seizing and holding prey, not chewing, so the stomach is in two parts—a muscular gizzard that grinds food and a digestive section.

possess mechanisms for conservation of solutes (such as sodium) and excretion of excess water.

Loss of sodium from crocodilians in fresh water is fairly low and there is some evidence that sodium conservation in renal/cloacal excretory processes is fairly effective and that the main route of sodium loss is through the skin. However, it appears that crocodilians are less efficient or specialized in conservation of sodium in fresh water than are turtles. Certainly there is no evidence of the active sodium uptake that occurs in some species of freshwater turtles.

In contrast to the relatively small amount of sodium loss from crocodilians, water loss while submerged in fresh water is substantial. Variation in water loss is considerable but does not seem to be related to external salinity. A large proportion of water turnover occurs through the skin, with the oral membranes being much more permeable than the epidermis. Interestingly the skin of alligators is considerably less permeable than that of many freshwater reptiles but is similar to that of the amphibious water moccasin; this probably reflects the great amount of time spent on land by crocodilians.

On land evaporative water loss occurs not

only from the respiratory tract but also from the skin and mouth. Detailed studies of evaporative water loss in alligators show that rates of water loss were directly related to temperature and inversely related to body size. The rate of evaporative water loss comes somewhere between that of aquatic and terrestrial reptiles; again emphasizing the amphibious nature of crocodilians.

The kidney and cloaca have minor roles in sodium chloride excretion but they are the primary route of excretion of nitrogenous wastes. Hydrated crocodilians excrete nitrogen primarily as ammonium bicarbonate; in dehydrated crocodilians uric acid becomes the primary means of nitrogen excretion. Apparently the kidneys themselves do not markedly regulate water and salt output but a regulation of water and salt absorption does occur in the cloaca. Sodium chloride is almost completely absorbed in the cloaca of hydrated American Crocodiles but is less completely absorbed after salt loading. This process may be important in terrestrial reptiles faced with periodic droughts.

The ability of crocodilians to tolerate salt water is related to their low rate of water loss (compared with other aquatic reptiles), their low

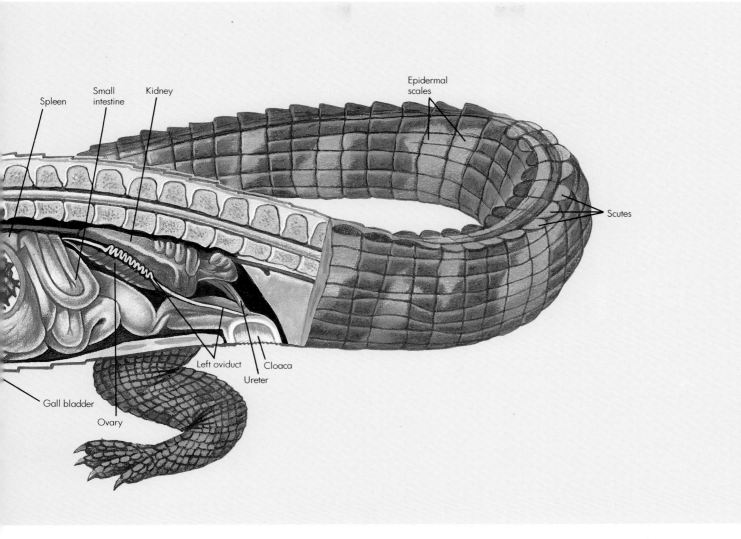

Spleen

Small intestine

Kidney

Epidermal scales

Scutes

Gall bladder

Ovary

Left oviduct

Ureter

Cloaca

rate of sodium uptake, their ability to excrete excess sodium, and their ability to osmoregulate behaviorally by not drinking saline water or by seeking fresh water after feeding in saline areas. As in thermoregulation, the ability of an animal to regulate its internal state in the face of fluctuating environmental conditions is a result of behavioral and physiological adaptations.

The most significant finding concerning how crocodilians are able to osmoregulate in saline water has been the discovery, by Gordon Grigg and Laurence Taplin at the University of Sydney, of salt glands in the tongues of crocodiles and their absence in the tongues of alligators and caimans. The ability of alligators to survive for considerable periods in saline water, as they do for example in the lower Florida Keys, is probably due to low rates of water loss and sodium uptake but is limited by their inability to excrete excess sodium. Importantly, hatchling crocodilians of all species are considerably less tolerant of exposure to salt water than even slightly larger juveniles, probably because the ratio of surface area to volume is so much greater in a small crocodilian and it takes considerable energy to excrete salt.

An interesting question is why do inland

species of the genus *Crocodylus* have salt glands if these are not used primarily as an adaptation for osmoregulation in salt water? The presence of salt glands in the tongue may function to eliminate excess salt accumulated during periods of prolonged exposure to a dry environment.

▼ Crocodilian body structure has changed relatively little over the past 200 million years. It comprises internal (below) and external elements — the dorsal armor (bony buttons or plates embedded in the skin) forms the external skeleton.

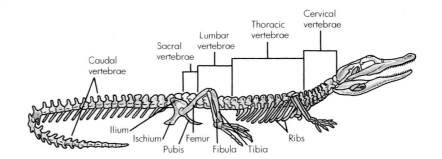

Cervical vertebrae

Thoracic vertebrae

Lumbar vertebrae

Sacral vertebrae

Caudal vertebrae

Ilium

Ischium

Pubis

Femur

Fibula

Tibia

Ribs

▶ The eye of an Indopacific Crocodile scans the horizon, its pupil a mere slit in the bright daylight. At night, the pupil can be almost round, maximizing light reception and giving the crocodile a visual acuity comparable to that of an owl.

David P. Maitland/Seaphot Limited Planet Earth Pictures/ Transglobe Agency

## THE SENSES

Crocodilians have a small but complex brain. The outer covering or cortex of the cerebrum contains nerve endings for intelligence or learning. The cerebrum also controls the senses and voluntary actions. The cerebellum controls the involuntary actions of muscular balance and coordination. The medulla controls the activity of internal organs and glands. The olfactory lobe is for the sense of smell and the optic lobe for the sense of sight.

Unlike other senses, which respond to physical stimuli, taste and smell are responses to chemical stimuli. The sense of smell in crocodilians is well developed. Olfactory nerve endings lie in nasal cavities that open into paired nostrils placed on top near the front tip of the upper jaw. A chemosensory organ in the roof of the mouth present in other reptiles is much reduced in crocodilians. In laboratory experiments juvenile alligators responded to airborne odors from the cloacal gland secretions of adult males. The role of glandular secretion in the biology of alligators in the wild is unknown and awaits further study.

Crocodilians have a fine sense of hearing and quite a variety of acoustic behaviors. They have external ear openings covered with a movable flap to reduce water intrusion during diving. The inner ear is well developed, and hearing is accomplished by a very thin rod (stapes) that extends from the inner ear to the eardrum (tympanum). Crocodilians vocalize (or respond to vocalizations) in a variety of contexts. Adults of some species bellow during the courtship season, larger animals hiss or snarl warnings at intruders, and smaller ones bark "distress calls" to adults. Tape recordings of hatchling crocodiles still in eggs have been used to elicit nest-opening behavior by adults attending nests. Adult crocodilians will also charge humans holding a vocalizing hatchling.

Crocodilians have typical vertebrate eyes with a rigid, spherical eyeball enclosing the light-responsive retina. The eyes are set laterally on the top of the head and are more prominent in alligators and caimans than in crocodiles. The eyes have a vertical pupil that can open wider at night to allow more light to enter than would be possible in a round pupil. An additional adaptation is the reflective layer (tapetum lucidum) that lies behind the retina. The cells of the tapetum contain guanin crystals, which form a mirror-like layer reflecting most of the incoming light back through the light-receptor cells of the eye (producing the characteristic yellow-orange-red eyeshine familiar to nighttime crocodile observers). Light receptors include both cones and the more numerous rods so presumably crocodilians can see colors. Crocodilians have well-developed movable eyelids and a transparent third eyelid called a nictitating membrane. Although covering the eye while the crocodilian is submerged the nictitating membrane does not allow the eye to focus underwater. Crocodilians apparently use vision to capture prey above the surface of the water but must rely on other sensory cues underwater.

▶ Through its flared nostrils an American Alligator can detect the numerous chemical signals in its environment. The sense of smell is difficult for researchers to study but is one of the means by which crocodilians detect prey and plays a part in reproduction.

Raymond A. Mendez/Animals Animals

# TOOTH REPLACEMENT IN CROCODILIANS

HANS-DIETER SUES

The teeth of living crocodilians have essentially conical crowns that are often separated from the cylindrical root by a slight constriction. The crowns are typically pointed and have thick walls. Each tooth is set in a deep socket in the jawbone and is held in place by non-calcified connective tissue. The dentition is usually more or less isodont, that is, all of the teeth are very similar in size and shape.

Radiographic studies on live American Alligators by the Canadian paleontologist A. Gordon Edmund have documented a lifespan of up to two years for an individual tooth, about half of which is spent in the functional position. Teeth at the front of the snout are apparently replaced more frequently than those closer to the back of the tooth row.

Replacement teeth develop from germinal material in a shallow pocket in the tooth socket on the tongue side of the functional tooth. In the early stages of development, each replacing tooth migrates through a hole in the cylindrical base of the old tooth so as to become situated within the pulp cavity of the latter where the new tooth crown matures to full size. As the replacing tooth approaches maturity, the remnants of the root of the old tooth become resorbed and its crown is eventually lost.

Replacement in young crocodilians proceeds in a pattern of "waves" that pass along alternately numbered teeth from back to front. Later in life, the direction of replacement is reversed. Edmund's work indicates that the regularity of tooth replacement decreases with advancing age. Neighboring teeth in a given tooth row are almost invariably in opposite phases of the replacement cycle.

The multiple episodes of tooth replacement in crocodilians and other non-mammalian vertebrates are thus clearly distinct from tooth replacement in mammals, which only have a deciduous ("milk") and a permanent dentition. The mammalian pattern of tooth replacement may have been an evolutionary consequence of the fact that opposing teeth in the upper and lower jaws of mammals meet in precise contact (occlusion). Recurrent tooth replacement would result in the addition of teeth larger than their precursors as the individual grows and would therefore disrupt occlusion.

David McGonigal/Photobank

Socket Line

Front of jaw

Back of jaw

Shed tooth

Functional tooth

Successional tooth

Dentine

Functional tooth

Successional tooth

Tooth socket

▲ All the teeth of this Indopacific Crocodile are intact and the staining around those at the front probably indicates the presence of leaves and therefore tannins in the water. The largest teeth in the bottom jaw (the fourth on each side) fit into a notch visible on the side of the top jaw — one of the major differences between crocodiles and alligators.

Tooth replacement in crocodilians occurs in ▲◄ "waves" with alternate (neighboring) teeth being replaced in separate waves. In a single wave (above) the functional teeth that sit high on raised bases will shortly be shed although the smaller successional teeth within the jaw have not yet erupted. The successional tooth, attached to dental lamina, moves through a hole in the base of the functional tooth (left) to mature to full size. The dentine of both teeth is shown by black and white bands.

# LIVING CROCODILIANS

CHARLES A. ROSS and WILLIAM ERNEST MAGNUSSON

Living crocodilians are found throughout the tropical and subtropical regions of the world wherever suitable habitat exists. The genus *Alligator* is, however, found in the warmer parts of the southern temperate region of North America and China.

Crocodilians are normally divided into three basic groups considered as subfamilies by most taxonomists. (Some recent research, supported by biochemical, physiological, and paleontological data conflicts with this approach but, for the time being, is inconclusive.)

The subfamily Alligatorinae includes four genera that have surviving species: *Alligator,* which contains the two species of true alligators; *Caiman,* consisting of several poorly defined species; *Paleosuchus,* with two species of dwarf caimans, and *Melanosuchus,* the Black Caiman. The subfamily Crocodylinae is split into three genera with surviving species: *Crocodylus,* the true crocodiles; *Osteolaemus,* the Dwarf Crocodile, and *Tomistoma,* the False Gharial. (Whether *Tomistoma* and *Osteolaemus* belong in this group has been questioned; the Dwarf Crocodile, for example, shares several distinctive characteristics with some of the caimans.) The third subfamily, Gavialinae, contains only one genus with one surviving species, the Gharial (*Gavialis gangeticus*).

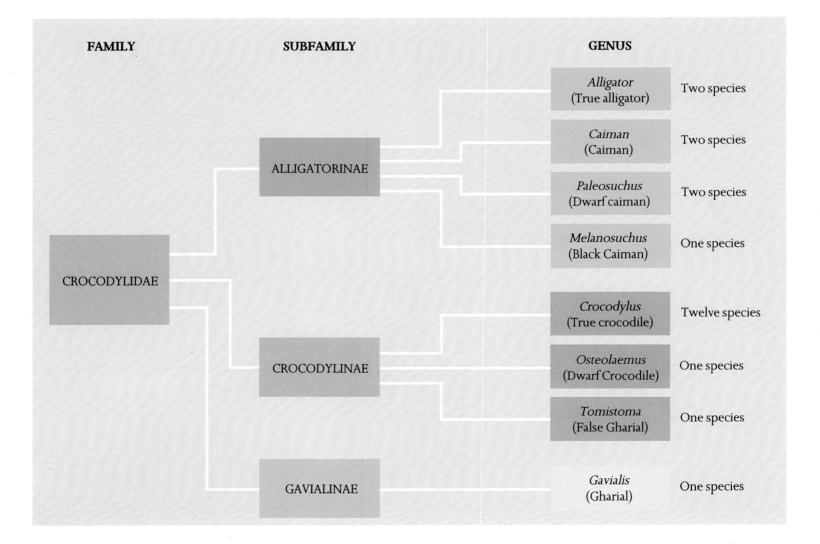

# SUBFAMILY ALLIGATORINAE

Living alligatorines are differentiated from other crocodilians by a combination of characteristics. The nasal bones extend forward to meet the premaxillary bones. There is a very short mandibular symphysis (the junction of the two mandibles or lower jaws as measured by how many teeth long the junction of the lower jaws are). The teeth of the lower jaw (mandibular teeth) are accommodated into pits in the upper jaw so that, when the mouth is closed, no mandibular teeth are visible. The ventral scales lack sensor pits.

**Black Caiman**
*Melanosuchus niger*

APPEARANCE Closely related to the Common Caiman and Broad-snouted Caiman but in general form it closely resembles the American Alligator. Unlike most crocodilians, which may be vividly marked as hatchlings but soon assume the drab colors of adults, the Black Caiman remains distinctively marked throughout life. Hatchlings have light gray heads and black bodies patterned with lines of white dots. As they grow, the gray on the head becomes brown and the lines of white dots may fade but even adults over 5 meters (16 feet) in length are more colorful than the hatchlings of most other species.
SIZE Attains lengths of over 6 meters (almost 20 feet), making it the largest predator on the South American continent.
HABITAT Adults are now most commonly found in the flooded forests around lakes and slow-flowing rivers, though juveniles are sometimes found around floating grass mats. Before extensive hunting for skins, the species was encountered frequently around open beaches and other habitats in which it is now rarely seen.

DISTRIBUTION Occurs throughout the Amazon basin and the coastal rivers of the Brazilian state of Amapa, French Guiana, and possibly Guyana but, strangely, has not been reported from Surinam. The well-defined distribution indicates very specific habitat requirements, poor dispersal ability, or both.
REPRODUCTION No reliable data on sizes of reproductive individuals but sizes at first reproduction are probably similar to those of the American Alligator. Mound nests are similar to those of the Common Caiman but may be much larger.
DIET Data on diet is limited but indicates that very small Black Caimans eat invertebrates and snails, larger individuals eat fish, and the largest Black Caimans include mammals, reptiles, and even other species of caiman in their diets. Although it is the only caiman that is regarded as dangerous to humans and domestic livestock, attacks are few as, like the American Alligator, it usually prefers other prey. It has certainly never attained the "man-eating" reputation of some of the similar-sized crocodiles.

## Chinese Alligator
*Alligator sinensis*

APPEARANCE Chinese Alligators differ from American Alligators in many subtle ways. In the Chinese Alligator the eyelids have a bony plate, which is absent in the American Alligator. The head is more robust and the snout is slightly upturned and tapered. The ventral scales of Chinese Alligators have osteoderms, which are occasionally found in large American Alligators. In coloration, juvenile Chinese Alligators are similar to American Alligators but have fewer yellow crossbands on the tail and body.

SIZE A smaller species than the American Alligator, early Chinese literature (going back to the seventh century B.C.) records lengths of up to 3 meters (almost 10 feet) but the largest specimens in accessible museum collections are less than 2 meters (6.5 feet) in total length.

HABITAT Found in marshland, ponds, and lakes, Chinese Alligators are known to make extensive use of caves or burrows, particularly during the colder and drier months (October–March) when they are dormant.

DISTRIBUTION Very restricted in distribution, it is known only from the lower Yangtze River and its tributaries. Distribution in the past was probably wider than it is today as suitable habitat was more extensive before pressure from agriculture and development.

REPRODUCTION The natural history is poorly known. It possibly comes out of hibernation in April, with courtship and copulation in June, and egg laying in July. Descriptions of the nest vary and early reports that the eggs are laid in a depression and hatch by the heat of the sun are probably in error. In a breeding program initiated at Rockefeller Wildlife Refuge in Louisiana, the Chinese Alligators built mound nests of vegetation similar to, but slightly smaller than, nests of American Alligators at the same locality. In other respects too, the reproductive biology of the two species appeared similar although clutch size is smaller for Chinese Alligators.

DIET Reported to eat snails, clams, rats, and insects. The teeth of adult Chinese Alligators suggest that this species is adapted to crushing hard objects. It is a relatively timid and inoffensive species of no danger to humans.

## American Alligator
*Alligator mississippiensis*

APPEARANCE Juvenile American Alligators are black with 10–11 narrow yellow crossbands on the tail and 4–5 on the body. As they grow larger the crossbands fade and, in adults, are rarely visible on the body. The eyes are normally silverish in color. The snout is moderately long and wide, generally uniform in width, with a bony nasal bridge. Some of the characteristics that vary among individuals are the presence or absence of bony plates or buttons (osteoderms) in the thoracic or ventral scales, the shape of the snout, and the massiveness of the skull.

SIZE American Alligators of 5–6 meters (16–20 feet) have been recorded in the past but today an adult male of 4 meters (13 feet) is considered large.

HABITAT Although a palustrine crocodilian, well adapted for marsh and swamplands, it occupies all available aquatic habitats from marshes and swamps to rivers, lakes, tidal areas, and, on rare occasions, the ocean.

DISTRIBUTION Found only in the United States along the Atlantic coastal plain from the border area of Virginia and North Carolina south through southern Florida and west to the Rio Grande in eastern Texas. It follows the Mississippi River drainage north to southern Arkansas and McCurtain County, Oklahoma. Human alteration of habitat in parts of Texas seems to be increasing the range of this species by providing water holes for cattle, which are utilized by American Alligators.

REPRODUCTION A mound nester with an average clutch size of about 45 eggs, mean hatchling length is 22 centimeters (9 inches). Parental care has recently been documented.

DIET American Alligators, like all crocodilians, are carnivorous. Hatchings, juveniles, and adults will eat a variety of insects. As they grow larger, snakes, turtles, snails, slow-moving fish, small mammals, and birds are included in their diet. Large adults sometimes take small calves and, very occasionally, people.

## Cuvier's Dwarf Caiman
*Paleosuchus palpebrosus*

APPEARANCE Differs from Schneider's Dwarf Caiman in that the snout is short and the skull high, smooth, and dog-like; the only crocodilian to have this head shape. The dorsal scutes are not as prominent as in Schneider's Dwarf Caiman and the double tail scutes are small and project vertically.

SIZE The smallest New World crocodilian, males reach about 1.5 meters (5 feet) and females about 1.2 meters (4 feet).

HABITAT This species seems to have fairly strict habitat requirements. In the Amazon system, it occurs in flooded forests around major lakes but does not penetrate far into streams under closed-canopy rainforest and is relatively rare in open grassy areas unless the banks are steep. It inhabits gallery forest along small savanna streams in the north and south of its distribution but does not occur in the llanos or the pantanal. Subadults are often found in isolated temporary water bodies and this species probably engages in a lot of terrestrial activity.

DISTRIBUTION Second only to the Common Caiman in its geographic range, Cuvier's Dwarf Caiman is found throughout the Orinoco, Amazon, and São Francisco river basins, and the upper reaches of the Paraná and Paraguay river systems. It is rarely found in high densities.

REPRODUCTION Mound nests have been found in areas near flooded forests and in savanna gallery forest but virtually nothing is known of the reproduction of this species in the wild.

DIET Limited data indicates that the species eats invertebrates and fish but it is an enigma as to why it has a dog-like skull.

## Schneider's Dwarf Caiman
*Paleosuchus trigonatus*

APPEARANCE The dwarf caimans of the genus *Paleosuchus* form a distinct offshoot from the rest of the caimans. Some of their physical characteristics may be adaptations for life in heavily forested areas. They are small, their skins are heavily ossified, and they lack the bony ridge (spectacle) between the orbits seen in all other caimans (hence the alternative common name, smooth-fronted caimans). Dwarf caimans have relatively short tails and brown eyes. When they walk they often carry the head high with the neck angled upward giving a mammal-like appearance.

Schneider's Dwarf Caiman has a snout that could be considered normal for a crocodilian and, in general, head shape is similar to some individuals of the Common Caiman. The scutes on the neck and tail are large, triangular, and often so sharp that it is difficult to hold a struggling animal. The tail is broad at the base and flattened dorsoventrally, unlike the tails of other crocodilians, which are flattened laterally. The double tail scutes also project laterally, making the tail appear even broader. The tail is so heavily ossified that it shows little of the flexibility seen in other crocodilians.

SIZE Most males do not exceed 1.7 meters (5.5 feet) in total length while females rarely exceed 1.4 meters (4.5 feet). For their size, they are much stronger than most other caimans.

HABITAT Rarely found in open habitats, the typical habitat is small streams in closed-canopy rainforest where mound nests are made.

Individuals rarely bask, even in captivity. The tiny streams, usually covering only the feet and belly of the caiman, offer little protection against predators. Adults spend much of their time away from water and often shelter in hollow logs or under fallen debris more than 50 meters from the stream. By the age of 10–15 years, adults have fixed home ranges extending along 500–1,000 meters of stream.

DISTRIBUTION Occurs in the forested areas of the Amazon basin, the Orinoco basin, Guyana, Surinam, and French Guiana. Considering the densities of this species that have been found along small streams, together with the number of small streams in rainforest habitats and the extent of the Amazonian rainforest, this is probably one of the world's most abundant crocodilians.

REPRODUCTION Most breeding females are about 1.3 meters (4 feet) in length. Nests are made at the end of the dry season and hatching occurs at the start of the rainy season. Most clutches contain 10–15 eggs. Males do not usually defend territories and probably do not breed until they reach 1.4 meters (4.5 feet).

DIET Hatchlings eat many insects but, from a small size, juveniles eat many terrestrial vertebrates such as snakes, birds, and lizards. Adults also eat many mammals such as porcupines and pacas (giant South American rodents). In contrast to other species of crocodilians, Schneider's Dwarf Caiman eats few fish or snails, probably because of its rainforest habitat and semiterrestrial life style.

**Broad-snouted Caiman**
*Caiman latirostris*

APPEARANCE In common with many other swamp-dwelling (palustrine) crocodilians in other parts of the world its head is wide, rounded, and heavy in appearance. Its generally dark coloring with dark blotches on the jaw is similar to that of the subspecies *Caiman crocodilus yacare* and the two have sometimes been confused in accounts of distribution.
SIZE Very large specimens up to 3.5 meters (11.5 feet) have been reported but it is probably rare for males to exceed 3 meters (10 feet) and for females to exceed 2 meters (6.5 feet).
HABITAT Occurs most commonly in shallow freshwater swamps though it is also found in mangroves around the margins of lakes and large rivers. One subspecies is apparently very adaptable, occurring in cattle ponds and heavily polluted rivers near major cities. However, dams, drainage for agricultural and coastal resorts, pollution, and highways have fragmented and degraded most of the former habitat of this subspecies.
DISTRIBUTION Occurs in coastal streams and swamps from the Brazilian state of Rio Grande do Norte south to Uruguay. It occurs inland in the basins of the São Francisco, Doce, Paraíba, Paraná, and Paraguay rivers in Brazil and Argentina.
REPRODUCTION Nests are mounds of vegetation, with 30 – 60 eggs per clutch. Nothing is known of the size or age at sexual maturity.
DIET This species eats insects and crustaceans when small, gradually changing over to water snails, fish, mammals, and birds as it grows.

**Common Caiman**
*Caiman crocodilus*

APPEARANCE *Caiman crocodilus* is the most generalized of the caimans and could easily be mistaken for a small crocodile. There are a number of widely recognized subspecies, differentiated on the basis of size, skull shape, or coloration.
SIZE Most populations do not reach 2.5 meters (8 feet) in length although some individuals exceeding 3 meters (10 feet) have been reported.
HABITAT An extremely adaptable species, it occurs in virtually all natural open habitats such as savannas, swamps, large rivers, and lakes, and readily invades open habitats created by humans such as cattle ponds, dams, and roadside borrow pits. It is probably the only crocodilian in the world that responds so favorably to human habitat modification.
DISTRIBUTION The most widespread species and the only species of caiman to range outside the South American continent, it occurs from southern Mexico south to northern Argentina, near the limit of crocodilian distributions in South America.
REPRODUCTION Common Caimans make mound nests of earth, litter, or fallen vegetation and females, depending on their size, lay 15 – 40 eggs. Most nests are among bushes or trees but some are made in open fields or on floating grass mats.
DIET Smaller individuals eat mainly insects, crabs, and other invertebrates; larger animals eat water snails and fish. Myths that caimans can reduce populations of water snails to the point that the snails cannot act as intermediate hosts for human parasites or that caimans control the numbers of piranha have not been proved. In fact, large populations of caimans usually indicate large populations of snails, and significant numbers of piranhas have not been found among the variety of fishes in caiman diets.

# SUBFAMILY CROCODYLINAE

Living crocodylines are generally unspecialized crocodilians with a moderately tapered snout that is not sharply set off from the posterior part of the skull. As in alligatorines the nasal bones are in contact with the premaxillaries. The lower teeth generally fit into pits in the upper jaw but, unlike alligatorines, the fourth tooth fits into a notch in the upper jaw and is visible when the mouth is closed. Ventral scales have sensory pits.

**Cuban Crocodile**
*Crocodylus rhombifer*

APPEARANCE The most distinctive of the New World *Crocodylus* species, the skull is remarkably short for the elevation of the snout between the eyes and the external nostrils. Elevations at the back of the skull are slightly reminiscent of horns. The flanks of the rear legs have heavily keeled scales unlike any other New World crocodile. Juvenile Cuban Crocodiles are light golden in color with black spotting and irregular black blotches and/or bands on the tail. Adult animals are dark gray or black with golden yellow spotting. The iris of juveniles is light in color but becomes darker in older animals.
SIZE A relatively small species, the Cuban Crocodile grows to 3.5 meters (11.5 feet) although there is a record from the nineteenth century of this species reaching more than 5 meters (16 feet).
HABITAT Presently restricted to pools and channels in interior freshwater areas of swamps.
DISTRIBUTION Restricted in distribution, this species is, as its name implies, found in Cuba, notably in the Zapata swamps and the Isla de la Juventud. In the nineteenth century it was found in the Havana area and west of Havana in Pinar del Rio Province, and there are subfossil remains (800 years old) from Grand Cayman Island. Reports of this species from Cayman Brac and the Archipelago de los Canarreos are as yet unsubstantiated.
REPRODUCTION Very little is known of the natural history of the Cuban Crocodile but it is a hole nester like the American and Orinoco crocodiles. American Crocodile – Cuban Crocodile hybrids have been reported in captivity and in the wild. These individuals share characteristics of both parent species, and some have been described where the hybrid resembles the Cuban Crocodile in coloration and the American Crocodile in skull characteristics. DIET Known to feed on fish, turtles, and small mammals.

## Morelet's Crocodile
*Crocodylus moreletii*

APPEARANCE Normally brown with black spotting and bands on the body and tail, it is generally darker in color than the American Crocodile. The iris is silver to light brown. Adults have a broader snout than similar-sized American Crocodiles and a raised flat promenade running down the nasal bones. The dorsal armor is irregular and the neck scales are heavy.

SIZE A small species that grows to 3–3.5 meters (10 –11.5 feet).

HABITAT A palustrine species, until recently it was thought that Morelet's Crocodile was restricted to ponds, lakes, freshwater marshlands, and the upper freshwater sections of rivers and streams, while the American Crocodile occupied the brackish and saltwater estuarine areas of these rivers. However, populations of Morelet's Crocodiles have recently been found in coastal habitats.

DISTRIBUTION Throughout much of its range — central Tamaulipas, Mexico, south through the Yucatan Peninsula and the interior of Chiapas to central Belize and the Peten region of Guatemala — it is sympatric with the American Crocodile.

REPRODUCTION Builds a mound nest of vegetation. Parental care has been observed and adult animals are known to guard nests. The parental female has been observed to open the nest and carry the eggs to the water, where they are gently crushed open.

DIET Known to feed on snails, mud turtles, small mammals, and catfish. Juveniles eat insects, snails, slugs, and other small animals.

APPEARANCE Juveniles are light in color, normally yellowish tan to gray with dark crossmarkings on the body and tail. As they grow older these markings fade and adult animals are usually olive-brown or tan (some populations or individuals are darker) with or without dark spotting or bands. The iris is normally silverish. Adults have a distinct hump in front of the orbits and irregular, asymmetrical dorsal armor.

SIZE The American Crocodile is known to grow to lengths of 6 meters (20 feet) or more and males are reported to grow larger than females.

HABITAT This species used to be a common resident of coastal habitats, large rivers, and lakes within its range. It is known to be dangerous to humans although authenticated records of attacks are very rare. It shares habitat with other crocodile species and caimans throughout a great part of its range, which has led to some confusion in specific identifications.

DISTRIBUTION This is the only crocodile species widespread in the Americas. It is found in southern Florida (primarily in the Everglades and Florida Keys); the Caribbean islands of Cuba (including Isla de la Juventud), the Caymans (Little Cayman and Cayman Brac), Jamaica, Hispaniola, Martinique, Trinidad, and Margarita; the eastern coast of Mexico from the Bay of Campeche south through the Belize Keys to Venezuela and Colombia. On the west coast it is found from Sinaloa, Mexico, and the Tres Marias Islands south to coastal Ecuador and the Rio Chira in Peru.

REPRODUCTION The American Crocodile makes a hole nest in which to lay eggs. In some instances, where sand or river banks are not available for nesting sites, a hole will be excavated in vegetation or marl with debris piled up on top of the eggs, reminiscent of the mound nest of an alligator or marsh-dwelling crocodile. Researchers report that several trial or false nests may be dug in proximity to an active nest, and it is presumed that nest sites are used repeatedly. In Florida, nests may be used by multiple females, whereas in Chiapas, Mexico, nesting females are reportedly territorial. Burrows of various sizes have been reported in the vicinity of nesting sites. Parental care has also been reported and adults appear to guard nests. Females excavate nests and transport the young to the water.

DIET Hatchlings eat aquatic and terrestrial insects; juveniles eat fish, frogs, turtles, birds, small mammals, and aquatic invertebrates. Large animals will eat larger mammals and birds as well as the food groups eaten by younger animals. Fish is a major part of the diet of adults in Mexico.

## American Crocodile
*Crocodylus acutus*

## African Slender-snouted Crocodile
*Crocodylus cataphractus*

APPEARANCE This narrow-snouted species differs from other members of the genus in several ways. Most *Crocodylus* have a distinct pattern of enlarged neck scales arranged dorsally in two rows of 4 and 2 scales, and separated from the dorsal armor. In the African Slender-snouted Crocodile the enlarged dorsal neck scales are arranged in three or four rows of 2 scales each and join the dorsal armor. This species has a series of blotches on its jaws, atypical of *Crocodylus* but reminiscent of *Tomistoma* and some caimans.
SIZE Up to 3 or 4 meters (10 –13 feet) in length.
HABITAT The habitat associations of this species are uncertain. It is known primarily from freshwater habitats but there are records of it in coastal areas and a single record on Bioko Island, 45 kilometers (28 miles) off the coast of Cameroon.
DISTRIBUTION Little is known of this apparently secretive crocodile of Africa's tropical forests. In most parts of its range, which includes much of West and central Africa from southern Mauritania and Senegal to northern Angola and extending eastward to Zaire, Zambia, and eastern Tanzania, it is sympatric with the Nile Crocodile.
REPRODUCTION Little was known of the reproductive biology of this species until a 1985 study in the Ivory Coast. It appears that nesting in this species is non-synchronous, even at one locality. Nests are constructed during the rainy season from March to July, so that some nests are still being constructed while others already have hatchlings. Nests are located along the banks of small forest streams. At hatching, the forest floor is flooded and the young can disperse. A mound nest of vegetation is built and clutch size is relatively small, only 13–27 eggs. An adult is known to frequent the nest and, in captivity, a parental female has been reported to defend the nest. Whether the parental adults assist with hatching is unknown.
DIET Little is known about the diet of this species but it includes crabs, shrimps, snakes, frogs, and, because of its narrow snout, probably also fish. It is likely that the young eat insects.

## Nile Crocodile
*Crocodylus niloticus*

APPEARANCE There appears to be considerable variation among populations of Nile Crocodiles. These variations can be seen in maximum size, presence or absence of ventral osteoderms, scales, reproductive habits, and other characteristics; numerous subspecies of the Nile Crocodile have been named. Juvenile Nile Crocodiles are dark olive to brown with darker, often black, crossbands on the tail and body. Adults are generally uniformly dark with darker crossbands on the tail. The abdomen is light in color.

SIZE Grows to large size, up to and possibly considerably greater than 5 meters (16 feet). The maximum known length of the Nile Crocodile extrapolated from hunters' accounts and game department records, is 5.5 meters (18 feet).

HABITAT Known to occupy a wide variety of freshwater habitats, this species also frequents coastal areas in West Africa, and in southern Africa one was sighted nearly 11 kilometers (7 miles) off the Zululand coast. From time to time crocodiles are washed out from East African river mouths to the sea; some of these have been able to cross to the island of Zanzibar and crocodiles are occasionally found on beaches or river mouths in Kenya.

DISTRIBUTION The widespread crocodilian of the African continent, it is found throughout tropical and southern Africa, and Madagascar. Its historical distribution included the Nile River delta and the Mediterranean coast from Tunisia to Syria. Isolated populations of the Nile Crocodile are known to have existed in lakes and waterholes in the interior of Mauritania, southeastern Algeria, and northeastern Chad in the Sahara Desert.

REPRODUCTION A hole nester, clutch size is large — from an average of 50 eggs up to 80 eggs. Parental care has been documented.

DIET Diet varies with age: juveniles eat insects, spiders, frogs, and probably snakes, lizards, and other small vertebrates. Fish make up a large part of the diet of subadults and adults. Very large animals eat antelope, zebra, warthogs, large domestic animals, and humans.

APPEARANCE A slender convex snout and symmetrically arranged dorsal armor differentiate it from the American Crocodile with which it can easily be confused.

SIZE A large species, it grows up to 6 meters (20 feet) or more. Early travelers' tales suggest that this species is dangerous to humans, which, owing to its large size, is possible, but there are no substantiated reports of this species attacking people.

HABITAT Details on habitat are often unreliable due to problems in differentiating this species from the American Crocodile. However, habitat is apparently riverine and freshwater.

DISTRIBUTION It has very restricted distribution, seemingly found only in the freshwater reaches of the Orinoco River drainage of Venezuela and Colombia, with the American Crocodile found at the mouth of the Orinoco River in coastal habitat.

REPRODUCTION Little is known of the natural history of this species. It is reportedly a hole nester like most American Crocodiles but parental care has not, as yet, been reported.

DIET Owing to its slender snout, it is assumed to feed on fish but probably also takes small mammals, amphibians, and reptiles.

## Orinoco Crocodile
*Crocodylus intermedius*

**Indopacific Crocodile***
*Crocodylus porosus*

APPEARANCE This species has a relatively large head and a heavy snout with a pair of raised ridges running obliquely from the orbits toward the center of the snout. The dorsal armor is regular and the scales more oval than in most species. In coloration the Indopacific Crocodile is quite variable. Normally juveniles are brightly patterned with black spotting and blotches on the tail, which often form bands. There are 4 or 5 dark bands on the body. Fully grown adults may be gray or golden tan; some adults lose the beautiful black markings/ bands while others retain them. The abdomen is uniformly cream to golden yellow in color. Melanistic (darkly pigmented) individuals are known.

SIZE It is known to grow to lengths of 7 meters (23 feet) or more. Some individuals in captivity weigh more than 1,000 kilograms (2,200 pounds). This species is the largest of living reptiles and is probably the most feared of all crocodilians. It is truly a "man-eating" crocodile and accounts for almost all crocodile attacks where it is found.

HABITAT Commonly encountered in marine habitats, the common names Estuarine or Saltwater Crocodile are, however, misleading since this species is often found in freshwater habitats such as large rivers and lakes.

DISTRIBUTION The most widely distributed of all living crocodilians, the Indopacific Crocodile is found throughout the tropical regions of Asia and the Pacific, wherever there is suitable habitat. Its distribution is still not fully known but recent research suggests that it is found from the islands of the Indian Ocean, coastal India and Sri Lanka, through mainland Southeast Asia, the Indonesian

and Philippine islands, northern Australia, New Guinea, as far as the Belau Islands and perhaps Fiji in the Pacific Ocean. The ability of this species to survive in the open ocean has enabled it to reach, and sometimes colonize, many small islands such as the Cocos Islands (nearly 1,000 kilometers from land) and the New Hebrides. Stories of these crocodiles out in the open ocean abound and some individuals have been seen with pelagic barnacle species attached to their scales. Throughout much of the range it is sympatric with other smaller, innocuous crocodile species, which are commonly found in (but are not restricted to) freshwater habitats.

REPRODUCTION A mound nester, females can lay large clutches of up to 60 – 80 eggs. Females nest during the wet season and parental care has been observed.

DIET Juveniles eat insects, crabs, shrimp, mudskippers, lizards, and snakes. Large animals eat whatever they want, including a variety of mammals and some birds. Fish also form part of the diet.

*This is the only crocodilian species for which the more commonly used names (Estuarine or Saltwater Crocodile) refer to a habitat association rather than an anatomical or geographic feature. As both the commonly used names are misleading, the geographic name Indopacific Crocodile has been adopted for this book.

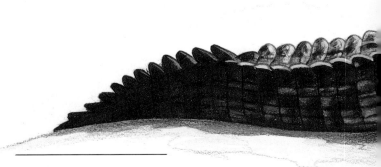

## Johnston's Crocodile
*Crocodylus johnsoni*

APPEARANCE Generally brown in color with a light venter, this species has black bands on the tail and spotted bands on the body. The snout is narrow, ventral scales are large, and the dorsal armor six scales wide.

SIZE A small, longirostrine species growing up to 3 meters (10 feet), most growth occurs during the wet season. Females grow more slowly and are smaller than males.

HABITAT Recent research has found that in the McKinley River area of the Northern Territory, Australia, this species occurs throughout the upstream freshwater habitat. Habitat size varies with the season: it may be extensive during the wet season when large areas of forest and grassland are inundated but, during the dry season, water may be limited to isolated deep pools in drying stream beds.

DISTRIBUTION Also known as the Australian Freshwater Crocodile, Johnston's Crocodile is restricted to the tropical regions of northern Australia (Western Australia, Northern Territory, and Queensland).

REPRODUCTION Johnston's Crocodiles make hole nests in somewhat exposed areas, which may be a response to particularly harsh living conditions, as nesting occurs during the dry season when they are often restricted to deep pools in drying stream beds where the lush vegetation available to swamp- or marsh-nesting species is not available. A high loss (up to 96 percent) of eggs and/or young during the first two years has been documented. This species displays a distinct homing ability.

DIET Johnston's Crocodiles are known to prey on fish, crustaceans, and both aquatic and terrestrial insects. Occasionally amphibians, reptiles, birds, and small mammals may be taken. Like most crocodilians, it is an opportunistic feeder, but its slender snout may allow it to capture small prey more easily.

## Mugger
*Crocodylus palustris*

APPEARANCE Juvenile Mugger or Marsh Crocodiles are a light tan or brown with dark crossbands on the tail and body. Adult animals are gray to brown, normally with no trace of darker bands. This species has a broad, heavy snout and regular dorsal armor.

SIZE A large species reaching a length of over 4 meters (13 feet).

HABITAT Known to inhabit freshwater habitats such as rivers, lakes, artificial water tanks, reservoirs, and irrigation systems. Occasional individuals have been sighted in brackish water.

DISTRIBUTION Widespread in the Indian subcontinent from eastern Iran, Pakistan, northern India, and Nepal (south of the Himalayas) to Bangladesh and south to Sri Lanka.

REPRODUCTION A hole-nesting species, single females in captivity have been reported laying two clutches of eggs in a single season. Average clutch size is 25–30 eggs but up to 46 eggs are known.

DIET Juveniles eat insects and small vertebrates. Larger individuals eat frogs, snakes (and possibly turtles), small mammals, and birds. Large adults have taken deer and buffalo species. Mugger are also known to take fish from nets.

### Siamese Crocodile
*Crocodylus siamensis*

APPEARANCE Juveniles are superficially similar to the Indopacific Crocodile in coloration — normally golden yellow or tan with black markings — and exhibit some similar patterns of the scales (squamation). This has caused confusion between these two sympatric species. However, Siamese Crocodiles have broader snouts than Indopacific Crocodiles and also have more transverse throat scales than any other species.

SIZE A small, less than 4-meter (13-foot) long, palustrine crocodile.

HABITAT Known to frequent freshwater lakes, rivers, and marshlands. Whether it occurs in brackish or coastal habitats is unknown.

DISTRIBUTION Restricted in distribution, found only in the tropical lowlands of mainland Southeast Asia (Thailand, Laos, Kampuchea, Vietnam, and Malaya) and some of the Indonesian islands.

REPRODUCTION Little is known of the natural history of this species, which is feared extinct in the wild, but it apparently builds a mound nest of vegetation and, in captivity, lays 25–50 eggs.

DIET Little is known, although it is said to feed on fish. However, the broad snout suggest a fairly generalized feeder and it is likely that snakes, frogs, insects, and other small prey species make up a large part of the diet.

## Philippine Crocodile
*Crocodylus mindorensis*

APPEARANCE This species has a broader snout, and heavier dorsal and neck scales than other crocodile species in the Pacific region.
SIZE A small species, its maximum known length is less than 3 meters (10 feet).
HABITAT Inhabits primarily freshwater habitats such as the tributaries of large rivers, small lakes, swampy depressions, and marshes.
DISTRIBUTION This species has a restricted range and is found only on the Philippine islands of Luzon, Mindoro, Masbate, Samar, Negros, Busuanga, Mindanao, and Jolo in the Sulu Archipelago. The

Philippine Crocodile was probably much more widely distributed than locality records indicate; for example, it was not until the early 1980s that its occurrence in the Visayan or central Philippine islands was recorded. It is believed that this species once occurred on other islands, which historically had suitable habitat that has now been converted to agricultural land.
REPRODUCTION The Philippine Crocodile builds a mound nest of vegetation and parental care has been observed.
DIET Little is known of the natural history of this species in the wild but it probably eats a variety of aquatic and terrestrial prey such as turtles, snakes, frogs, insects, and small mammals.

## New Guinea Crocodile
*Crocodylus novaeguineae*

APPEARANCE These crocodiles have a tapered snout that is not as elongate or slender as Johnston's Crocodile. Brown with black to dark brown bands on the tail and bands or spots on the body, coloration is similar to the Philippine and Johnston's crocodiles.
SIZE Of medium size, up to 4 meters (13 feet) in length.
HABITAT Usually found in freshwater rivers, lakes, marshes, and swamplands not inhabited by the Indopacific Crocodile with which this species is sympatric. Individuals are known to enter brackish or coastal habitats on occasion.
DISTRIBUTION Separated from Johnston's Crocodile by the Torres Strait, the New Guinea Crocodile was first described from the Sepik River drainage on the north coast of New Guinea. A morphological analysis of a large number of "freshwater" crocodiles from both coasts of New Guinea, indicates that the south coast (Papuan)

population is distinct but is as yet unnamed. These populations are separated by mountains running along the center of the island. There are no records of "freshwater" crocodiles from the extreme eastern tip of New Guinea and, in the west, the Papuan population inhabits the Jazirah Doberai Peninsula. It is unlikely that there is any genetic interaction between these populations.
REPRODUCTION This species builds a mound nest of vegetation but in the Papuan population nesting occurs during the wet season, whereas in the northern population nesting occurs during the dry season. Parental care has been observed and, in the Papuan population, both parental male and female have been observed to open the nest and carry the young to water.
DIET Opportunistic feeders and stomach contents include insects, amphibians, snakes, birds such as rails and grebes, and fish.

**Dwarf Crocodile**
*Osteolaemus tetraspis*

APPEARANCE The Dwarf Crocodile is heavily armored, from its osseous eyelids, heavy dorsal and neck armor, bony-plated ventral and side scales to the bony covering of its tail. Juveniles are dark brown with black crossbands on the tail and body, and a bright yellow pattern laterally. Adults are uniformly dark. The iris is brown.
SIZE A small crocodilian reaching lengths of 2 meters (6.5 feet).
HABITAT The Dwarf Crocodile is poorly known but apparently prefers slow-moving water and avoids major waterways. It has been reported from aquatic forest and savanna habitats but there are no records for brackish or saltwater areas. It is reported to be basically nocturnal and does not spend long periods basking in the open like many other crocodilians.

DISTRIBUTION Known only from the tropical forest zone of west and central Africa, where its distribution nearly parallels that of the African Slender-snouted Crocodile although, unlike the latter, it is not found as far north as Mauritania, Chad, and Mali or as far east as Tanzania. Two populations exist, one of which ranges from Senegal to Angola while the other is restricted to northeastern Zaire and Uganda (where the African Slender-snouted Crocodile is not found). The exact distribution and region of contact or overlap between these populations has still to be examined.
REPRODUCTION This species builds a mound nest of vegetation and apparently has a small clutch size of less than 20 eggs.
DIET Diet is reported to be crabs, frogs, and fish.

**False Gharial**
*Tomistoma schlegelii*

APPEARANCE The only living species of this ancient genus, which can be traced back to the Eocene of Africa and Asia, the False Gharial is a slender-snouted, longirostrine species. It is dark in coloration with broad black bands on the tail, and dark bands and blotches on the body. The mandibles also have dark blotches. One of the few living crocodilians where the adult is almost as distinctly marked as the juvenile.
SIZE Grows to a length of 4 meters (13 feet) or more.
HABITAT The False Gharial is found in freshwater habitats, swamps, lakes, and rivers. No records of occurrence in brackish water or coastal habitats are known. Captive individuals sometimes utilize burrows.
DISTRIBUTION Restricted in distribution, being found only on the

Malay Peninsula of Thailand and Malaysia, Sumatra, Borneo, Java, and possibly Sulawesi. Recent research by Chinese scientists and the unearthing of two skulls from excavations in Guangdong (Kwantung), China, indicate that the range was much larger in the past, possibly until as recently as the Ming dynasty (1368–1644).
REPRODUCTION Little is known of the natural history of this species but it is known to make a mound nest of vegetation and clutch size has rarely been reported.
DIET Feeds on small vertebrates and fish.

# SUBFAMILY GAVIALINAE

In living gavialines the snout is very slender, rounded dorsally, and sharply demarcated from the rest of the head. The nasals do not meet the premaxillaries. The teeth are slender and the teeth of the upper and lower jaws interlock.

## Gharial
### *Gavialis gangeticus*

APPEARANCE Most individuals have a slender, parallel-sided, attenuate snout with adult males having a distinctive knob on the tip. However, there is considerable age-related variation in snout shape. Hatchlings and very large Gharials have proportionately wider snouts than juveniles and young adults. Gharials are generally light in color, olive to tan with oblique dark blotches or bands on the tail and body. The neck and back armor are contiguous. The Gharial has extensively webbed rear feet and relatively weak legs; it does not make the extensive overland journeys of many other species.
SIZE A large crocodilian known to grow up to 6.5 meters (21 feet).
HABITAT It is apparently restricted to river habitat and, as such, is extinct in parts of its range.
DISTRIBUTION The genus *Gavialis* is known from the Miocene to the present. Fossil taxa are known from South and North America, Africa, and Asia, where the sole remaining species is found. The Gharial is now restricted to the northern part of the Indian subcontinent. Its recent distribution includes the Brahmaputra, Irrawaddy, Bhīma, Ganges, Mahānadi, and Kaladan river drainages of Pakistan, India, Nepal, Bangladesh, Bhutan, and Burma.
REPRODUCTION This species digs hole nests in sandbanks along rivers or on midriver islands. Mean clutch size varies from 28 to 43 eggs, according to locality.
DIET Primarily a fish eater, it is probable that the feeding behavior of very young and old animals differs from that of juveniles and young adults, which have narrower snouts. This would account for past records of large adult Gharials eating animals that would literally snap the snout of younger individuals. Although the Gharial grows very large, it is not known to attack people. Early accounts of this species concentrated on the occurrence of human artifacts found in the stomach. Most crocodilians are known to ingest and retain hard objects (gastroliths), which possibly aid digestion. Along the Ganges and some other rivers where the Gharial occurs, it is the custom to cremate or float human bodies on rafts and thus human artifacts such as bracelets, rings and so on are introduced to the river environment. It is more likely that the Gharial ingests these secondary materials rather than directly feeding on people.

A female American Alligator
stands guard over her brood of newly
hatched young.

# BEHAVIOR AND

# ENVIRONMENT

# FOOD AND FEEDING HABITS

A.C. (TONY) POOLEY

▲ To pull its prey apart a Nile Crocodile needs only to "tear along the dotted line" of puncture marks made by its teeth. Stained and worn with use, the teeth on this animal are regularly replaced by new ones growing underneath.

T. Pooley

With their powerfully constructed armor-plated bodies, stout limbs, streamlined tails, impressive bony heads, and tooth-studded jaws, crocodilians appear to be, and are, highly efficient predators. While they are opportunistic hunters, taking whatever prey they can find when foraging for food, they can also exercise more advanced behavior when dealing with different prey in various habitats.

## ANATOMY AND PREY SPECIES

Crocodilians have stout conical and cylindro-conical teeth. The enlarged canines are sharp with cutting edges and are well adapted to puncturing and gripping prey. The short, blunt molars are used to crush prey; there are usually 28–32 teeth in the lower jaw and 30 – 40 teeth in the upper jaw. Prey once seized has little chance of escape. However, the teeth are not rooted but fit into sockets in the mandibles and can be dislodged. There is no sideways movement or chewing action of the jaws and, as food is easily impaled on their sharp canines, crocodilians gulp their food whole.

Most crocodilians are mainly nocturnal hunters, preferring to spend the daylight hours basking, so field observations on actual prey species taken are not numerous. Temperature also plays an important part in both feeding behavior and rate of digestion. Food intake is minimal in the cooler winter months but increases steadily during spring and summer months.

In Africa many hundreds of Nile Crocodile (*Crocodylus niloticus*) specimens were killed from habitats in several countries in order to examine their stomach contents. It was thought that these predators were voracious feeders consuming a full

▶ The jaws of a mighty predator! Every tooth in this Indopacific Crocodile's prickly array is adapted for catching, and holding prey. The jaws can be closed with extraordinary force by the bulging muscles at their base while the armor of the head and back can withstand attack from almost any natural enemy.

Reg Morrison/Auscape International

◄ Crocodilians rely largely on gravity to move food from their jaws to the gullet; first juggling each food item until it is placed comfortably in the mouth then tossing back the head so the food literally falls down the throat.

▼ Analysis of Nile Crocodile stomach contents reveals a direct relationship between the length (and thus age) of a crocodile and the size of its prey. In this study, the stomachs of all the Nile Crocodiles up to half a meter included insects and up to 40 percent of the stomachs also included frogs and spiders. Of the stomachs of the fully grown, mature animals, 60 percent contained mammal prey but none contained the smaller prey species suggesting that mature animals do not expend energy pursuing small prey that does not provide a worthwhile energy "return," if larger prey is available.

FOOD OCCURRENCES BY SIZE OF NILE CROCODILE:

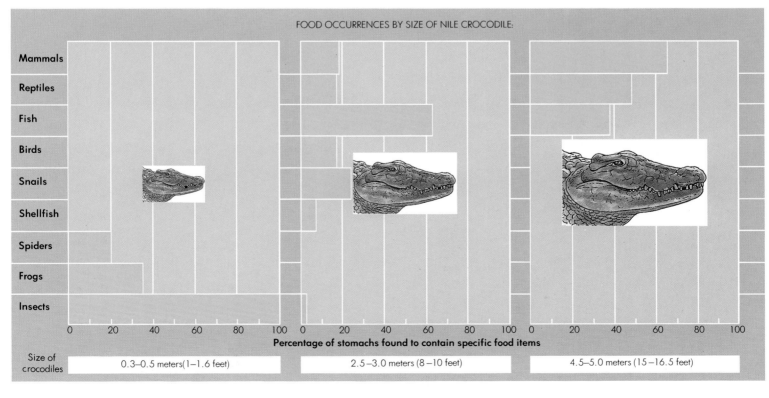

Mammals
Reptiles
Fish
Birds
Snails
Shellfish
Spiders
Frogs
Insects

Percentage of stomachs found to contain specific food items

Size of crocodiles: 0.3–0.5 meters(1–1.6 feet) | 2.5–3.0 meters (8–10 feet) | 4.5–5.0 meters (15–16.5 feet)

meal every 24 hours and that their diet of mainly fish was detrimental to both sporting and commercial fishery interests. In wildlife sanctuaries they were blamed for taking too many antelope and for being responsible for an imbalance in predator-prey relationships. Analysis of the stomach samples, however, revealed that 30 percent of all stomachs examined were empty. Researchers therefore concluded that adult animals probably ingest no more than 50 full meals a year.

The American Alligator (*Alligator mississippiensis*) was also considered to be detrimental to fish species palatable to humans and to valuable fur-bearing animals such as the mink. This was similarly disproved and, in fact, nutria (a species of otter found in Louisiana and Florida) was shown to form the bulk of the mammalian prey taken by large alligators throughout their range.

Further examination of hundreds of stomach samples from all sizes and from many species of crocodilians shows, not surprisingly, that the young subsist largely on aquatic and shoreline insects of many species. Their food includes tadpoles, frogs, snails, crabs, shrimps, and small fishes in increasing numbers as the animals approach a size of 1 meter (3 feet) or more.

Crocodilian diet also changes considerably with habitat. In brackish water, estuaries, and lagoons, young crocodilians feed principally on mud and fiddler crabs, mud prawns, shrimps, mollusks, mudskippers, and a variety of small marine fishes that shelter in the mangrove root systems, as well as on insects. In freshwater marshes and swamps, they eat tadpoles, frogs, freshwater snails, fishes, small mammals, and possibly a greater variety of insect life.

► These feet belong to a rapidly disappearing painted reed frog. Seconds earlier it was sitting peacefully on the water lilies, now it has made its contribution to the diet of a growing Nile Crocodile. Insects, frogs, and other small aquatic or amphibious animals are the mainstay of hatchling crocodiles.

▼ From a very early age, stealth and surprise are the main elements of successful food gathering by crocodilians. This fish is probably too large for the young Common Caiman but a smaller fish would be snapped up by a twitch of the caiman's head.

Jane Burton/Bruce Coleman Ltd.

T. Pooley

Diet also changes markedly with the size and age of crocodilians in the subadult and adult classes. There is an increase in the fish intake (probably up to 70 percent of the bulk in the diet of most species) as well as a greater intake of crabs, birds, reptiles, small and large mammals, terrapins, and turtles.

It is important to remember, however, that in every habitat crocodilians will capture whatever prey is available. Even reptiles in excess of 3–4 meters (10–14 feet) in length may include small prey such as snails, crabs, frogs, and small fishes of a variety of species and sizes in their diet. Although they seek out larger prey, they do not lose the ability to subsist on smaller prey.

Long- or slender-snouted crocodilians such as the Gharial (*Gavialis gangeticus*), False Gharial (*Tomistoma schlegelii*), Johnston's Crocodile (*Crocodylus johnsoni*), New Guinea Crocodile (*Crocodylus novaeguineae*), and African Slender-snouted Crocodile (*Crocodylus cataphractus*) are principally fish eaters, although they also take shrimps, crabs, frogs, snakes, birds, and small mammals. A flattened snout offers little resistance when sweeping and snapping sideways in the water at prey such as fish — the more slender the snout, the faster and more effective the sideways snap. These species are also agile and can catch fish, bats, and birds by leaping into the air. The long thin snout is, no doubt, also effective in probing for crabs in subterranean burrows.

▲ The slender snout of an African Slender-snouted Crocodile is too fragile to take large prey on land but is equipped with teeth capable of subduing fish of substantial size in the water.

► Even the turtle's strong bony shell is no defence against the jaws of an adult American Alligator. The ability of crocodilians to eat almost any animal they can overpower has contributed to their success as predators.

Glen Threlfo/Auscape International

▲ Tropical waterbirds are always vulnerable to attack from beneath. There can have been little warning for this Magpie Goose when the Indopacific Crocodile erupted from the lilies behind it.

Joanna Van Gruisen/Ardea London

◄ Schools of tiny fish make an easy meal for this Mugger as it sweeps its head through the water. Great opportunists, no morsel is too small if it takes little effort for a crocodilian to catch it.

The more robust, heavier, and broad-snouted species tend to take larger prey and include more mammals in their diets. The Black Caiman (*Melanosuchus niger*) takes capybara (South American waterhog), otters, dogs, pigs, small deer, and cattle. The adult Mugger (*Crocodylus palustris*) preys on sambar (deer), gaur (wild ox), squirrels, and monkeys. The Indopacific Crocodile (*Crocodylus porosus*) preys on crab-eating monkeys, squirrels, flying foxes, wallabies, cattle, horses, and buffalo. The Nile Crocodile has an extremely wide range of mammals in its diet ranging from cane rats to Cape buffaloes, which can be as heavy as itself. Mugger, Indopacific, and Nile crocodiles also include humans in their food range.

◄ With little more than nose, eyes, and ears exposed, this American Alligator can smell, see, or hear any potential prey items within range. When it submerges before attacking, the weed on its snout will be left on the surface without a ripple.

▼ As Africa's dry season sets in many mammals have no option but to drink at places where Nile Crocodiles are abundant. Each visit to the water hole becomes a terrifying lottery for survival as there is little an animal such as a zebra can do to avoid the lunge and bite of a large crocodile.

Jonathan Scott/Planet Earth Pictures

## HUNTING AND FORAGING BEHAVIORS

Crocodilians are usually regarded as idle hunters that lie in wait in the offshore shallows for the approach of unsuspecting prey. They rely on camouflage and an ability to lie submerged with only their nostrils, eyes, and ears above the surface to scent, see, and hear approaching prey. From this concealed position they can launch themselves out of the water with astonishing speed, and may make a rush of several meters up a beach to snap at prey approaching the shoreline. Even large crocodilians are capable of vaulting almost vertically out of the water to a height of more than 1.5 meters (5 feet) to snap at birds or animals on river banks above them. Hatchlings will actually leap into the air to snap at hovering dragonflies.

▶ Pelicans are heavy birds and slow to get airborne, too slow for this lunging Nile Crocodile — the acceleration provided to the crocodile by a thrust of its tail was greater than the pelican could generate by flapping its wings.

T. Pooley

# EFFICIENT METABOLISM

STEPHEN GARNETT

Many crocodilians are found to have empty stomachs because they use the energy in the food they eat more efficiently than almost any other animal. They manage this partly by the way they obtain their food, partly by being cold-blooded, and partly from the thoroughness with which food is digested.

Most crocodilians are "sit-and-wait" predators, that is, rather than actively seeking out food they wait for the food to come to them, thus saving energy. When something appetizing does present itself at the water's edge the crocodile may use a quick burst of energy as it lunges and twists but expends nothing like the amount of energy it would need to scour the countryside for food.

Being cold-blooded means that crocodilian temperature varies with the temperature of its surroundings. In cold weather crocodilians are sluggish and sometimes warm themselves by basking on a sunny bank. This means that, unlike mammals and birds, crocodilians do not need to expend energy keeping their body temperature at the same level.

The crocodilian digestive system is remarkable for several reasons. Firstly, the stomach is the most acidic recorded for any vertebrate, allowing the crocodilian to digest all the bone it consumes. Secondly, about 60 percent of the energy contained in the food it eats is stored away as fat in the tail, in mesenteric organs in the abdomen, along the back, and almost anywhere it can be stored. Even some of the energy contained in protein is converted to fat in crocodilians.

This allows crocodilians to survive for exceptionally long periods with no food at all. A newly hatched crocodile can survive for more than four months without eating, by using the fat from the remains of the yolk sac tucked away in its belly. A large crocodile, which may weigh more than 1 tonne, can probably last for up to two years between meals. Alligators and some crocodiles regularly fast through the cooler months but the larger animals probably need to eat little even during the summer, provided they do not waste too much energy on breeding.

Naturally, there are costs of such efficient metabolism. The first cost is the rate of growth. When food is constantly available crocodiles can grow nearly half a meter (1.5 feet) a year but in the wild this growth rate is often much lower. Because the young are storing so much of their food as fat, in case they have to go for a long time with none, fewer resources are directed into increasing length and muscle size.

The other cost comes when crocodilians have to expend energy quickly, as when they capture food. Using energy requires oxygen in the blood but, because the crocodilian system is geared to using energy slowly, it can never get much oxygen in the blood at any one time. Without oxygen, exertion produces lactic acid, which gradually breaks down after activity ceases and more oxygen becomes available. The levels of lactic acid in the blood that can be tolerated by crocodilians have astonished researchers; their blood reaches an acidity level that would easily kill most other animals. However, it also means that crocodilians are easily exhausted and take a long time to recover from exercise of any kind.

Despite these drawbacks, the efficiency of crocodilian metabolism has undoubtedly helped it to survive as long as it has. Very little of any prey species eaten will be wasted.

Animals drinking at the water's edge are vulnerable to attack if the shoreline is muddy and they sink into the soft substrate. The steep slope of the shore may also be a disadvantage to an animal attempting to leap backwards when attacked. Most antelope species are obliged to splay their front legs when drinking so that their muzzle can reach the water, but from this stance they are unable to leap backwards speedily. When a herd of antelope is drinking there is also considerable bunching and confusion at the unexpectedness of a crocodile attack and in these circumstances the crocodilian is usually successful.

When an animal's muzzle is seized in the crocodile's powerful jaws and gripped by its sharp, curved teeth, it often offers little or feeble resistance. The sensitivity of the nerves in the nostrils and lips coupled with the pulling, shaking, or jerking of the crocodile is undoubtedly extremely painful. Gripped like this around the muzzle, domestic animals and antelope alike have been seen to walk out into the water without resistance until, with a final tremendous spin, the crocodile flips the victim over and holds it under by the muzzle until it drowns.

◄▼ With the powerful jaws of a Mugger clasped over its head (left) this sambar fawn is forced to walk into the water. By choosing such a sensitive point of attack the crocodile wastes a minimum of energy in capturing its prey. A few moments later the fawn's snout is pulled beneath the water (below) and the animal drowned.

Sue Earle/Planet Earth Pictures

Sue Earle/Planet Earth Pictures

▶ With wing feathers too short for flight this young egret has nowhere else to go but down. Waterbird colonies provide easy pickings for American Alligators such as this one — not only do the alligators take young birds that fall from their nests but they also catch the fish that congregate to feed on the birds' droppings.

▶▼ On their long migrations vast herds of African wildebeest have to cross many streams and rivers. With so many animals to choose from this Nile Crocodile does not even bother to submerge before attacking (below). In a similar attack (right) another wildebeest, selected as victim from a group, flails for a grip in the shallows in an attempt to escape from the Nile Crocodile raking its back with sharp teeth.

Jonathan Scott/Planet Earth Pictures

Sometimes the crocodile erupts from the water into the midst of a herd of drinking antelope then uses its massive bony head to deliver sledge-hammer side-to-side blows to stun prey, break limbs, or knock an antelope into the water. Several crocodile species have been reported to use their tails for the same purpose when ambushing animals along game trails but there is no concrete evidence of this.

Many of the larger crocodilians are known to take advantage of the habitual behavior of their prey, taking up position in the water on regularly used game trails, or at well-used river crossings or watering sites for humans and livestock, particularly if previous attacks at these sites have been successful. In the same way, they will lie in wait beneath the nests of cormorants, herons, and storks for days on end, ready to snap at unwary birds straying from nests or alighting on branches low over the water. The Indopacific Crocodile has

Jonathan Scott/Planet Earth Pictures

Ian Beames/Ardea London

▶ Crocodile attacks are usually directed at the most readily accessible parts of their prey's anatomy but this Nile Crocodile's grip on the scruff of the warthog's neck has succeeded in rendering its sharp tusks harmless.

also been found to lie up in the mangroves beneath colonies of flying foxes in some regions of Australia. Johnston's Crocodiles catch flying foxes and other bats as they come down to drink.

Crocodilians also display their versatility as master predators in their methods of capturing fish. Lying in the shallows, often with jaws agape, the crocodile probably detects vibrations in the water from approaching fish prey. It snaps at and seizes the fish in its jaws; then with a simultaneous sideways and downward motion of its head, the crocodile pins the fish in the shallows to prevent its escape. Once the crocodile has a firm grip, it lifts its head high above the water and, after a series of bites, maneuvers the fish in its jaws and swallows it head first to prevent the sharp dorsal spines from injuring its throat and gullet. Very large fish may be taken ashore and held firmly until they cease to struggle or they may be battered on the ground.

An alternative tactic is for the crocodile to leave some unwanted part of the prey outside its mouth and jerk the rest of the tissue away from it with a series of vigorous shakes of its head. This maneuver is used to break off the heads of catfish.

The African Slender-snouted Crocodile hunts fish by swimming slowly parallel to a river bank with its tail curved toward the bank. Small shoalfish and other fishes in the shallows move along ahead of the disturbance but, when the crocodile turns its head around to the bank, the

fish are trapped and are seized by a sideways sweep of the open jaws. Nile Crocodiles have been seen to use their tails to bend reeds and flip nestling weaver birds out of their nests into the water where they are snapped up.

## COOPERATIVE AND SOCIAL FEEDING BEHAVIORS

Well-documented accounts of the Nile Crocodile support the belief that crocodilians have a socially advanced feeding system.

In Lake St. Lucia, Natal, South Africa, there are annual migrations of shoalfish out of and into the lake from the Indian Ocean either to spawn or to feed. Species include kob, spotted grunter but, more importantly, striped mullet (*Mugil cephalus*). The annual movement of the mullet shoals is fairly constant, and between mid-April and mid-May each year large numbers of crocodiles move down from northern and open stretches of the lake in response to the fish shoaling; others move up from river systems to the south.

They congregate in an area known as the Narrows, a channel less than 500 meters (550 yards) in width. Numbers peak during May but decrease rapidly thereafter. Examples of cooperative feeding can be observed with several crocodiles spreading out in a semicircular or line formation, which blocks the passage of the fish. Each crocodile maintains its place in the line and

Michael Cermak

Jeff Foott/Survival Anglia Ltd.

▲ Curlews are wading birds and share their water's edge habitat with crocodiles. Not surprisingly wading birds are common prey items in places where Indopacific Crocodiles, like this one, are abundant.

◄ Fish are streamlined to move easily through the water. This shape also makes them easy to swallow provided they are correctly positioned and despite appearances this American Alligator will have no trouble swallowing its catch.

snaps at approaching fish. There is no fighting over prey; shifting position and leaving a gap in the ranks would lessen the chances of successful prey capture.

In other Zululand rivers similar behavior may be seen in summer when rivers flood and water spills over into channels leading to natural pans. The crocodiles form a barrier where a channel enters the pan, facing the inrushing water and snapping up river fishes such as bream (genus *Tilapia*) and catfish.

Jonathan Scott/Planet Earth Pictures

▶ With stomachs about the size of a basketball, Nile Crocodiles do not usually consume wildebeest and other large prey at once. Prey is often left to be finished off later although crocodiles prefer fresh meat and, certainly in captivity, will not eat putrified flesh.

Peter Davey/Bruce Coleman Ltd.

Other examples of cooperative feeding may be seen when Nile Crocodiles gather to feed at the carcass of a large animal such as a buffalo or a hippopotamus. The teeth and jaws of the crocodile are not suitable for opening up a tough-skinned carcass unless it is putrescent enough for penetration of the soft parts of the body. (This inability to deal with a freshly killed, thick-skinned carcass has led to the erroneous belief that the crocodile prefers its meat "high" and will deliberately store or lodge a freshly killed animal under a ledge, in a cave, or between the tangled

▼ The carcass of an Indian elephant provides plenty of food for several Mugger. The scent of flesh will sometimes entice crocodiles to come right out of the water to feed on land.

Dieter and Mary Plage/Survival Anglia Ltd.

roots of a tree on the river bank to allow the carcass to putrefy.)

Up to 30 or 40 adult crocodiles may arrive at a buffalo carcass, and there is a record of 120 sharing the carcass of a hippopotamus in the Luangwa River, Zambia. Here, because of space limitations, not all the crocodiles were able to feed at the same time. They encircled the carcass awaiting their turn, moved in to procure a portion, then

retreated to the outer edge of the circle to devour the morsel. Despite the considerable movement to and from the carcass, there was no evidence of fighting among the large group of crocodiles.

When a large crocodile seizes the leg of an antelope it has drowned, it spins or rolls over repeatedly in the water until the seized portion is torn away. However, this does not work with prey species that are not very large. When the crocodile spins, so does the prey. In such circumstances, a second crocodile bites the carcass and holds it while the first reptile rotates, or both may rotate in opposite directions. Each crocodile, and there may be several, eats what it tears off without any hostility to the others, then waits its turn again.

This specialized and advanced social feeding behavior is quite unlike the rather stereotyped hunting behavior of most species of reptiles.

▲ A fresh zebra kill attracts Nile Crocodiles from all around, the animals probably alerted to its presence by the splashing. Such a large prey item would be too difficult for a single killer to defend and, in any case, is more easily dismembered if eaten cooperatively.

# MORTALITY AND PREDATORS

A.C. (TONY) POOLEY AND CHARLES A. ROSS

Crocodilians are most susceptible to death, through natural causes and from predators, while embryonic in the nest or during the first few months (or years) of life. While in the nest the eggs are subject to fluctuations of environmental parameters and direct predation. During the first six months, and up to several years of life, hatchling and juvenile mortality from predators is high. In fact several African and Pacific crocodile management programs justify harvest of eggs and/or juvenile crocodiles as recruitment of this segment of the population into the adult breeding population is so low. Some wildlife management specialists estimate a death rate as high as 90 percent during the first year of life. However, as a crocodile successfully runs the gamut of early-life predators and reaches adulthood, the number of predators and the causes of mortality diminish rapidly. An adult crocodile has little to fear but its peers and humans.

► Hunting crocodilians has long been an "exotic" sport. This Nile Crocodile, having survived numerous predators to reach adulthood, finally met death at the hands of the most skilled predator of all in Lake Victoria, in central Africa.

Nick Gordon/ Ardea London

◄ Crocodilian mortality is highest during the early stages of life. These Chinese Alligator (*Alligator sinensis*) eggs and hatchlings are at the stage of greatest risk — the natural elements as well as numerous predators will decimate their numbers so that only a small percentage will survive to reach adulthood.

## NEST MORTALITY

Unlike most species of birds that lay relatively small clutches of eggs but may produce two or three broods each breeding season (thus increasing the chances of survival of at least one brood) crocodilians normally lay a large number of eggs but do so only once a year. Mean clutch size varies both within and between species but analysis of clutch size for most species indicates that between 20 and 80 eggs are laid.

Incubation periods for crocodilian eggs tend to be lengthy in comparison with those of birds, and vary from 35 days for small species to 90–100 days for larger species. Most female crocodilians guard their nests from predators and may fast for the entire incubation period in order to remain close to the nest. Birds incubate their eggs and therefore have some control over the results. They can rapidly rebuild a nest to lay another clutch of eggs in the event of a natural disaster or loss through predation. Crocodilians, however, are not so fortunate. The eggs once laid — either in a hole in the ground or within a mound of debris — are subject to the elements and crocodilians have no control over nest conditions, such as temperature of the eggs, humidity in the egg chamber, flooding, or a multitude of other environmental parameters.

Heavy rainfall or even a prolonged cloudy period can drop incubation temperatures below the level required for the embryos to survive. The developing embryos, which depend on oxygen diffusion through the porous eggshells, may drown during prolonged periods of heavy rain.

Conversely, lack of rainfall causing lowered moisture and humidity levels in the nest during extended hot, drought periods will lead to overheating or desiccation of the eggs and a large percentage, or even whole clutches, may perish.

Nests are often built on river banks, marsh impoundment dikes, floating mats of vegetation, lake shores, and other sites subject to flooding and devastation by tropical storms, hurricanes, or typhoons. Although the female may have laid the eggs at a time when substrate and air temperatures were ideal and when water levels were suitable, and although the eggs may have been laid above the normal high-water flood levels, an entire season's crop of eggs can be destroyed by flooding or lakeside wave action.

Bill Green

◄ Although female crocodilians take maximum care to site their nests above the high-water flood level, abnormal rain or tropical storms can destroy nests and eggs with devastating results for the season's hatchlings. The eggs in this flooded mound nest in Arnhem Bay in the Northern Territory of Australia would have died through lack of oxygen.

Climate, however, is not the sole cause of egg and embryo mortality. Excessive dampness in the nest can encourage fatal fungal growths on the eggs. Noxious gases emanating from putrid eggs in tightly packed and mud-covered nests can cause mortality of healthy eggs in the same nest. Mortality, particularly at colonial nesting sites, can also be attributed to females inadvertently digging up and destroying clutches previously laid by other females. Occasionally a large percentage of eggs in a clutch are pierced by the sharp claws of the female's hind feet, and several eggs in a clutch may be squashed or dented by the female's careless nesting habits. Turtles utilize the nests of some crocodilian species to lay their own eggs and may damage some of the crocodilian eggs.

Thin-shelled eggs that crack or dent easily and even unshelled eggs are occasionally found; these have usually been laid by either very young or very old females. There are also instances of complete hatching failure because the female has not returned to release her offspring, imprisoned beneath a hard-baked layer of clay from which they cannot dig out unaided.

## PREDATION OF EGGS

Predation of eggs in nests is high, even though nests may be guarded by parental females or other adult crocodilians. A large number of reptilian, avian, and mammalian predators of crocodilian eggs have been reported. Predators on eggs vary geographically and are normally not species specific, that is, if more than one crocodilian species is found in an area, a nest predator will prey on eggs from all of the species.

In North America, American Alligator (*Alligator mississippiensis*) nests are subject to predation from raccoons, opossums, skunks, pigs, black bears, and possibly otters. In Central America, the introduced mongoose predates crocodilian nests as do raccoons, coyotes, foxes, and dogs. There is even a record of a Gila monster (*Heloderma horridum*), a venomous lizard, digging into the nest of an American Crocodile (*Crocodylus acutus*). In South America, caiman nests are preyed on by the coati, crab-eating fox, tegu lizard, and capuchin monkey.

Asiatic crocodilian nests are heavily preyed on by monitor lizards (genus *Varanus*). In addition, civet cats, mongooses, jackals, sloth bears, dogs, wild pigs, and probably a variety of other small mammals eat crocodilian eggs. Rats are known to tunnel into nests and eat eggs.

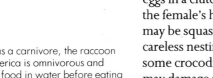

▼ Classed as a carnivore, the raccoon of North America is omnivorous and immerses all food in water before eating it. The location of American Alligator nests near water is therefore ideal for this nest predator.

Des Bartlett/Bruce Coleman Ltd.

▶ The coati (genus *Nasua*), related to the raccoon, are confined to South America where they survive on a diet of insects and eggs. Opening a caiman nest with its well-developed claws and scooping out the exposed eggs is a relatively easy task for a coati.

Michael Freeman/Bruce Coleman Ltd.

In Africa, Nile Crocodile (*Crocodylus niloticus*) nest predators have been described from various countries and habitats. These include water and white-tailed mongooses, honey badgers or ratels, olive and chacma baboons, otters, warthogs, bushpigs, and spotted hyenas. Avian predators of nests include the Marabou Stork, which has learned to probe through the sand with its stout bill to remove eggs from unattended crocodile nests. However, the Nile or water monitor lizard is undoubtedly the major predator of crocodile eggs throughout the African continent and, over some nesting seasons, these lizards may be responsible for stealing up to 50 percent or more of all eggs laid.

Monitor lizards are widespread throughout Africa, the Indian subcontinent, Asia, Australia, and the Pacific islands. Wherever these lizards and crocodilians are sympatric, the monitor lizards are either confirmed as, or suspected of, taking a heavy toll on crocodilian eggs and are likely to be the primary predator on crocodilian nests.

▲ Elegant Marabou Storks, seen here cooling by a lake in Kenya, use their bills to probe through the sand to gain access to the crocodilian nests below. Nest-guarding adults keep a sharp eye on avian predators but an unguarded nest is likely to get the unwanted attention of the storks.

◄ A major predator of eggs on the African continent, the monitor lizard is widespread with a distribution ranging beyond Africa to Asia and Australia. With its large size, elongated snout, and extensible forked tongue, it is ideally equipped to seek out crocodilian nests.

There are some other dangers to nests that are neither climatic nor predator related. In Botswana, Africa, reed beds and papyrus stands are burned, during the crocodilian nesting season, to provide grazing for livestock. In Natal, South Africa, the cocktail ant (genus *Crematogaster*) has been found to seek out eggs and destroy embryos in the underground nests.

In several African countries, humans are a major threat to the breeding success of all three species of African crocodiles — Nile Crocodile, African Slender-snouted Crocodile (*Crocodylus cataphractus*), and Dwarf Crocodile (*Osteolaemus tetraspis*). Nests are raided for eggs, which are collected either for their medicinal properties or, mainly, for food. A similar situation exists in several other regions such as the Philippines and New Guinea. On Cape York peninsula in Australia, eggs of the Indopacific Crocodile (*Crocodylus porosus*), according to local Aboriginal law, can only be eaten by certain old men, effectively protecting many nests. In some other areas, even though the eggs are not eaten by humans, crocodilian nests are destroyed wherever they are found. This is true even of crocodilian hunters who find nesting females, kill them on the nest for their skins, and then destroy the nest (and their own future harvest).

▶ Cocktail ants destroy crocodilian eggs as well as embryos and hatchlings at nesting beaches on the shores of Lake St. Lucia, Zululand. Following the scent trail of an addled egg, the ants tunnel beneath the surface and may destroy the entire clutch of eggs while the unsuspecting adult crocodile remains nearby unaware of the tiny predators.

▼ An adult Nile Crocodile is no match for fast-spreading fire in papyrus reeds. It is likely that this female was caught while trying to flee the fire but others will have managed to escape.

T Pooley

Anthony Bannister/NHPA

## PREDATORS OF THE YOUNG

Newly hatched crocodilians are a source of food for numerous predators in the tropics and subtropics. Most predators of crocodilian eggs will also take newly hatched young, which are, unlike the eggs, subject to danger from aquatic predators as well. These predators vary geographically.

The young of the American Alligator are reported to be preyed on by frogs, snakes, probably turtles such as the snapping and soft-shelled turtles, Great Blue Herons, caracaras, raccoons, and black bears. Central American crocodile hatchlings are preyed on by some fishes, the larger herons such as the Bare-throated Tiger Heron, cormorants, and some birds of prey such as the Roadside Hawk (*Buteo magnirostris*) and the Laughing Falcon. The young are also eaten by raccoons and cats. In southern Asia, young crocodilians are eaten by turtles, fish (such as bugaries), jackals, monitor lizards, Adjutant Storks, and birds of prey.

In Africa, in particular, the variety of hatchling predators in different ecosystems is quite impressive. Mammalian predators include a small nocturnal cat — the rusty spotted genet — selous mongoose, and leopard. Avian predators include wading birds such as the Goliath Heron, Gray Heron, Great White Egret, Little Egret, Sacred Ibis, Marabou and Saddle-bill storks together with birds of prey such as the Fish Eagle, Black Kite, Fishing Owl, Palm-nut Vulture, and Raven. The African soft-shelled turtle is reported to eat juvenile crocodilians. Fish predators include the catfish and, no doubt, the tiger fish as well as the Zambezi shark and other scavenging sharks in the estuaries. It is also very likely that other marine fish species are predators during times when newly hatched young are washed out to sea when rivers are at peak flood levels.

Konrad Wothe/Bruce Coleman Ltd.

◄ The long-necked Goliath Heron shares habitat with Africa's crocodiles but, as with other avian predators, the predation works both ways — the herons may make a meal of crocodile hatchlings but adult crocodiles will take herons, large or small, should the opportunity arise.

At the nesting beaches, prowling monitor lizards take a heavy toll of young in the nests, particularly when the parent crocodiles leave these open and unattended while they transport part of their brood to the crèche area.

There are always weak and abnormal hatchlings that do not stand a chance of survival. Congenital abnormalities include blindness, twisted or rudimentary tails, scissor-shaped mandibles, tumours, and runts. In some prematurely hatched crocodiles, the yolk sac is distended and has not been absorbed into the abdomen, limiting movement. Some abnormalities occur because the eggs were incubated at high temperatures. These hatchlings have a poor chance of survival and are often taken by predators.

G.D. Plage/Bruce Coleman Ltd.

◄ Largely fish-eating, the aptly named African Fish Eagle dives for fish in the Okavango swamps in Botswana but is not averse to crocodilian hatchlings in the same vicinity.

97

# BIRTH DEFECTS IN AMERICAN ALLIGATORS

MARK W.J. FERGUSON

Crocodilians exhibit a mixture of primitive characteristics (for example developing in an external calcified egg) and advanced characteristics (for example, the presence of an intact palate separating the nasal and oral cavities, a four-chambered heart, and a mammalian-like diaphragm). This unique combination makes them an extremely valuable model in human biomedical research.

Research currently being carried out on American Alligator embryos has shown that spontaneous malformations occur and are nearly always fatal, with the exception of some mild disorders, such as in pigmentation. Among the more serious malformations are spina bifida, cyclopia (one eye) and monorhiny (one nasal passage), microphthalmia (small eyes) or anophthalmia (absent eyes), hydrocephalus, and incomplete twinning. Careful study of the eggs produced by female alligators of different ages shows that very young and very old females have the highest spontaneous incidences of birth defects in their offspring; this pattern exactly matches that seen in humans. The percentage of spontaneous malformations among these females can be manipulated by altering the maternal diet — alligators fed a diet rich in fish will produce many more birth defects than those fed a diet rich in red meat because the fish-rich diet is deficient in such fat-soluble vitamins as vitamin E and in trace elements like selenium. (It is now recognized that maternal diet may also be important in human birth defects.)

Environmental conditions during egg incubation can also give rise to spontaneous malformations. Essentially, embryos incubated at the limits of the viable incubation range — 29° C (84° F) and 34° C (93° F) — produce high numbers of spontaneously malformed embryos or embryos that, although viable, do not grow very well and eventually end up as the runts of the population. If the eggs are allowed to dehydrate during incubation this also has an adverse effect on embryonic development. Malformations observed in eggs incubated at the extremes of incubation temperatures, include scoliosis of the spine and duplication of limbs.

It is also now well established that the temperature of egg incubation also determines the pigmentation pattern of the hatchling. Embryonic alligators incubated at 33° C (91° F) have one extra stripe compared with their counterparts incubated at 30° C (86° F). The mechanism underlying this pigmentation difference relates to the larger size of the embryos (incubated at the higher incubation temperatures) at the time when the wavelike pattern of pigmentation initiation passes down the embryonic body.

Since alligator embryos can be manipulated much more easily than mammalian embryos they are an extremely good model for biomedical research into the molecular mechanisms of sex determination, birth defects, and embryonic development. It is possible to monitor the development of an alligator embryo as it actually occurs in the egg. This can be achieved either by explanting the embryo and growing it under sterile-culture conditions or by removing the top one-third of the eggshell and incubating the lower two-thirds of the eggshell in a sterile incubator. This semi-shell-less culture results in normal development of the alligator embryo and this development can be watched, filmed, and experimentally manipulated in the same embryo as development progresses; such experiments are impossible to do in mammals. Furthermore, by combining this semi-shell-less technique with precise microsurgical removal of the cells that would normally form the mandible (lower jaw) of the embryo it is possible to develop embryos in semi-shell-less culture with almost no lower jaw and tongue but with a completely normal palate. In this way it is possible to film the development and closure of the palate as it would happen normally. These so-called "longitudinal studies" of palatal development are the first ever to have been conducted on any animal. Naturally occurring malformations, where the embryo has virtually no lower jaw or tongue, are common and fatal. It is also possible to add various compounds to the developing embryo to produce specific malformations, such as cleft lip or cleft palate, enabling the development mechanisms that are disturbed to be studied and the surgical repair of these defects in embryos to be carried out.

▼ Defects such as incomplete twinning (left) or reduced development of the lower jaw and tongue (right) can be induced in the laboratory, but are also normal occurrences in the wild where variations in incubation temperature, deficiencies in maternal diet, or other factors produce malformations that are almost invariably fatal.

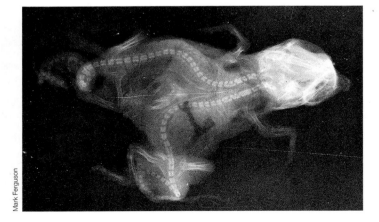

Martin Wendler/NHPA

## MORTALITY OF SUBADULTS AND ADULTS

Natural mortality of crocodilians of more than 1 meter (3 feet) in length is relatively rare. Adult Nile Crocodiles are sometimes preyed on by lions, particularly when caught on land at night. Hippopotamuses have also been known to kill adult Nile Crocodiles, presumably in defense of their own calves, and African elephants are known to kill crocodiles found on dry land.

In Central and South America, anacondas (large constricting snakes) have been reported to take medium-sized caimans and jaguars have been observed killing crocodiles. In southern Asia, leopards and tigers may occasionally take subadult or adult crocodilians.

Bill Green

▲ The anaconda (*Eunectes murinus*) is a semi-aquatic, South American constrictor that reaches lengths of 7.5 meters (25 feet) — longer than many of its caiman victims. Anacondas, however, are not major predators of caimans.

◄ The remains of a rope around its snout and tied to the bank identified the predator of this 1.5-meter (5-foot) long Johnston's Crocodile (*Crocodylus johnsoni*) as human. Whether its death was as a result of drowning or shotgun wounds is unknown but the amateur hunter or poacher never returned to skin the carcass.

◄ A lone male hippopotamus basks, apparently peacefully, next to a 3.5-meter (12-foot) long Nile Crocodile in a river in Kenya. But who is the prey and who the predator in other such encounters — especially when a large group of crocodiles is involved — cannot always be predicted although the hippopotamus will usually emerge the victor in a one-to-one confrontation.

Richard Matthews/Seaphot Limited/Planet Earth Pictures

T. Pooley

▲ Although mortality among adult crocodilians is not common during territorial combat in the breeding season, subdominant males are occasionally killed, usually by larger, more aggressive males. Almost totally submerged, the victor guards the carcass of a rival killed in just such an encounter.

## CANNIBALISM

Cannibalism in natural populations of crocodilians is considered rare by some researchers but is thought to be common by others. It is the only predation that is seemingly worldwide but difficult to quantify.

It appears that cannibalism does not occur between parental crocodilians and their offspring, or perhaps even between adult males and females. However, there is some evidence that subadult individuals sometimes eat juveniles and adults eat subadults. (On the other hand, adults are known to respond quickly to the distress cries of juveniles,

and subadults are sometimes gently chased away from crèche areas.) One population of Indopacific Crocodiles in Australia was described as its own worst enemy. After 30 years of overhunting all hunting was stopped. The number of juveniles increased rapidly for the first few years. This rate of increase soon slowed as the juveniles of these first few years began to eat the next generation of hatchlings.

In Nile Crocodiles, and possibly other species, combat mortality during the breeding season and among rival males also occurs. The carcasses of these freshly killed males are seldom found and, as

a result, the incidence of mortality from these encounters cannot be determined.

In the Okefenokee National Wildlife Refuge in southern Georgia, the incidence of serious wounds and missing limbs and tails in the alligator population is exceedingly high. (One young alligator collected was missing three legs and half of its tail!) Whether this high rate of maiming is the result of attempted cannibalism or predation by other organisms is unknown.

Interspecific predation between crocodilian species has not been documented. It is possible that the Indopacific Crocodile preys on other

smaller sympatric crocodile species throughout its range. (This interspecific competition may account, in part, for there being so many isolated populations or species of closely related crocodiles in the Indopacific region.)

The primary predators on crocodilians at present are, of course, humans. Killing crocodilians out of fear, spite, or for commercial purposes is widespread. No size class is immune from human persecution. Natural predation and mortality of these ruling reptiles pales into insignificance compared with the toll from hunting and habitat alteration by human beings.

# SOCIAL BEHAVIOR

JEFFREY W. LANG

▲ Mistakenly regarded as primitive, crocodilians owe much of their success as predators and their continued survival to a surprisingly complex and sophisticated social life. In this social life highly ritualized behaviors, such as the snout rubbing by this female American Alligator, play an important regulating role.

Crocodilians have a reputation for ferocity but a closer look reveals that these unique reptiles exhibit many subtle and complex behaviors on a par with those of birds and mammals. Perhaps the most unusual and interesting behaviors are social, and these are surprisingly diverse and sophisticated. The voices and sounds of crocodilians terrified early explorers and still intrigue scientists today. Alligators and crocodiles routinely guard eggs, liberate young from the nest, and then protect the hatchlings for weeks or months. The remarkable social life of crocodilians clearly sets them apart from turtles, lizards, and snakes, and even provides a glimpse of how the dinosaurs, their closest relatives, may have behaved.

At first glance it is hard to imagine how an alligator or crocodile could really be a social creature. These carnivores are supposedly solitary predators, patrolling waterways or waiting in ambush, when not lying about basking in the sun. But a quiet stroll along a trail through the Florida Everglades quickly dispels any doubts. In this open grassland dotted with tree islands and hummocks, the water is knee-deep. On a warm morning in early October, a group of one-month-old alligators lie motionless on lily pads in a shallow depression. Well camouflaged in the weedy vegetation, they escape detection until an unmistakable vocalization, a soft but distinctive guttural sound — "ungh, ungh, ungh" — is heard. Soon the lone caller is joined by its neighbors in a gentle chorus of identical calls. Within minutes, about two dozen hatchlings are evident; several swim about, climb onto fallen branches, or slip slowly into the water. Then the deeper calls of several yearlings, basking among the younger alligators, are heard. Suddenly a loud, startling hiss followed by churning water reveals the presence of a 2-meter (6-foot) long alligator behind a nearby bush. We have disturbed a female alligator with her young from this and the previous season. Family groups like this are commonplace in Everglades habitat and reveal the complexity of crocodilian social interactions.

Prior to 1970, our understanding of crocodilian behavior relied heavily on relatively few detailed natural history accounts. American Alligators (*Alligator mississipiensis*) in the southern United States and Nile Crocodiles (*Crocodylus niloticus*) in eastern and southern Africa were the subjects of these investigations but most of the remaining species were unstudied. Investigating crocodilian behavior is not an easy task since many behaviors occur at the surface of the water or underwater in an environment alien to humans. However, an increasing number of studies have been conducted during the past two decades, due in large part to current efforts to conserve endangered species and to manage wild populations. The systematic depletion of many species in their natural habitats has led to the establishment of breeding programs in zoos and farms. In these captive facilities, it is possible to examine, at close range, many behaviors performed by animals habituated to humans. Although the high densities in outdoor enclosures lead to frequent social encounters, many interactions are typically stereotyped and species-specific. Behavior that would be rare, if not impossible, to observe in the wild has now been documented for the first time in such settings.

Behavior may be conveniently categorized in terms of its primary functions — maintenance (day-to-day activities associated with survival), social, or reproductive. This chapter outlines key features of crocodilian social life — communication, group living, dominance hierarchies, territoriality, and courtship.

Jeff Foott/Auscape International

▲ Alligators are inactive much of the time — basking in the sun or leisurely patrolling the waterways — but they are capable of immediate response to a variety of stimuli, some of which are not detectable to humans.

Jeffrey W Lang

◄ An alligator's social life begins before hatching — the young communicate with each other while still in their eggs. Nest mates spend most of their first months after hatching together, relying on their mother for protection against predators.

## COMMUNICATION

Crocodilians convey social messages with sounds, postures, motions, odors, and by touch. All of the crocodilian species examined so far use various combinations of vocal, acoustic, and visual messages coupled with tactile and chemosensory cues in particular social contexts. Certain behaviors, especially courtship and territorial displays, have meanings that are species-specific. Each species' repertoire is composed of three types of signals: discrete signals that do not vary, graded signals that vary according to situation, and complex signals, that is, displays that are composites of vocal, acoustic, and visual elements.

Communication begins in the egg and continues throughout a crocodilian's life. Bird embryos are known to communicate while still inside their eggs but the idea of eggs "talking" to one another is often treated with some skepticism. However, in an experiment in which eggs of alligators and American Crocodiles (*Crocodylus acutus*) were being incubated (under controlled conditions in a laboratory), eggs of both species responded to sounds made near the eggs as well as to sounds coming from within nearby eggs, during the final two weeks of incubation. Tapping lightly on the container resulted in "pecking" sounds from within individual eggs. Later, a microphone buried with the eggs revealed that tapping sounds from inside one egg were answered within seconds by similar sounds from adjacent eggs. Because the young emerge from the nest together on a single night, often aided by one or both parents, it is possible that communication among eggs helps to synchronize hatching of the clutch.

Once liberated from its egg, a hatchling vocalizes spontaneously or in response to any disturbance or novel stimulus. The young of all species produce similar but distinct yelps and grunts. It is likely that the young emit several different types of calls, each with a different message. Picking up a hatchling often provokes a "distress" call, which serves to alert other nearby individuals of an intruder or potential predator. Typically, adults respond with threatened or actual attacks. (This protective tendency is so strong that these sounds are often imitated by poachers to attract otherwise wary animals to within shooting range.)

Provoking a large adult to attack is a frightening experience. While staff at a crocodile farm in Papua New Guinea were walking around the breeding pens of freshwater New Guinea Crocodiles (*Crocodylus novaeguineae*) they heard a stray hatchling calling along a fence line. After some searching they found and picked up the hatchling. It called loudly, and immediately the previously quiet pond nearby erupted with the frantic activity of some twenty adults plunging into the water and swimming in the direction of the staff and hatchling. The dominant male responded by dashing to their corner of the enclosure. He headslapped repeatedly in the water at the base of the bank and then charged out of the water straight into the chainlink fence where they were standing. Females swam nervously about, vocalized with deep guttural calls, and also headslapped frequently. Several nights later, the "experiment" was repeated by approaching other pens with a calling young in hand. In an enclosure

► Adult crocodilians, such as the Mugger shown here, respond to vocalizations from within the nest to assist the hatchlings to escape, and will move quickly to the aid of a hatchling that emits a distress call. Threatened young may be sheltered, picked up by adults, or actively defended against predators.

Jeffrey W. Lang

Ernest Neal/Seaphot Limited/Planet Earth Pictures

containing a female and her young from two previous years, the calls from the hand-held captive readily elicited lower frequency calls from juveniles throughout the pen. In a nearby rearing pen full of juveniles, the hatchling's calls were immediately answered by a loud synchronous chorus of grunts.

In many species, other vocalizations produced by young function as "contact" calls, to bring the young together and maintain the cohesion of the group. When baby alligators are fed, they vocalize frequently. Introducing youngsters to a new pen frequently stimulates them to call as they move about and explore their surroundings. Recent studies of groups of young alligators in marsh habitat in Florida indicate that individuals disperse in the evening to feed, and then gather together during the daytime when they spend much of their time basking in a tightly knit group. Vocalizations are most frequent as the group disperses in the evening and when it forms again the next morning. Adults nearby, presumably the parents, may signal to hatchlings with vocalizations or sounds when predators approach or when there is food in the vicinity but little is known at present about the role of adults in promoting the cohesion of hatchling groups.

The different species of crocodilians have distinct vocalizations, and the tendency to vocalize varies with species. In nearly all species, juveniles

and adults are able to vocalize and handling often provokes the deep, guttural "whaa" calls characteristic of older animals. Alligators and caimans are notoriously noisy species whereas some species of crocodiles rarely call under any circumstances. Alligators are notably the most vocal, and are renowned for the bellowing choruses of breeding males and females that reverberate through the marshes and swamps in the late spring. Among Indopacific Crocodiles (*Crocodylus porosus*), Siamese Crocodiles (*Crocodylus siamensis*), and New Guinea Crocodiles, adult females produce a throaty, repetitive vocalization, sometimes called a "roar," when approached closely by another adult. Nile Crocodiles also produce roars or growls in a similar situation. Mugger (*Crocodylus palustris*) are less vocal but, on occasion, roar during assertive displays or aggressive encounters. Even adult Gharials (*Gavialis gangeticus*) make sounds, albeit infrequently. In a sequence recorded during the filming of nest opening by a female Gharial, the parent was approached by a male and another female. As the other female approached the nest being uncovered, the parent chased her away and vocalized softly. The differences apparent between species may be related to their particular habitats. Species living in open water, in lakes, and along rivers vocalize less often than species living in marshes and swamps.

▲ Young Nile Crocodile hatchlings, like most species of crocodilian typically gather in "crèches" as they bask during the day. They maintain contact by vocalizing when they disperse to hunt in the evening and when they reunite in the morning.

# VOCALIZATION

Crocodilians are the "loudmouths" of the reptile world. Various sounds, mostly low frequency, are produced by vocal cords located in the throat. Forceful contractions of the chest muscles push air continuously or in pulses through the voice box (larynx). The sounds range from very low volume, barely audible coughs and hisses, to high volume roars and bellows. Individuals communicating by means of vocalizations are able to convey an array of social messages with particular meanings, depending on the identity of the performer and the context of the performance. Within the past several decades, promoted by concerns for conservation and management, detailed studies (primarily in captivity) have begun to reveal that these vocal messages play a crucial role in the diverse and complex signaling systems unique to crocodilians.

The bellow of the alligator is a loud, throaty roar that lasts for one or two seconds. It is performed repeatedly (from five to seven times) at intervals of about 10 seconds, by both males and females. Bellowing is a long-distance signal easily heard at distances of 150 meters (165 yards). The sound is intense — about 84–92 decibels at 5 meters (16 feet) — almost as loud as standing next to the engine of a small propeller aircraft. Bellowing is a contagious behavior. Although one animal typically begins bellowing, most of its neighbors soon join in. During the spring when alligators congregate in breeding groups, bellowing choruses last from ten minutes to more than half an hour, usually in the early morning and late afternoon. Alligators bellow with voices that are easily identified by a trained observer, so each animal is probably able to recognize and keep track of its friends as well as its foes. The bellow-growl, a lower intensity single bellow, identifies an individual as a female.

Other alligator vocalizations are surprisingly subtle. During courtship, both partners exchange "chumpfs," cough-like, low-intensity purrs that only carry a few meters. Low growls are produced during aggressive interactions and signal an animal's intent to escalate the encounter. Adult alligators also vocalize with grunts in response to the calls of juveniles and hiss defensively when approached by an intruder. Hatchlings and juveniles vocalize with a variety of grunts that vary in character with an animal's size and age. Grunts occur in many social situations. Young alligators grunt when they hatch, when they feed, and when they form groups or disperse. The distress call of a juvenile alerts its peers to impending danger, and elicits approach and possible attack by any adults nearby.

Although American Alligators are the most vocal "singers and talkers," all crocodilians vocalize to some extent. In most species, hatchlings are noisy and respond by frequent vocalizing in many stimulus situations. But as juveniles and adults, certain species, such as American Crocodiles, rely heavily on visual cues, and call infrequently. Others, including Siamese Crocodiles and Common Caimans, rival alligators in vocality. Chinese Alligators (*Alligator sinensis*) emit from two to eight explosive roars that sound similar to the bellow-growls of female American Alligators. The African Slender-snouted crocodile (*Crocodylus cataphractus*) roars repeatedly, sounding like a truck exhaust backfiring. Nile Crocodiles reportedly produce six vocal signals, including a loud, repetitive roar.

Ecological factors probably influence the kinds of calls and the ways in which these are used, and may explain similarities and differences among species. The marked vocality of American Alligators may be related to living in vegetated habitats in contrast to the open environments inhabited by several, relatively silent species of crocodilians. Low-frequency sound travels over long distances with minimal distortion. Repetitive calls facilitate locating the sender. There is evidence that some vocal signals produced by crocodilians are heard underwater where sound travels four times faster and at greater sound pressures than in air.

▲ Vocal or acoustic communication may signal "honorable intentions" during courtship when the male and female expose the vulnerable throat while bellowing to each other (right) or submission to a more dominant adult whether male or female (left).

Communication in the water is well suited to the amphibious lifestyle of crocodilians. A wide variety of sounds are produced that are acoustic rather than strictly vocal. Most notable of these is the headslap or jawclap performed at the surface of the water. The headslap is performed by lifting the head above the water so that the lower jaw is just visible. Often an animal will remain motionless in this position for minutes before swiftly opening then closing its jaws in a biting motion directed at the surface of the water. The result is a very sudden, loud popping sound as the jaws are closed, followed immediately by a resounding splash; the sound is similar to that produced by slapping a flat shovel on the water. In many species, this behavior is typically followed by head submergence and the production of copious bubbles from around the head. Bubbles are produced by exhaling through the throat and nostrils (nares) on the tip of the snout. Some species vocalize with a series of roars just after headslapping and/or thrash the elevated tail from side to side in the water. The entire display, consisting of the headslap and associated behaviors, is an instant attention getter and announces, rather dramatically, the presence and location of its performer.

The exact form and context of headslapping varies somewhat with species but it has been observed in nearly all species studied to date. In the American Crocodile, dominant males headslap two or three times in rapid succession from positions within their own territories. Most other species produce only one headslap rather than a series in rapid succession. But headslapping is a contagious activity, and an initial headslap is usually answered almost immediately by headslaps from other individuals nearby. The acoustic signal produced by the headslap and accompanying loud splash is both an aerial and aquatic message. Animals emerge from underwater, those in the water respond by approaching or retreating, and those on land move into the water. Headslapping, like bellowing, is associated with establishing and maintaining long-term social relationships and is most obvious during seasonal reproductive activities. In captivity, loud noises and

disturbances, such as a vehicle backfiring or a gunshot, sometimes elicit headslaps.

One of the slender-snouted species, the False Gharial (*Tomistoma schlegelii*), is known to headslap but the Gharial of the Indian subcontinent apparently does not. In the latter species, underwater jawclaps have been observed during the reproductive period. Individuals nearby and underwater seem to respond to these signals, which may be analogous to the headslaps of other species. Interestingly, in both species, bubbling behavior is frequently performed by both sexes when courting.

Another type of acoustic message, barely perceptible to humans, is the subaudible vibrations, sometimes referred to as "infrasound," produced by many crocodilians. The trunk muscles are rapidly contracted just beneath the surface of the water, radiating waves pulse out from the body, and the shallow water across the back bubbles up and bounces off the back. These extremely low frequency signals (1–10 hertz) are close to the limits of human hearing but at close range resemble the sound of distant thunder. Male American Crocodiles and Nile Crocodiles use subaudible vibrations during courtship. In alligators and caimans, similar vibrations are produced immediately before bellowing or roaring. These vibrations also precede headslaps in a number of species, including the Mugger. Such signals travel rapidly and over long distances underwater. However, they are difficult to record and document, particularly in the wild, and have not yet been adequately studied.

Other acoustic signals include a variety of sounds produced by exhalations from the throat or nasal chambers. Alligators emit soft, purring "chumph" sounds by expelling air through the nostrils during short-range courtship encounters. In many species, exhalations underwater produce bubbles, ranging from a steady stream of fine bubbles to an explosive expulsion of several large bubbles. Out of the water, loud exhalations produce low, guttural sounds from the throat and hisses from the nostrils. The Gharial relies heavily on hisses and snorts when communicating in or out of the water. Male Gharials develop a

◄ This territorial American Crocodile advertizes his dominance by headslapping at the surface of the water two or three times in rapid succession.

▼ After the ritual headslap courting males, such as this Indopacific Crocodile, will often submerge and produce bubbles while the female (in this case, with a damaged jaw possibly as the result of some previous social encounter) remains with her head out of the water.

◄ Male American Alligators produce subaudible vibrations using the muscles of the trunk. Although detectable at the surface only by the bubbles and ripples they produce, the vibrations can easily be detected underwater.

conspicuous bulb-like structure on the end of their slender snouts where the nostrils are located. The protuberance is a convoluted cavity with connections to the nasal chamber and appears to change hissing exhalations into buzzing sounds as air resonates in the enlarged nasal cavity.

Body postures (in and out of the water) and specific movements are the principal visual communicating signals. In all species, the exposure of the head, back, and tail above the water surface conveys important information about an individual's social status and intent. Dominant animals advertise their large size by swimming boldly at the surface. Conversely, submissive individuals usually expose only the head and readily retreat by submerging underwater. Fighting occurs infrequently, even in high-density breeding groups. In many species, a threatening individual inflates the body and assumes an erect, static posture to exaggerate body size.

In many species, snout lifting is an easily recognizable behavior because the movement is slow and exaggerated. When approached by a dominant male, an animal lifts its snout out of the water at an acute angle, opens its jaws, and holds its head stationary for a period of time. Further approach usually elicits deliberate movements of the snout upward until the approach is halted. In Indopacific Crocodiles and New Guinea Crocodiles, females snout lift and then vocalize repeatedly. In Nile Crocodiles, females and subdominant males snout lift. In American Crocodiles, only females snout lift during daily social encounters and do so silently. This signal clearly indicates submission, probably conveys information about the performer's sex, and may aid in individual recognition. In many of these species snout lifting is a prominent behavior during the initial stages of courtship. In courtship preliminaries, both sexes often lift their snouts in unison and sometimes cross snouts while touching the partner's head.

Tail thrashing is a dynamic visual signal that involves movement of the tail from side to side. This behavior commonly follows headslaps in the water and is also employed on its own during aggressive encounters. Dominant animals on land move the tail from side to side just prior to aggressive encounters. Sometimes just the tip of the tail is moved quickly back and forth before an animal either moves away from an attacker or chases another individual.

Crocodilians also employ tactile and chemosensory messages but little is known about how these signals are sent and received, or what they mean. Courtship entails prolonged tactile contact prior to mating, particularly around the head and neck areas of both partners. Touch receptors are concentrated in these areas and may facilitate not only the perception of physical

▼ Dominant males maintain feeding and breeding territories by chasing away rivals. While the risk of actual attack and injury to this pursued Common Caiman is slight, it does not hesitate to flee, leaping almost out of the water in its haste.

Jeffrey W. Lang

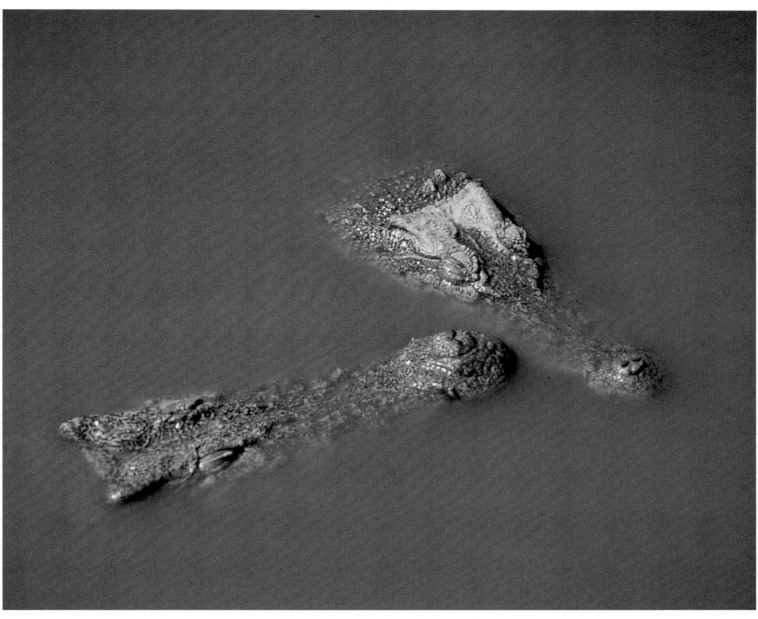

Jeffrey W. Lang

contacts such as snout rubbing but also of other tactile behaviors such as bubbling.

Secretory glands are located under the chin and in the cloaca. The oily secretions from these glands may function as defensive compounds to repulse potential predators and/or may be employed as chemical messages between individuals. Other kinds of reptiles locate one another, mark territories, find mates, and assess reproductive condition using chemical cues. Yearling alligators recognize the glandular secretions of adult males, and young caimans are able to sense the glandular products of other caimans. In breeding enclosures, adult crocodilians exhibit many behaviors that strongly suggest that odors may be an important mode of communication.

It is apparent that adults of the same species living together recognize each other and respond accordingly. Individual recognition may be incorporated into some signals and displays,

particularly vocalizations, which differ in predictable ways for each animal. With a little practice, it is easy to pick out the individual bellow of a particular alligator. Large male alligators have deeper, more resonant voices than smaller ones; among the older males, each voice has a unique quality. Likewise, the headslaps of American Crocodiles are distinctive and recognizable because of minor differences in the way in which each male performs the combination of behaviors.

Even hatchlings may be able to recognize individuals or at least be able to distinguish siblings from other hatchlings. On the basis of mark-recapture studies, most family groups do consist of siblings. New techniques, such as "genetic fingerprinting" using DNA markers, reveal a unique "bar code" for each animal. This information, in turn, reveals the degree of genetic relatedness among individuals, and provides a means of assessing objectively how kinship affects behavior.

▲ Social encounters between crocodilians (in this case adult Siamese Crocodiles) may not be related to aggression, dominance, or courtship. Indeed, crocodilians' social behavior is so complex that it is tempting to believe some encounters are motivated only by social recognition.

## GROUP LIVING

Hatchlings frequently remain in the vicinity of the nest site in crèches and nurseries where they form social groups or pods. Although this behavior is usually associated with the presence of a parent or other adults nearby, hatchling groups persist in assembling even when adults are not present. Presumably, group living decreases an individual's risk of predation and it is therefore not surprising that such behavior is pronounced in hatchlings, which are especially vulnerable to predation. The young of all crocodilian species exhibit this behavior to some extent but there are differences among species in the length of time hatchlings remain together. In addition, there may be differences within a species, which are related to different habitats and/or seasonal regimes. In the Florida Everglades, American Alligators stay in family groups for years and it is not uncommon to

find a female at her nest surrounded by young from several previous seasons. In other parts of their range, however, juvenile alligators disperse at earlier ages. In some species, hatchlings remain together for only weeks or a few months before dispersing. Although in many species nesting females typically care for the young once they have hatched, males of some species remain near the nest site and have been observed guarding young.

Hatchling calls attract other adults, subadults, and even juveniles. Large males (especially dominant males in captive-breeding groups) and females respond demonstratively by approaching, threatening, and sometimes attacking intruders. Intraspecific defense of young has been observed. In captivity, juveniles, subadults, and other adults may be actively excluded from the vicinity of hatchling groups by protective parents. In one captive situation, juvenile Morelet's Crocodiles (*Crocodylus moreletii*) were repeatedly threatened and attacked by a female guarding her young. This behavior typically resulted in juveniles fleeing from the nursery area. If retreat was not immediate the female grabbed the juvenile, held it firmly in her jaws, and shook it vigorously before releasing it.

Juveniles and adults are less gregarious than hatchlings but they also associate in loosely organized social groups. Some species, including American Alligators and Nile Crocodiles, frequently assemble in basking groups on land at particular times of day. Other groups form to exploit locally concentrated food, such as schools of fish. In southwest Louisiana, groups of alligators, ranging in size from 1 to 3 meters (3–10 feet), were recently observed feeding on small fish in the late evening. Every several hundred meters along a coastal canal, the telltale bright red "eyeshines" of eight to twelve alligators were spotted within several meters of one another. Stopping the boat right in the middle of several of these groups, observers were able to sit and watch them feed as they moved leisurely through schools of fish jumping at the surface of the water.

In habitats subject to periodic droughts, crocodilians aggregate in mixed-age groups at sites where there is permanent water. Social interactions, particularly territorial and/or dominance-motivated, are often suspended or diminished in these circumstances. In northern Australia, Johnston's Crocodiles (*Crocodylus johnsoni*) retreat to the deep billabongs in river and stream channels at the height of the dry season. Even though a billabong may be temporarily inhabited by numerous adults and subadults, social interactions are rare and animals generally ignore each other. In the Venezuelan llanos, Common Caimans (*Caiman crocodilus*) move long distances overland as the extensive wetlands recede during the dry season. Large aggregations assemble in the few remaining bodies

▼ Remaining with the female parent reduces the risk of predation for New Guinea Crocodiles (below). Caimans (bottom) congregate in large groups at permanent water, during the dry season. However, groups of animals of varying ages associate for long periods in situations other than these.

Jeffrey W. Lang

Richard Matthews/Seaphot Limited /Planet Earth Pictures

Gordon Langsbury/Bruce Coleman Ltd

of permanent water. In one such situation, more than 200 adult caimans were living in a water hole only 50 meters (165 feet) in diameter and less than 2 meters (6 feet) deep. Although individuals would literally bump into one another as they swam about, most social interactions were amiable. Several large males established dominance in the group but chases and fights were infrequent.

▲ It is not uncommon for young American Alligators from a succession of seasons to stay together in a group with their mother, while juveniles and adults form less tightly knit social groups.

Jeffrey W. Lang

◄ Even in crowded conditions in the dry season, when few large bodies of water remain, Common Caimans maintain amiable social relationships. Large males may dominate such aggregations, but fights are fewer than normal — possibly due to limited food resources and the absence of courtship behavior in response to the crowded circumstances.

## DOMINANCE HIERARCHIES

Systematic studies of captive groups of adults and subadults indicate that dominance hierarchies are a regular feature of crocodilian social life. Large body size and an aggressive temperament appear to be the most consistent characteristics of dominant individuals. Dominant animals control access to mates, nest sites, food, and living space. Challenges may occur but physical combat is rare. Dominance relationships are most obvious during seasonal reproductive activities but, typically, persist throughout the year. Dominance is asserted and maintained by social signals and displays that vary with species. Dominant animals are usually conspicuous and frequently expose the head, back, and tail when approaching other individuals. Submission is signaled by submerging the body, retreating underwater, or moving away.

Large captive males dominate breeding groups and females normally display submissive behaviors in the presence of a dominant male. Females also form dominance hierarchies but challenges among captive females are most frequently related to disputes over nesting sites rather than access to mates. Subadult males and small females occupy low-ranking positions in hierarchies. Less is known about dominance relationships among wild crocodilians but hierarchies based largely on size and sex are formed when adults assemble in breeding groups or in permanent water areas during the dry season. In captive groups, particularly when densities are high, low-ranking animals may be denied access to food, water, shade, and places to bask or nest. Dominant individuals attack submissive animals by grabbing and biting at the base of the tail, just behind the legs. Scarring and injuries usually indicate low-ranking animals that are unable to escape repeated attacks.

Groups of larger juveniles and subadults may form hierarchies in which larger animals control access to available food and shelter but such behavior appears to be both species-specific and density-dependent. In captivity, dominance relationships may contribute to the often marked differences in growth rate among pen mates.

## TERRITORIALITY

Territorial behavior is an expression of site-dependent dominance. In wild populations, dominant males defend territories from which they exclude other males. The defended resources vary with species and include access to mates, nesting sites, foraging areas, basking locations, winter sites, or some combination of these. In some species (for example, Indopacific Crocodiles) territories are defended all year round although these territories vary in size with seasonal changes in aquatic habitat and with seasonal reproduction. In some areas male Nile Crocodiles maintain home ranges, with little overlap, along sections of river throughout the year and territorial behavior is most evident during the breeding season. Females maintain overlapping home ranges, which include nesting sites. In other areas, such as Lake Rudolf in Kenya, this species assembles in large breeding groups near nesting sites. In these aggregations, large male Nile Crocodiles defend territories only during the reproductive season. Females of some species defend territories that include their nesting sites, while in other species females nest close together at communal nesting grounds defending only their own immediate nest sites.

▼ Most dominance displays consist of only ritual behavior but fighting is not uncommon among some species such as the Indopacific Crocodile and the American Alligator. Even in such situations serious injury is rare although adults may show considerable scarring, especially around the base of the tail.

◄ Crocodilians' territorial and defensive behaviors are most pronounced during the breeding and nesting season. Females of even timid species will defend their nests vigorously. In captivity, males such as the Dwarf Crocodile shown here, will also sometimes guard the nest but the extent to which this occurs in the wild is unknown.

In captive breeding groups, territorial defense is density-dependent as well as species-specific. When densities are low, dominant animals maintain separate territories, which may vary in size and location with social status. Females and subadult males may be tolerated within a male's territory but other adult males are excluded. In high-density situations, maintenance of exclusive territories becomes increasingly difficult. Dominant individuals may continue to limit access to defended resources while permitting subordinates to remain nearby. Dominance hierarchies typically replace territorial behavior at high densities.

▼ High-density situations, such as in this pen of captive juvenile New Guinea Crocodiles, dampen dominance and territorial behaviors although larger and more dominant animals may substitute control over access to food and water for territories.

## COURTSHIP

In all species studied to date, the mating system is polygynous; that is, each breeding male mates with a number of females. In some species, large or small aggregations of adults form during the breeding season. At these gatherings, large males set up mating territories or establish dominance hierarchies. In other species, breeding takes place within territories occupied throughout the year. The number of reproductive males relative to the number of reproductive females is known as the operational sex ratio. In crocodilians, this ratio varies with social structure and group size. In Nile Crocodiles, it is about 1 male to 20 females in the large breeding groups, which form on Central Island in Lake Rudolf, while in other habitats, such as rivers, the operational sex ratio is 1 male to 5–10 females. For some territorial species, the operational sex ratio is much lower — 1 male to 1-3 females. Territorial defense in all species intensifies during the breeding season.

Establishment of territory and dominance precede courtship and mating. A large male advertises his dominance by swimming conspicuously within his territory with much of his body exposed on the surface, periodically engaging in species-specific assertion displays. Headslapping or an explosive jawclap performed at the surface of the water is often accompanied by vocalizations, exhalations, and/or subaudible vibrations. Large males dominate breeding groups by patrolling territorial boundaries and by approaching other animals. Subdominant males are actively challenged and excluded by vigorous chases and open-mouthed lunges. Combat between males contesting dominance involves

Jeffrey W Lang

▲ Subtle changes in relationships occur during courtship when males are prepared to fight any other male that threatens their territory. This female American Alligator, however, can approach the male (here with a tag) in a manner that will redirect his aggression into courtship displays.

▶ Nile Crocodiles are polygymous, males mating with a number of females to maximize their chances of breeding successfully. However, it is often the female that initiates courtship and copulation, which may last for several minutes.

Adrian Warren/Ardea, London

Jeffrey W. Lang

head-to-head physical contact; for example, sparring with the jaws or head ramming and posturing with raised, inflated bodies.

Head ramming is a particularly brutal display of strength characteristic of Indopacific Crocodiles. Two similar-sized males align themselves with their bodies parallel and facing in the same direction. The two first swing their heads sideways and away from their sparring partner to gain momentum then bash their heads together with a loud "thud." These contests apparently do little permanent damage and often go on for an hour or more. Among American and Nile crocodiles, males contesting dominance fight with open jaws directed at a rival's jaws. "Bites" during these encounters usually do little damage but serve to hold a rival while he is being overpowered.

Females are tolerated within territories and indicate submission upon approach by snout lifting, vocalizing with sex-specific calls, and/or by submerging. In some species, females tolerate other females during courtship but sometimes a group of females form their own dominance

hierarchies within male territories. In other species, several females defend individual territories within one male's territory.

Receptive females typically initiate courtship and tolerate other females nearby as they court and mate. Dominant males interfere with courtship attempts by subdominant males. After such an interruption, a female often resumes courtship with the dominant male once he has displaced a subordinate. In large aggregations, females move with impunity between the territories of different males, and may court and mate with several territory holders in succession. In captivity, dominant males often court and mate with receptive females in serial sequence, repeatedly courting and mating with one female for days and subsequently consorting in similar fashion with another. Although female-female aggression is more subdued during courtship than during nesting, social hierarchies among females during the courtship period are evident and may affect when and how often a female mates with the dominant male.

▲ Aggression is so constant a part of a male crocodile's behavior in the breeding season that even a potential mate must divert it with submissive displays. To initiate courtship or indicate submission, this female American Crocodile reduces a large male's aggression by snout lifting as she swims past.

Courtship and mating consist of a sequence of attraction or advertisement behaviors followed by pair formation, precopulatory behaviors, and finally copulation. Dominant males approach females to initiate courtship or females approach a dominant male, often after a male-male aggressive interaction or an advertisement display. During pair formation and precopulatory activity, males and females engage in a variety of species-specific behaviors, which include snout contact, snout lifting, head and body rubbing and riding, conspicuous male displays, vocalizations, exhalations, narial and guttural bubbling, circling, and periodic submergence and reemergence. Mating occurs when the male mounts the female by moving onto her dorsum, positions his tail and vent underneath the female's tail, and inserts the anteriorly curved penis into the female's cloaca. Copulation is difficult to observe because it occurs underwater but successful copulation appears to take several minutes and may last 10–15 minutes or longer. In captive groups, a pair may copulate on repeated occasions for several days.

Differences among species in courtship and mating behaviors are readily apparent. In some species, such as the American Crocodile, there is a determined order to the sequence — copulation predictably follows once the couple engage in certain precopulatory behaviors. In others, such as the American Alligator, the sequence is more flexible and less predicatable — precopulatory behaviors occur repeatedly but many sequences are interrrupted before mating occurs. These behaviors probably function primarily to enable individuals to assess the attributes of potential mates and also to synchronize reproductive activity. Courtship behavior may also serve as a premating mechanism to prevent interbreeding and ensure reproductive isolation although, in captivity, hybridization between related species has been documented.

▲▶ Courtship and mating may occur in a strict sequence or in a more casual manner. In the New Guinea Crocodile pre-copulatory behaviors such as pair formation (top) and underwater bubbling by the female (above) are followed by copulation (right). During copulation the female shown here holds her snout out of the water but in many instances the female too will submerge.

▶ The vocalizations, snout lifting and open-mouthed displays that form much of crocodilian social behavior may look ferocious but are no more lethal than territorial and reproductive displays of birds or terrestrial mammals such as deer or mountain goats. Such behaviors are designed to impress, establish status, or indicate intentions that are not necessarily aggressive.

# REPRODUCTION

WILLIAM ERNEST MAGNUSSON, KENT A. VLIET,
A.C. (TONY) POOLEY, and ROMULUS WHITAKER

Field studies, both in the wild and on captive animals, have revealed that the reproductive cycle of crocodilians is protracted, complex, and the most advanced among reptiles.

Sexual maturity in crocodilians is both size and age dependent. There is sexual dimorphism in size in most species of crocodilians, with males growing faster and reaching a larger size at maturity than females. In general, alligatorines and some small crocodylines become reproductively mature at relatively small sizes while the big crocodylines and Gharials delay reproduction until they are larger.

Unlike birds and mammals, the sex of whose embryos are determined at the moment of fertilization, the embryo held within a newly laid crocodilian egg is without gender. The temperature at which the egg is incubated during the first few weeks in the nest determines if the embryo will develop into a male or female. The critical temperature varies among species but all species of crocodilians, whether they live in Himalayan mountain streams, tropical jungles, or temperate swamps, incubate their eggs at temperatures close to 30° C (86° F). Prolonged exposure to temperatures below about 27° C (81° F) and above about 34° C (93° F) kills embryos of most species. It is far from clear just how crocodilians manage to make nests that function as fairly precise incubators when they must work with such a variety of materials and in conditions that range from full exposure to sunlight, wind, and rain to almost complete protection against the elements under dense forest canopies.

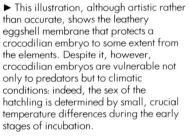

▶ This illustration, although artistic rather than accurate, shows the leathery eggshell membrane that protects a crocodilian embryo to some extent from the elements. Despite it, however, crocodilian embryos are vulnerable not only to predators but to climatic conditions: indeed, the sex of the hatchling is determined by small, crucial temperature differences during the early stages of incubation.

From *Encyclopedie de Diderot*/Roger-Viollet, Paris

Michael Cermak

◀ While caiman nests are large, carefully constructed mounds of vegetation hidden in swamps or forest undergrowth, Johnston's Crocodiles simply excavate a hole nest in sand in exposed river banks. There is comparatively little parental care of the nest and egg mortality is high.

## CAIMANS

Courtship of wild caimans has been studied only in savanna populations of the Common Caiman (*Caiman crocodilus*). In the llanos of Venezuela and the pantanal of Brazil, Common Caimans become concentrated in isolated ponds during the dry season. Courtship and copulation take place at the end of the dry season, preparatory to dispersal and nesting. At this time large animals, presumably males, are seen to lift their heads high and hold their tails almost vertically out of the water. Sometimes the tail is waved sideways. Normally copulation takes place with the male above water level and the female completely submerged but, under conditions of low water, the female may mount the male and twist her tail under his.

Common Caimans may use less vocal communication during courtship in the llanos or the pantanal, presumably because visual signals are much more effective than vocal signals at close quarters in open habitat. The Black Caiman (*Melanosuchus niger*), like the American Alligator (*Alligator mississippiensis*), is known to bellow during the courtship period and there are unconfirmed reports that the Common Caiman also bellows in Amazonia. As far as is known dwarf caimans (genus *Paleosuchus*) do not use loud vocal signals during courtship.

Caimans and all other alligatorines make mound nests out of fresh vegetation, soil, and leaf litter. No alligatorine makes hole nests in exposed beaches or friable soil as many crocodylines and gavialines do. This is surprising as many sea turtles and giant freshwater turtles nest in this way along South American ocean beaches and the extensive sandbanks exposed in the Amazon system during the season of low water.

The size and composition of caiman nests appear to depend more on the habitat and the availability of material than on the species involved. Nests are generally 1.5–2 meters (5 – 6.5 feet) in diameter and 40 –100 centimeters (16–39 inches) high. Nests made in swamps where there are abundant grasses and sedges are generally larger than nests made in forests where leaf litter and soil are the only materials available.

In both the llanos and the pantanal, the Common Caiman nests during the season that the low-lying plains are covered by floodwaters. The llanos floods in the Northern-Hemisphere summer and the pantanal floods during the Southern-Hemisphere summer so the caiman populations in these areas nest asynchronously. In the Amazon basin, the Common Caiman has been reported to nest during the dry season, during the wet season, or all year round, depending on the locality. Although the southernmost populations might not be able to nest in winter because of low temperatures, breeding season seems to be linked to the cycles of rainfall and river levels over most of the range. Much more work needs to be done on the factors affecting reproductive cycles of the Common Caiman.

Information on the nesting season of the Black Caiman, Cuvier's Dwarf Caiman (*Paleosuchus palpebrosus*) and Schneider's Dwarf Caiman (*Paleosuchus trigonatus*) is limited but it appears that all three species nest at the end of the dry season and the beginning of the rainy season in areas with warm climates. Much of the range of the Broad-snouted Caiman (*Caiman latirostris*) is subject to low winter temperatures. Its pattern of nesting in spring probably evolved to take advantage of the warm seasons for egg incubation

# SEX DETERMINATION

JEFFREY W. LANG

The sex of a bird or mammal is determined at conception by particular sex chromosomes. Not all vertebrates, however, have sex chromosomes; in some vertebrates, sex is determined at a later stage of development or growth — certain fish, for example, change sex even as adults, depending on the social situation or the environment. In reptiles, sex determination has been characterized as being either genetic or environmental. In crocodilians, many turtles, and some lizards, the temperature experienced by the embryo in its egg is a major determinant of hatchling sex, a type of environmental sex determination referred to as temperature-dependent sex determination (TSD). By simply altering or controlling egg temperature during development, it is possible to produce in a predictable manner the desired sex or a predetermined sex ratio.

Among crocodilians, TSD was first reported in 1982 for American Alligators, based on artificial incubation of eggs at constant temperatures in a laboratory and on studies of natural nests in coastal Louisiana. High temperatures of 32°–34° C (90°–93° F) result in male American Alligators; low temperatures of 28°–30° C (82°–86° F) yield females. At intermediate temperatures over a narrow range, both male and female American Alligators are produced in varying proportions. This result helps to explain some puzzling reports about the sex ratios of juvenile alligators from Louisiana. In the wild, males comprised 60–80 percent of the young alligators sampled, whereas, among farm-reared animals, only 10–25 percent were male. In this instance, artificial incubation of the eggs had evidently resulted in "cooler" temperatures and, consequently, a preponderance of females.

To date, TSD has been demonstrated in five species of crocodilines and in three species of alligatorines. Since all species of crocodilians lack sex chromosomes it seems likely that TSD will eventually be demonstrated in all species. However, there are important differences in the pattern of sex determination exhibited by each species. In all species, exclusively females are produced at low incubation temperatures. In crocodiles, high incubation temperatures also produce mostly or only females; males are produced at intermediate temperatures. In American Alligators and in Common Caimans, only males are produced at high temperatures. Species differences such as these are relevant for management because the conservation and/or utilization programs for each species must be designed and implemented differently.

For every species, very small differences of 0.5°–1° C (1°–2° F) in incubation temperature result in markedly different sex ratios. The critical period of thermal sensitivity (when temperature affects sex) begins early in development and extends throughout the first half of incubation. Where the female builds her nest and when she lays her eggs both have major effects on the sex ratio of her offspring. A nesting female often makes "trial" nests and appears to be very selective in choosing a nesting site. Thermal cues probably play a major role in nest-site selection and construction. In Louisiana, some

American Alligators build mound nests on warm levees; others nest in cool marshes. The warm nests produce predominately male hatchlings, whereas the cool nests yield females. In south India, female Mugger that nest early produce mostly female offspring because nest temperatures in the soil are cool. When soil temperatures are warmer later in the nesting season, the hatchlings are mostly males.

It is not surprising that, in many crocodilian nests, all of the siblings are the same sex. Sometimes incubation temperatures vary enough within a nest to produce males in the top layer of eggs and females below or vice versa. Despite the diverse habitats and climates in which crocodilians live, incubation conditions for all species are remarkably similar whether they build mound or hole nests. During the two or three months of incubation, egg temperatures are still strongly dependent on prevailing weather conditions. Droughts and low water levels result in drier, hotter incubation temperatures; rain and high water levels lower incubation temperatures. In the wild, sex ratios are strongly skewed in favor of females in most years but also fluctuate from year to year. Conceivably, a changing climate might lead to the overproduction of one sex and the eventual extinction of the species. But crocodilians are an ancient lineage, and their continued survival argues against such simple scenarios.

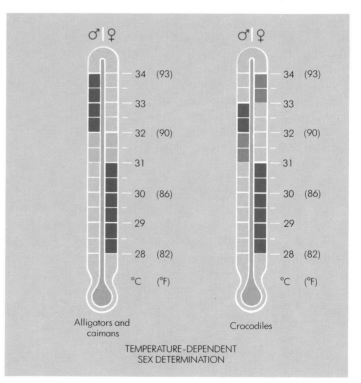

TEMPERATURE-DEPENDENT
SEX DETERMINATION

▲ The patterns of temperature-dependent sex determination for American Alligators and Common Caimans (left) show that females are produced at low temperatures and males are produced at high temperatures. The alligator-caiman pattern involves a single transitional (or pivotal) temperature yielding mixed sex ratios. The patterns for five species of *Crocodylus* (right) are less clear-cut. Exclusively females are produced at low temperatures and predominantly females are produced at high temperatures. Males, in varying proportions around a peak intermediate temperature, result at mid-range incubation temperatures.

William E. Magnusson

William E. Magnusson

and growth of hatchlings. Nesting is also probably costly in terms of energy expenditure. Female Schneider's Dwarf Caimans do not breed every year and it is likely that other species also require a year or more to recover after each nesting. Well-fed captive crocodilians can breed annually.

It is extremely time consuming for researchers to find the nests in the first place, let alone construct heat budgets for crocodilian nests. Also, disturbance by the investigator often attracts predators to the nest, which ends the experiment prematurely. Despite these problems, study of the thermal relations of caiman nests promises to be an exciting area of future research. Preliminary studies of the Common Caiman, Schneider's Dwarf Caiman, and Cuvier's Dwarf Caiman indicate that they generally incubate their eggs at temperatures between 28° C (82° F) and 32° C (90° F) but an attempt to quantify the various sources of heat for eggs has been made only for nests of the Common Caiman in the Venezuelan llanos and for Schneider's Dwarf Caiman in the Amazon rainforest.

The Venezuelan llanos is a very open habitat dominated by seasonally flooded grasslands. Many caimans make nests of grass in exposed situations but some also make nests of earth, sticks, and debris at the bases of isolated trees or in patches of forest. Heat from decaying vegetable matter and heat obtained from solar radiation should be greater in the exposed nests and researchers have found that these nests do, in fact, maintain temperatures about 0.5°–3° C (0.9° – 5° F) higher than earth nests, depending on the time of day.

While solar radiation and decomposition of vegetation are thought to contribute to nest temperatures, the insulation of the mound itself acts to isolate the eggs from extremes of heat or cold. The effects of different materials, and hence temperatures, on the sex of caiman offspring have not been studied.

Many predators have been reported to prey on caiman eggs, including tegu lizards, coatis, foxes, and monkeys, though the tegu lizards and coatis appear to be the principal predators. Females of the Common Caiman, the Broad-snouted Caiman, the Black Caiman, and Schneider's Dwarf Caiman remain near their nests and defend them from predators, at least in the early part of incubation when the fresh nests are easily detected. In captivity, males have also been observed protecting the nests. Flooding, which is a major source of egg mortality in other crocodilians, appears to be of only sporadic importance for

▲ One consequence of nesting so close to termite mounds is that termite workings may cover the eggs of Schneider's Dwarf Caiman. If this happens, as it did with this clutch of eggs, the female caiman will scratch away the hard "termite earth" coating; without such assistance this young hatchling would never have hatched.

◄ The Common Caiman is the most widely distributed caiman species, its breeding cycle appears to be closely linked to fluctuations in water levels. In the Amazon basin this species prefers to build nests in the grass mats that cover the shallow parts of large lakes.

# TERMITE MOUNDS AS NEST SITES

WILLIAM ERNEST MAGNUSSON

Schneider's Dwarf Caiman is only known to nest in dense, closed-canopy rainforest. Therefore direct solar radiation has little potential for contributing to nest temperatures. Most nests of this species are built beside termite mounds where they are warmed by the metabolic heat generated by the termites. Originally, it was thought that in the cool shaded rainforests the caimans were totally dependent on the heat generated by the termites to maintain temperatures high enough both for survival of the eggs and for production of offspring of both sexes. However, it has since been shown that air temperatures, metabolic heat production by the embryos, and possibly metabolism and decay of the vegetable material in the nest also play important roles in the maintenance of nest temperatures.

The critical temperature for the production of males is 31°–32° C (88°–90° F) in Schneider's Dwarf Caiman. In fact, many nests that attain such temperatures early in incubation are not associated with termite mounds or are associated with mounds in which the termite colony has died out and, therefore, no longer generates significant amounts of heat. These nests are built on top of nests that have been used in previous years. Apparently, the extra insulation between the nest and the cool soil provided by the old nest is sufficient to allow other sources of heat to maintain the temperature of the eggs above 31° C (88° F).

By the end of 100 days or more of incubation the eggs are usually enclosed in a tight mat of roots, which have grown in response to the large quantities of nutrients offered by the mound of decomposing vegetation. Often the termites extend their mound outward around the eggs, cementing them into the mound with hard workings that no hatchling could break through unaided. Parental assistance is therefore vital to release the young from the egg chamber.

▲ Because it builds its nest in dense rainforests, Schneider's Dwarf Caiman cannot make use of sunlight to regulate nest temperatures; instead, it makes use of the heat generated from termite mounds. Eggs are laid near the mound where the optimum temperature prevails.

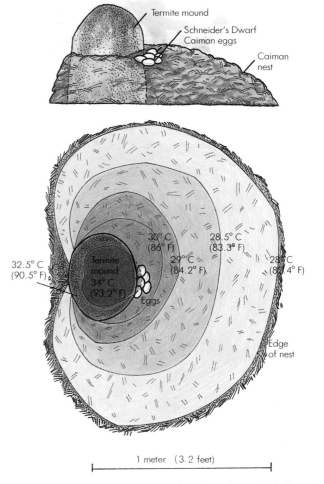

1 meter  (3.2 feet)

▲ A temperature profile through one nest shows how the metabolic heat of the termites helps to maintain the temperature of the nest. The center of the termite mound, at 34° C (93.2° F), is probably too hot for the eggs; the edge of the nest, at 28° C (82.4° F), is probably too cold. The eggs have therefore been laid at the edge of the termite mound where the 32° C (89.6° F) temperature is just right for the development of hatchlings.

caimans. For the smaller caimans defense of the nest against large predators, and for the Black Caiman defense of the nest against humans, may be dangerous. There is a report of a Common Caiman killed by a jaguar and numerous reports of other caimans shot while guarding nests.

In captivity, female Common Caimans, Broad-snouted Caimans, and Cuvier's Dwarf Caimans open the nest in response to hatchling calls and carry the young to water. Male Common Caimans have also been seen to assist with nest opening and carrying hatchlings. In the wild, however, it is usually the female that has been observed to open the nest. Although hatching and emergence from the nest may occur unaided many young cannot make it out of the nest without the help of an adult. This is especially true for Schneider's Dwarf Caiman, which nests in dense rainforest and often deposits its eggs beside termite mounds.

Jany Sauvanet/NHPA

◀ ▼ The female parent of the Cuvier's Dwarf Caiman hatchling (left) and the Common Caiman hatchling (below) may well have assisted them to hatch by opening the nest and carrying them to water. Vocalizations from the batch of eggs in her nest are the signal for action.

Jane Burton/Bruce Coleman Ltd.

William E. Magnusson

▶ In Brazil, newly hatched Schneider's Dwarf Caimans are popularly known as "crowned caimans" because of the gold patch on their heads. Hatchlings are otherwise well camouflaged, blending into the background of the leaf litter in shallow stream beds; their ability to remain motionless underwater for several minutes also helps them to avoid predators.

The degree of parental care after hatching varies with the species and the local conditions. Female Schneider's Dwarf Caimans remain with the hatchling group for only a few weeks before the hatchlings disperse, even though there is no change in the water levels in their nesting streams at this time. In the llanos and the pantanal, female Common Caimans remain with their hatchlings until falling water levels force them to disperse; this period varies from two weeks to four months or more. In Surinam, the female may remain with the young for seven months and the young remain in groups for up to 18 months. One study in the pantanal has described the behavior of the female and her young in detail. During the day the hatchlings remained relatively inactive, often with their eyes closed, near or sitting on the female at the mouth of a small inlet of a lake. At night the hatchlings dispersed around the shore of the inlet to feed on insects. While the hatchlings were feeding the female moved further out into the mouth of the inlet where she could intercept other caimans or large predators trying to enter the inlet. At dawn, the hatchlings started to vocalize and moved back down the inlet to meet the female at their daytime rest site. It is likely that protection of the hatchlings by adults is an important factor in the survival of the hatchlings in their first few weeks or months outside the egg.

Not only the parents defend hatchlings. Other adults and even subadults respond to hatchling distress calls. One researcher reported that he and three companions had their inflatable boat sunk by an adult Schneider's Dwarf Caiman responding to human imitations of the distress calls of hatchling Common Caimans — quite a feat for one of the world's smallest species of crocodilian.

## ALLIGATORS

The alligator is the most temperate of all the crocodilians. The alligator requires warm temperatures for the proper development of the embryos. The seasonal fluctuations in temperature in temperate climates restrict the alligator to reproducing only during the warm summer months. As a consequence, the breeding season of the American Alligator is far shorter than that of any other crocodilian. In February and March, as the temperature begins to rise and the days get longer, hormones begin racing through the blood of the males and the testes begin to enlarge. The females also respond to changing conditions with increased levels of hormones. Female reproductive hormone levels peak in early April. The increased hormone levels stimulate the liver to produce vitellogenin, which is the precursor of egg yolk. The follicles within the females' ovaries begin growing, ultimately

FEMALE UROGENITAL SYSTEM

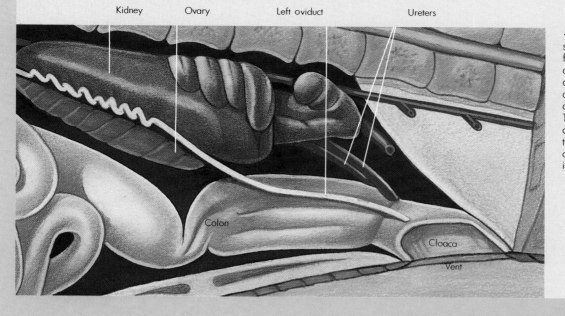

Kidney    Ovary    Left oviduct    Ureters

Colon

Cloaca

Vent

◄ In the female reproductive system, at ovulation, the ova pass from the ovaries into the convoluted oviducts where they are fertilized. In the oviduct, albumen, the eggshell membrane, and eggshell surround the ova. The two oviducts open into the cloaca slightly nearer the tail than the ureters, which, in the absence of a bladder, also open directly into the cloaca.

MALE UROGENITAL SYSTEM

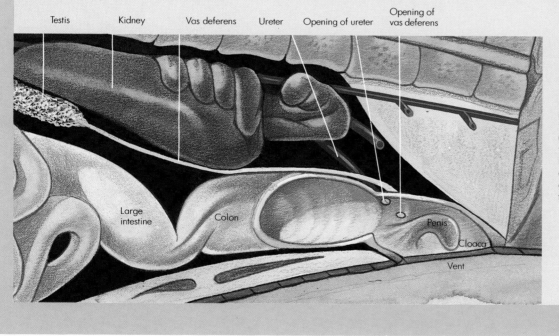

Testis    Kidney    Vas deferens    Ureter    Opening of ureter    Opening of vas deferens

Large intestine

Colon

Penis

Cloaca

Vent

◄ The reproductive organs of male crocodilians show certain distinctive features. The penis, always bent and relatively solid, is attached to the ventral surface of the cloaca inside the body. Muscles and tissue in the cloaca force the penis outside the vent (cloaca) during mating. The two vasa deferentia ducts open at the base of the penis and sperm is conducted along a single, open groove on the dorsal surface of the penis.

increasing tenfold in diameter. The males' maximum sperm output occurs in late May, just at the time that the females ovulate.

In Florida, virtually the entire population of reproductive females lay their eggs within a two-week period in early June. In other areas, egg deposition has also been found to occur in a discrete two-week period but the timing of this period is influenced by temperature and length of daylight, and varies slightly from year to year. Rainfall does not appear to be a factor although if some nesting habitat is covered with water this has an adverse effect on overall reproductive effort. A

maximum of two-thirds of adult female alligators reproduce each year. This is a much smaller proportion than has been found to be the case in many crocodile species. The reasons for this reproductive quiescence are unknown: perhaps the energy requirements of producing a large clutch of eggs are simply too great for most females to build up their reserves each year.

Alligators become sexually mature at 1.9 meters (over 6 feet) in total length. Males grow a little faster than females so they reach this length at a younger age. In Louisiana, males reach maturity in about seven years while females may

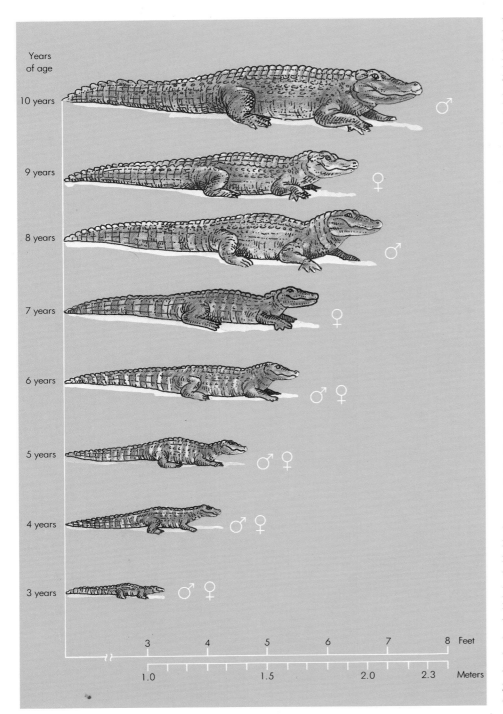

Years of age

10 years ♂

9 years ♀

8 years ♂

7 years ♀

6 years ♂ ♀

5 years ♂ ♀

4 years ♂ ♀

3 years ♂ ♀

3    4    5    6    7    8 Feet

1.0    1.5    2.0    2.3 Meters

to interact. Courtship may continue for several hours in some cases. Both partners attempt to press the other under water; this apparently allows partners to assess each other's size and strength. The male then presses the female under and pulls himself up into a mounted position. Mating takes place in the water and usually lasts only a minute or two before they separate. Alligators are polygamous and may mate with several partners during the courting season. Although courtship-associated behavior may last for two months, males have viable sperm for only about one month, and in females the time between ovulation and nesting is only 3 – 4 weeks.

The female alligator scratches dirt and vegetation from the immediate area into a pile, repeatedly dragging her body over the nest until it is compacted into a mound. In the center of the mound she prepares an egg chamber, scooping out a cavity in the mound with her hind feet. Once prepared, she begins to lay her clutch of eggs. With her hind feet positioned in the nest cavity, she drops the eggs (one every half minute or so) until the clutch is complete. Some say that the female alligator actually catches the eggs with her feet as they drop into the nest; if this is true, it certainly is not always the case. The female becomes completely quiescent during the egg-laying process. Humans can approach the female and even catch the eggs as they are being deposited without fear of attack.

The eggs are large, about the size of a goose's egg, and creamy white in color. An average-sized female lays about 35–40 eggs. Larger, older females produce more eggs. Nests containing up to 100 eggs have been found, although these probably represent the combined clutches from more than one female. In about a day, a small white spot forms on the top of the egg as the developing alligator embryo attaches to the eggshell. This spot soon becomes a complete band around the middle of the egg. As the embryo grows, the band increases in width until it encompasses the entire eggshell.

▲ Alligators grow most rapidly during the first four years of life. Both sexes reach sexual maturity at around 1.9 meters (over 6 feet) in length, although males become sexually active at a younger age because they reach this length sooner than females.

▶ Crocodilian eggs — such as those being laid here by an Indopacific Crocodile — are up to 10 centimeters (4 inches) long, creamy white in color and generally have a smooth, hard shell, although the eggs of some species, such as the American Alligator, have pitted shells.

require nine or even ten years to become sexually mature. In the northern extreme of the alligators' range, where the growing season is much shorter, it takes males about 15 years and females as long as 18 years before they reproduce for the first time. Social interactions, however, tend to prevent adult males from breeding until they are 2.4 –2.8 meters (8–9 feet) in length.

Courtship begins in the first few days of April and intensifies until it peaks in the last two weeks of May. Courtship is a slow, languid affair in alligators, consisting of nudges, bumps, and presses to the head and neck of the partner. Females, typically, initiate courtship encounters (at least during the peak of the activity), enticing males

Frithfoto/Australasian Nature Transparencies

As the embryos grow within the eggs, they exhale carbon dioxide into the nest chamber. This gas dissolves in the humid air within the chamber and forms a weak acid that coats the surface of the eggs. It is possible that this acid slowly degrades the shell, making it thinner and increasing the size of the pores through which the embryo respires. Larger embryos need more oxygen to survive and the enlarged pores would allow more oxygen to reach the embryo. At the end of the 65-day incubation period, as the young alligator pushes its snout through the shell, the weakened eggshell will often fall away easily.

Alligators court during the end of the dry or start of the wet season. Nesting occurs at the start of the wet season, and nests are located so as to avoid flooding by the anticipated rising water levels. The embryos develop as the rains fall so that the new alligators emerge from the nest at a time of peak water levels when food is plentiful.

Parental care behaviors are well developed in crocodilians and the alligator is a typical example. Following nest construction and deposition of the eggs, the female frequently remains with the nest through the incubation period and protects the eggs from predators. When the young are ready to hatch they emit grunts from within the egg. These sounds encourage the female to tear open the nest. The female then lifts each unhatched egg from the nest in her mouth and gently rolls the egg against the roof of the mouth with her tongue, cracking the shell from the egg and releasing the young. Once all of the young are liberated, with or without assistance, the female may carry them to water and often remains with them for several months or, in some circumstances, years.

David Hughes/Bruce Coleman Ltd.

Anthony Bannister/NHPA

▲ Alligator courtship is protracted and casual, and is commonly initiated by females. After a series of nudges and slow bumping movements, either partner (here a captive female) may test comparative strength by attempting to press the other under water.

◄ Curled tightly inside the egg, this Nile Crocodile embryo plays an active role in its own development. It exhales carbon dioxide which, through chemical reaction, may help to make the shell more porous to oxygen as it grows.

Dale Jackson

◄ Female crocodilians display a degree of parental care unusual among reptiles. This American Alligator is guarding her nest and may, when hatching time comes, gently crack the eggshells to help the hatchlings break free.

## NILE CROCODILE

In the tropics of Africa, in countries such as Uganda and Kenya, Nile Crocodiles (*Crocodylus niloticus*) may lay eggs at two separate times of the year — some females lay in August or early September and others in December or January — because there are only slight variations in temperature throughout the year near the equator and different rainfall patterns. However, in much cooler climatic regions, such as subtropical Natal, South Africa (the present southern limit of the species range) there is only one laying season — from late September through to mid-December. Crocodile eggs that incubate in sand nests at 28°–34° C (82°–93° F) and at high humidity levels, would never survive in the subtropics other than over the hot summer months.

In the subtropics, preliminary courtship and stimulative behavior may commence some four or five months prior to egg laying and over this period animals may travel many kilometers from their regularly used winter basking grounds to the nesting beaches. Courtship activity intensifies in the early spring (August–September) triggered by a rise in air and water temperatures, increased humidity, the onset of rains, and perhaps the lengthening of daylight hours.

Arriving at the nesting grounds, the larger males compete for dominance and establish their territories, regularly patrolling their areas and advertising their presence in a variety of behaviors. Dominant males are usually large and aggressive in

◀ After hatching is complete, female American Alligators remain with their young for several months to protect them from predators, including other alligators, herons, snakes, opossums, and raccoons. The young often bask on her head or back, secure from attack.

▼ Male Nile Crocodiles establish dominance at their breeding grounds with a range of aggressive behaviors. Smaller males are attacked and chased well away from sexually receptive females, and most wait until they grow large enough to "win" a territory of their own.

Adrian Warren/Ardea London

▼ In response to the croaks, yelps, and grunts from her young beneath the surface, this female Nile Crocodile digs the nest open with her front feet. She will use her sharp teeth, if necessary, to tear away roots that have grown in between the eggs.

▲ Signaling acceptance of the male by lifting her head out of the water — a submissive gesture that exposes the vulnerable throat and indicates that she will not respond aggressively by attacking her "suitor" — the female Nile Crocodile emits a prolonged low, warbling growl.

▶ The female Nile Crocodile delicately picks up unhatched eggs between her teeth. The unbroken eggs are cracked by repeatedly rolling them between tongue and palate.

temperament. At the approach of an intruder they may respond by executing a headslap, rearing high out of the water with jaws agape, then falling back with a tremendous splash and simultaneous snapping of the jaws audible for a considerable distance. In this manner, a territorial male can advertise his presence at night.

Another behavior designed to intimidate an adversary is to lift the head and much of the forebody above the surface of the water. The aggressive male's neck swells, his jaws partly open then he gives chase in a high burst of speed, causing waves as the powerful tail strokes propel him through the shallows. The adversary may be forced to beach in order to escape and may well be bitten across the tail during the pursuit. If a subdominant male is chased in this manner he may submit by lifting his head almost vertically out of the water baring his throat and remaining passive. He may be circled threateningly or even seized across the base of the tail and thoroughly bitten and shaken before being released. If he does not submit he may suffer serious injury or, very rarely, he may be killed by the dominant male.

Courtship may be initiated by the females who move freely from one territory to another. A female may approach a male and present by submerging both head and tail underwater, showing only the rump. The male circles the female; there is mutual rubbing of snouts, he may submerge and partly lift her out of the water, and will often repeatedly rub the underside of his throat and jaws across her head and back. This may serve to apply pressure on the glands beneath his mandibles and possibly the musk released acts as an olfactory stimulus to the female.

The female indicates acceptance of a courting male by lifting her head high out of the water in the submissive posture, partly opening her jaws, and at the same time uttering a prolonged, low, throaty growl. However, a male may court a female unsuccessfully for days before she accepts his advances; in the meantime he may be courting and mating with four or five other females.

Copulation takes place in water about 1 meter (3 feet) in depth. The male mounts the female then twists his tail slightly downward and sideways so that the base of his tail is brought opposite her cloaca. Copulation may last from only 30 seconds to more than several minutes.

Nests are generally sited about 1–50 meters (3–160 feet) from water and above the normal high-flood levels at lakeside, sandy beaches, or on river banks. Hippopotamus paths or game trails are often used to allow easy access to or egress from the water.

Females may haul out to the nesting beaches a week or more before actually laying and, at times, there is competition for nest sites. This involves two females standing up shoulder to shoulder on raised forelegs, each trying to push the other over

Occasionally, severe bites are inflicted across the nape of the neck by aggressive individuals and usually the larger, heavier females win these contests. Nest sites are scent-marked by repeated rubbing of the mandibles over the sand and grass and, it is thought, also by exudate from the glands in the cloaca.

The nest burrow is excavated by digging out and scraping sand backward with alternate movements of the powerful, webbed hind feet. Once the cavity has been dug to the required depth — the length of her hind limbs — the female shuffles forward until her cloaca is over the cavity. The hind limbs are stretched backward and laying commences. This may take 20–30 minutes for a young female laying only 16–20 eggs but can take nearly one hour for a large, older animal depositing 80 or more eggs. Once laying has been completed, soil is scraped back over the eggs and periodically packed down by tamping motions of the hind feet and claws.

The female appears to fast over the long 84–90 day incubation period, lying up under the shade of small bushes and trees during the heat of the day, close to her nest ready to defend it from predators. Females only move away from their nests for short periods to drink in nearby lakes or rivers. During heavy rains they remain right over the nests to shelter the eggs.

Toward the end of the incubation period some females become torpid and sluggish in their movements but some females aggressively defend their nests from human intruders. They exhale loudly when first approached, and partly open their jaws and growl loudly if the approach continues. They then either snap their jaws two or three times in rapid succession or lunge threateningly at the intruder. The majority, however, slip quietly away from their nests long before a human reaches the nest area.

Despite their nest-guarding efforts, egg predators such as the Nile monitor lizard and others succeed in destroying some 50 percent of all eggs laid over most seasons. These predators

Anthony Bannister/NHPA

Tony Pooley

wait patiently under cover near the nests until the female moves away to the water to drink.

Nest opening is triggered by the yelps, croaks, and grunts of the buried young some 20–30 centimeters (8–12 inches) below the surface. The female begins to scrape away the soil with her front feet and may even use her teeth to sever roots that have grown in between the eggs. Once the sand has been scraped away to expose the eggs, the hatchlings burst out of the eggs. They continue to yelp loudly, raising themselves up high and repeatedly flicking their tails from side to side. The female then lowers her head into the nest cavity and delicately picks up the hatchlings, as well as unhatched eggs, between sharp pointed teeth and gulps them into her mouth. Their weight depresses her tongue to form a pouch capable of holding up to 20 eggs and live young. Once inside the pouch, the young continue vocalizing and during the hours of darkness this enables other hatchlings to locate the mother more easily.

Hatchlings are transported to water, usually to a quiet pool overhung by reeds and grass. There the female releases her brood by submerging her head, opening her jaws and, with side-to-side motions of the head, she washes them out. Unhatched eggs are repeatedly rolled delicately between the tongue and palate with gentle pressure applied every so often to crack the shells. This behavior may continue for about 20 minutes

before the hatchling is freed from the egg.

Over the first few weeks the hatchlings remain close to the mother, often using her back as a basking platform. At the slightest sign of danger, such as a bird of prey circling overhead, the mother rapidly vibrates her trunk muscles and the young immediately dive underwater and remain submerged. The female as well as the male, who remains in the vicinity of the hatchling group, may leap out of the water and snap their jaws should the predatory bird descend too low. When satisfied that danger has passed, the female

▲ The Nile Crocodile's ferocity is belied by its assiduous care of its young. The female carries eggs and hatchlings to the water in a pouch in her mouth (bottom). Both parents guard the hatchlings against predatory birds, Nile monitors, and other dangers.

submerges, probably communicates with her offspring underwater, and, one by one, they climb onto her scaly back to resume basking.

In the early weeks the young feed on shoreline and aquatic insects, small frogs, and crabs. They keep together by uttering contact calls, but, should an individual stray from the crèche area and become separated from the group, it will utter loud double-syllable distress calls. The female parent, or any other female in the vicinity, will respond immediately and often the stray will be captured, taken back to the crèche, and released from the female's jaws.

The young may remain in the crèche area for several weeks, moving away in search of food but keeping under cover of reed beds or overhanging riverside vegetation. However, once they have left the protection of the crèche area, they fall prey to numerous predators. When the young have dispersed, the parents move away from the breeding beaches to feed again — the female, in particular, is usually famished after a long spell of abstinence.

Despite the amount of time, energy, and parental care invested in ensuring survival of

offspring, it is estimated that only about 2 percent of all eggs laid survive the many predators, and environmental and human hazards to reach maturity. But clearly, without this care, we would no longer have the pleasure of viewing these splendid animals in the wild.

## MUGGER

Mugger (*Crocodylus palustris*) are medium-sized crocodiles closely allied in habit and appearance to the better known Nile Crocodile. They are at home in habitats as different as cool hill streams, wide rivers, reservoirs, and coastal salt pans.

Male Indian Mugger mature when they are about ten years old or 2.5 meters (8 feet) in length, and each December they establish their respective territories by a series of activities. They will cruise the perimeter of their territory with back and tail out of the water, leaving no doubt as to their dominance should a smaller male stray into the area. Their most dramatic display — the jawslap or headslap — serves to deter other males but its primary purpose could be to attract females who often respond by coming to the male, sometimes responding with their own jawslap.

▼ Like the Nile Crocodile, the male Mugger is an aggressive competitor for access to breeding females and will drive away rivals that stray into his territory.

G. Ziesler/Bruce Coleman Ltd.

When a female Mugger is ready to breed (in January or February in India) she will often initiate courtship with a male by swimming around close to him with head upraised. She may even mount the male. Sometimes the male starts the courtship by circling, snout rubbing, and submerging, often blowing bubbles under the female. If she seems agreeable, the male proceeds to mount. If she is receptive the couple will start to mate on the surface, with the male on top, and then submerge for 5–15 minutes with only bubbles and stirred up mud to indicate what is happening.

Within about 40 days of mating the female has usually already chosen the area of the bank where she will lay her eggs and will defend this chosen area from other encroaching females. The success of her defense depends on her size, experience, and a quality that can only be termed "spunk." For a few nights before she lays her eggs she will dig trial nest holes, a manifestation of the nesting urge that may be used to check for an optimum temperature.

This greatly increased terrestrial activity may also be helpful in inducing the eggs. Then, when the ambient temperature is about 27°–28° C (80°–82° F) the female digs an L-shaped hole as deep as her hind legs. Here she deposits her 25–35 eggs, each weighing about 85 grams (3 ounces). She then laboriously (for an hour or more) covers and camouflages the nest hole with sand or earth. For the next two months she stays in the vicinity and a "good" mother Mugger will aggressively defend her nest from any intruder. (While this may at one time have contributed to the survival of the species, the appearance of humans soon turned protective behavior into a death warrant as it is easy for a skilled hunter to deal with a crocodile out of water.)

While the reproductive biology of the Mugger is similar to that of other crocodiles, one aspect demonstrated by the captive breeding colony at the Madras Crocodile Bank stands out as unique — up to 80 percent of the nesting female Mugger at the Bank will lay two clutches of eggs each breeding season. So far there is no documentation of any other crocodilian double clutching (except as an aberration). This phenomenon is apparently the result of two distinct peaks in mating activity between December and April each year. It is likely that the consistently high temperatures of Madras and regular feeding induce double clutching.

Both parents will excavate the nest at hatching time, in response to chirping calls emerging from the eggs underground. The parents will hatch the young in their mouths by pressing on the eggs and then transfer the hatchlings to the water. The male may claim exclusive rights to hatch a nest, chasing away all other crocodiles including the mother.

Both parents will guard and then, after one or two years, tolerate the presence of the young in their habitat. It appears, at least in captivity, that the presence of the young inhibits breeding in subsequent seasons. In general the Mugger is a sociable animal and, in both wild and captive situations, large numbers of adults and subadults get along well even in dense concentrations. The young find it safer to stick to their own alternative microhabitats within the parents' territory for the first few years of life.

◄ ▼ Nest making (left) is a laborious process for a female Mugger, starting only after a number of trial nest holes have been dug. Between 25 and 35 eggs are laid (below), then the nest is meticulously covered and camouflaged. During the actual laying females, in a trance-like state, will allow humans to approach but will defend their nests aggressively after egg laying has been completed (bottom).

S. C. Bisserot

▲ Although it can grow as large as a Nile or Indopacific Crocodile — males can reach more than 7 meters (23 feet) in length — the Gharial is a relatively inoffensive fish eater. Females react aggressively to human interference only while guarding their nests.

▶ Male Gharials reach sexual maturity at around 4 meters (13 feet) in length or 15 years of age. When the adult male is patrolling or courting, the *ghara* or nose knob, which gives this species its name, is used to produce a buzzing noise that repels rival males; an audible warning system used effectively in the absence of strong jaws and large teeth.

Romulus Whitaker

## GHARIALS

Considering the very endangered status in the early 1970s of Gharials (*Gavialis gangeticus*) — strangest of all the crocodilians — we are lucky to have them still around.

A large male can reach more than 7 meters (23 feet) in length and a female more than 4 meters (13 feet), putting the species in the top size class along with the Nile Crocodile and Indopacific Crocodile (*Crocodylus porosus*). The minimum breeding size of a female Gharial is 2.6 meters (8–9 feet), a size reached at 7–8 years. A sexually mature male is 4 meters (13 feet) and 15–18 years.

When the male is about 10 years old it starts to develop the distinctive nose knob or *ghara* (Hindi for mud pot). This cartilaginous growth eventually forms a lid on the nostrils that flaps when the male exhales, making a very audible buzz. Hissing and buzzing are conspicuous activities when an adult male Gharial is patrolling territory and courting females. While they occasionally perform weak jawslaps on the surface at courtship time, both sexes also produce an underwater jawslap — a hollow clap that can be heard quite clearly from beneath the water. It is assumed that the jawslap is used as a deterrent to rival males and as an attraction to females, and that subsonics are likely to play a role in this form of communication.

Gharials court with a lot of snout rubbing, mounting by both partners, circling, and following prospective mates around a territory until the right moment and partner arrive. Courtship starts in December and mating takes place in January and February — dry, low-water winter months. The female will indicate willingness to mate by raising her snout skyward and the male will mount. They then submerge for up to 30 minutes.

Gharials are riverine reptiles of northern India, Pakistan, Nepal, and Bangladesh, with a liking for wide, deep stretches of water with plenty of basking security. Being a hole nester, like the Mugger, the female Gharial's preferred nest site is in a high, steep, sandy bank. Nesting is also strongly seasonal, taking place in late March to early April. Like the female Mugger, the female Gharial may make many trial holes in her chosen nest bank before laying her eggs at night, 3–5 meters (10–16 feet) from the water line. She lays 35–60, 100-gram (3-ounce) eggs in a hole about 50 centimeters (20 inches) deep, dug with her hind feet. Gharials, being the most aquatic of all crocodilians, are awkward out of water and the female looks especially vulnerable and out of place during the nesting process. She may spend several hours covering her nest and will then remain in the vicinity for the 60–80 days of incubation. She visits the site at night with increasing frequency as hatching time approaches, and this is the only time that a Gharial may be aggressive toward humans who come near the nest.

The parents are probably unable to pick up their young at hatching time — their teeth are sharp and they have been observed to have difficulty in picking up fish from the ground. But they certainly dig up the nest and help the young to hatch in response to the hatchlings' little grunts. For several weeks (or longer if the annual monsoon floods do not disrupt the area too much) the young remain in a hatchling group protected by the female and, sometimes, by the male. For example, at one nesting site on the Chambal River in Rajasthan, a 4.5-meter (15-foot) female Gharial was observed in mid-July in the shallows with 34 hatchlings around her, on her head, or on the nearby bank.

Monsoon generally means dispersal time and this no doubt adversely affects the survival chances of the delicate young Gharials as they are so soon without the security that their parents and their own grouping behavior gave them.

Romulus Whitaker.

Mike Price/Bruce Coleman Ltd

▲ ◄ ▼ Female Gharials prefer to excavate their nests in steep, sandy banks (above). Like the Mugger, the female Gharial will often dig trial nests before depositing her 35 – 60 eggs. Although the female cannot carry hatchlings in her mouth she helps to dig up the eggs at hatching time (left). She also protects her young until they disperse at the time of the monsoon (below).

Mike Price/Bruce Coleman Ltd.

# HABITATS

ANGEL C. ALCALA and MARIA TERESA S. DY-LIACCO

Simply stated, a habitat is the place where an organism lives. It includes the physical, non-living or abiotic environment (such as soil and water) and the living or biotic organisms (such as plants and animals) normally associated with the organism. Through the life-sustaining phenomena of nutrient circulation and energy flow the living organisms of the habitat are inextricably linked with crocodilians and with each other. To the extent that human beings interact with crocodilians, directly or indirectly, they too are part of the habitat and have emerged in many parts of the world as the crocodilian's major competitor for space and other resources.

Living crocodilians are, typically, animals of the tropics. The exceptions are the two species of alligators — the American Alligator (*Alligator mississippiensis*) that inhabits the southeastern part of the United States and the Chinese Alligator (*Alligator sinensis*) found in the lower Yangtze River in China — and five other species of crocodilians whose ranges extend from the tropical zone to warm regions beyond it. In recent times, crocodilians have been restricted to lowlands and probably never lived at elevations at or above 1,000 meters (3,280 feet), where the mean annual temperature is 5°– 6° C lower than it is in the tropical lowlands.

Crocodilians are amphibious vertebrates, spending part of their lives in water and part on dry land. They inhabit rivers, lakes, ponds, marshlands, swamplands, and estuaries. These habitats, varying in water quality, salt concentration, and other characteristics, are ecologically linked with terrestrial communities that include deserts, grasslands, savannas or wooded grasslands, and forests. Most of these habitats are found in the tropics, although a few extend to the subtropical regions of the world.

▼ The preferred habitat of the Black Caiman, the largest of the South American caimans, appears to be flooded forests (as shown here) or quiet backwaters in large lakes.

William E. Magnusson

## AQUATIC HABITATS

The edges of freshwater lakes and ponds, where the water is shallow, receive abundant sunlight and therefore abound in rooted and floating plants that in turn support a diverse fauna. These edges of lakes and ponds, or marshes, are favorite haunts of crocodilians, since they rely on both water and land for their activities. The still waters of the lakes and ponds offer crocodilians a habitat that is rich in food organisms.

The lower reaches of rivers, where the water is slow moving, relatively warm, more saline, and well-stocked with plant life, also provide adequate cover and a good supply of food for larger aquatic organisms, including crocodilians. Freshwater and mangrove swamps are often well developed in these lower reaches. In the upper reaches of rivers the water is cooler, fast flowing, and usually clear of silt. Here fewer plants can gain hold on the bottom of the swift-moving streams; as a consequence, fewer higher forms of life are found in this habitat.

Bill Green

◀ Mangroves for shade, broad mudbanks for basking, and waters teeming with fish and mudcrabs make the tidal rivers of Northern Australia ideal habitat for the Indopacific Crocodile.

▼ The American Alligator, seen here in clear, upstream water surrounded by a ready food supply, is able to survive the lower temperatures of the temperate southeastern United States.

Peter Parks/Oxford Scientific Films Ltd

► The underwater world of Schneider's Dwarf Caiman encompasses swift-flowing streams where the water is cooler than that preferred by many other crocodilians.

Xavier Desmier

Freshwater microhabitats thus span a wide range of conditions to which different species of crocodilians have adapted. But this range of habitats is undoubtedly more restricted now than it was in the past. The present habitat of any living species does not reflect the diversity of possible habitats for that species but merely indicates the habitat in which it has managed to survive.

The two species of dwarf caimans now commonly live in clear, swift-flowing South American streams. They are frequently found near waterfalls and seem to prefer cooler water than most other crocodilians. Other South American caimans inhabit the warmer, quieter, and turbid waters of lakes, ponds, and the lower reaches of rivers. Both the true Gharial (*Gavialis gangeticus*) and the False Gharial (*Tomistoma schlegelii*), which have evolved long slender snouts adapted to catching fish, often live in swift-flowing rivers, with the Gharial inhabiting deep pools and the

► Gharials favor river habitat where fish, the mainstay of their diet, is in abundant supply. However, they must compete for space along the rivers of the Indian subcontinent with humans — settlement, development, and river traffic all reduce the habitat available to the Gharial.

Peter Jackson/Bruce Coleman Ltd.

Joyce Wilson/Seaphot Limited/Planet Earth Pictures

False Gharial sometimes being found in more sluggish water. The Chinese Alligator lives in turbid river waters of grassy flood plains or marshes while its closest living relative, the American Alligator, occupies a variety of habitats from rivers and lakes to swamps, in clear to turbid water. Most species of *Crocodylus* also inhabit the fresh water of rivers, lakes, and marshes. A few *Crocodylus* species, however, are at home in more saline environments, such as mangrove swamps and estuaries.

A hazard of staying in a saltwater medium is that salt ions enter the body through the skin and through the mouth when eating, and water is lost to the environment, resulting in dehydration. It takes a lot of energy to pump out the unwanted salt ions. Although all *Crocodylus* species have salt

glands that excrete salt from their body fluids, only a few have the ability to catch enough food to make it viable for them to live largely in salt water. The Indopacific Crocodile (*Crocodylus porosus*) appears to have exploited this salt-excreting mechanism best. The large amounts of energy needed to catch food and to excrete salt have apparently prevented other *Crocodylus* species from competing successfully with the Indopacific Crocodile in its saltwater habitat.

If, however, the Indopacific Crocodile was absent from its habitat, other *Crocodylus* species — including Johnston's Crocodile (*Crocodylus johnsoni*), the Philippine Crocodile (*Crocodylus mindorensis*), the Siamese Crocodile (*Crocodylus siamensis*), the New Guinea Crocodile (*Crocodylus novaeguineae*), and possibly the

▲ Habitat requirements for American Alligators are not as circumscribed as those of other crocodilian species and they are at home in habitats as diverse as clear, sparkling rivers and turbid swamps.

▶ The Indopacific Crocodile has successfully invaded saltwater habitats. Whether this is solely because of its highly developed salt-excreting mechanism or its aggressive exclusion of other species from saltwater habitats is unclear.

Rod Salm/Seaphot Limited/Planet Earth Pictures

# SALT GLANDS

LAURENCE TAPLIN

The crocodile is one of many vertebrates able to live in salt water and, like all of them, has to cope with the problem of too much salt and not enough fresh water in its environment. The salts the animal absorbs through its skin and its food tend to make its body fluids too saline, and these salts have to be excreted. Crocodiles and other reptiles, however, have inefficient kidneys, incapable of excreting much salt without plenty of fresh water to flush it through their systems.

Crocodiles, turtles, sea snakes, and other marine reptiles solve this problem by having salt glands that can excrete very concentrated salt solutions with a minimum of water loss. In turtles, the salt glands are former tear glands, accounting for the doleful appearance of the nesting turtle. The marine iguana of the Galapagos Islands has nasal salt glands and expels a salty spray from its nostrils. The Indopacific Crocodile has salt glands on its tongue. This might seem a strange place to have excretory organs but the glands are modified salivary glands and the crocodile's mouth is really part of the animal's external surface, sealed off from the throat by a cartilaginous flap.

A major puzzle in crocodile biology is the presence of salt glands in typically freshwater crocodiles worldwide. Such glands should hardly be necessary in fresh water — leading some biologists to suggest that, historically, the glands developed in a stock of saltwater crocodiles that subsequently invaded fresh waters. Interestingly, the American Alligator and the caimans appear to have no salt glands and never successfully invaded or bred in saltwater habitats in their long history.

Laurence Taplin

▲ In this close-up view of the mouth of an Indopacific Crocodile, minute drops of salty fluid secreted by the salt glands in the tongue are visible. Also visible is the flap at the back of the palate that blocks off the entry of water, allowing the crocodile to breathe while almost totally submerged.

Mugger (*Crocodylus palustris*) — would probably occupy saline microhabitats. Evidence of this was provided in northern Australia, where the hunting of the Indopacific Crocodile in the 1950s and 1960s greatly depleted their population, enabling Johnston's Crocodiles to extend their range well downstream. As the Indopacific Crocodile population recovered during the 1970s and 1980s, however, fewer Johnston's Crocodiles were seen downstream.

Seasons can affect the crocodilian's local distribution within the aquatic habitat. Dry seasons tend to concentrate riverine populations in river pools. In some regions of South America, caimans can be confined to river pools for 4 – 5 months of the year until floods return in the wet season. In the Venezuelan llanos, during the wet season, up to 95 percent of the savanna can be flooded and caimans are widely dispersed. During the dry season these caimans are restricted to permanent pools or lagoons, which are reservoirs for other aquatic organisms, and caiman population density can be extremely high. On the Philippine island of Negros, where little or no rain falls during the four-month period from December to February, remnant populations of the Philippine Crocodile were found in the 1950s and 1960s in the deeper pools of rivers, which at the time usually harbored large mullets. In some parts of the southern Philippine island of Mindanao, where rainfall is evenly distributed throughout the year and forest cover is still good, rivers do not dry up or flood and the concentration of crocodilians in pools is not evident at any time of the year.

▼ During the dry season large concentrations of Common Caiman gather in the few remaining permanent water sites in the Venezuelan llanos. Despite the sometimes overcrowded conditions at such sites, social interactions are generally amiable.

Sullivan and Rogers/Bruce Coleman Ltd.

▶ The buoyancy effect of water allows this Indopacific Crocodile in Kakadu National Park, Australia, to conserve energy. Water also allows the crocodile to keep most of its body hidden from potential prey.

By living in aquatic habitats crocodilians have taken advantage of two basic properties of water. The first property is the ability of water to absorb large amounts of heat with little increase in water temperature. This has a buffering effect, allowing the crocodilians to remain active within optimal temperature limits in the water, in spite of wide temperature fluctuations in the atmosphere. The other property of water that is beneficial to crocodilians is its buoyancy effect on objects within it. Buoyancy enables crocodilians to move around with greater ease in water than on land and, consequently, they expend less energy.

▶ In the Florida Everglades American Alligators maintain "gator holes" that retain permanent water, even during the dry season, providing a reservoir for aquatic species that would otherwise perish.

Francois Gohier / Ardea London

## TERRESTRIAL HABITATS

Dry land is no less important than water to crocodilians. It serves as a site for basking, which results in the raising of body temperature to optimal levels for their activities. Periodic excursions to dry land are particularly beneficial for crocodilians inhabiting estuaries and mangrove swamps for it allows them to minimize their intake of salt ions.

Crocodilians find shelter from extremes of temperature on dry land. They can cool themselves there by letting moisture evaporate from their opened mouths. Mugger escape hot and cold weather by retreating into burrows. American Crocodiles (*Crocodylus acutus*) escape periods of drought by digging holes or burrows. Some crocodiles have been reported to estivate (remain inactive) when their pools dry up during hot seasons. Both Chinese and American alligators retreat in winter into burrows under river banks and in mud holes, surviving cold temperatures that other crocodilians cannot tolerate. Observations on Indopacific and Philippine crocodiles reveal that they resort to burrowing on land to escape human population pressures.

Dieter and Mary Plage/Bruce Coleman Ltd

▲► Nile Crocodiles gain warmth with the minimum of effort by basking on land where the heat of the sun raises their body temperatures (right). The Mugger cools by letting moisture evaporate through its opened mouth (above).

Anthony Bannister/NHPA

Dry land serves another important function for crocodilians: it is the site for egg laying. Many New Guinea and Indopacific crocodiles nest on floating grass mats. These nests may be affected by flooding or by overheating due to the type of vegetation used in their construction. In some areas of northern Australia, buffalo graze and trample on the banks where the floating vegetation is partially anchored and the mats float away, forcing the crocodiles to find less satisfactory nesting sites or preventing them from nesting at all. The common egg-laying sites, however, are river sandbanks and higher ground or mounds above water. Some crocodilians need vegetation to build their mound nests. The heat generated by the decomposing vegetation actually accelerates incubation of the eggs. Other crocodilians need sandbanks that do not flood in which to dig their

# TURTLES' USE OF ALLIGATOR NESTS

DALE JACKSON

In the southeastern United States, American Alligators build their nests in late May and June, just as spring turns to summer. Situated on low berms of land or among aquatic vegetation within lakes and marshes, and consisting largely of plants and mud gathered by females and piled as high as 1 meter (3 feet), alligator nests often represent the highest points in the extensive wet "prairies" that typify this region. The potential utility of such large, elevated mounds within aquatic ecosystems has not gone unnoticed by other members of the reptile community, many of which reproduce at approximately the same time as the alligators. The nests not only provide convenient basking sites for aquatic turtles and snakes but also serve as fortuitous locations for such animals to deposit their own eggs or young. At least three species of turtles, one species of snake, and one species of lizard are known to lay eggs in alligator nests.

In Florida, where freshwater turtles reach their highest diversity in the western hemisphere, one species in particular makes a regular practice of using alligator nests for its own nesting sites. The Florida red-bellied turtle (*Pseudemys nelsoni*) may reach very high densities within some marshy habitats where suitable nesting sites can be very limited. Recent studies conducted at three separate localities within the state have documented that females of this turtle species regularly seek out and utilize alligator nests for laying their own eggs. In fact, in one such study nearly half of the alligator nests examined were found to contain red-bellied turtle eggs. One of the nests was opened by investigators only after a raccoon (*Procyon lotor*) — a mammal that commonly feeds upon unguarded turtle and alligator eggs — had excavated and eaten several alligator eggs and exposed others. Although no turtle eggs had been exposed, the investigators had recorded the predation of four clutches of turtle eggs prior to laying by the alligator. Within the next eight days red-bellied turtles had laid four more clutches of eggs in the nest. In total, more than 200 turtle eggs had been deposited in the nest within a two-week period!

Laying eggs in alligator nests probably has many advantages for turtles. The presence of large numbers of alligator and turtle eggs at the same site may be sufficient to satiate predators, thereby allowing at least some eggs to survive. In addition, the nest provides easy digging, reducing the time the female turtle is exposed to terrestrial predators while allowing her to bury her

Dale Jackson

▲ Surrounding the central cluch of larger alligator eggs are seven clutches of red-bellied turtle eggs, probably laid by seven separate females, and a single clutch of Florida soft-shelled turtle eggs (bottom right).

eggs more deeply. The relatively high, stable temperature and humidity within the nest are ideal for incubation of turtle eggs, which also receive increased protection from flooding. Furthermore, the turtle eggs receive inadvertent protection against predators from the nest-guarding behavior of adult alligators. However, the relationship is not wholly without cost. Clutches of turtle eggs laid prior to the alligator's own are often destroyed by the restructuring activities of the alligator. Aggressive adult alligators have also been observed to attack and drive off red-bellied turtles attempting to lay in their nests; the high-domed thick shell of this turtle is an important adaptation that helps it to survive most such attacks.

Jean-Paul Ferrero/Auscape International

▲ The fragility of the ecology means that if surrounding forests or mangroves are destroyed, the water adjacent to them and the microhabitats within them are also indirectly destroyed.

nests. Eggs laid in holes in the sand derive warmth from the sand.

Both mound nests and hole nests are subject to flooding, due either to early rains in the dry season or to abnormal flooding in the wet season, and the eggs may fail to hatch. There are other difficulties encountered when venturing onto land — eggs and hatchlings are more exposed and frequently fall prey to mammals, birds, and other reptiles.

The type of vegetation in the terrestrial environment encompassing crocodilian habitats is mostly humid tropical forest. Mangrove forests surround tidal estuarine areas of the humid tropical zone but also extend beyond the tropics. In monsoon regions of the tropics, where a wet season contrasts with a prolonged dry season, typical forest cover is deciduous, that is, the trees shed their leaves during the dry season. Lowland forests, including mangrove, monsoon, and tropical rainforests, are of prime importance to most crocodilians. Forests make equable conditions possible for habitats adjacent to or within them as they ensure the presence of water all year round. When the equable conditions of a habitat are disrupted the wildlife that plays an important ecological role in the microhabitat is also disturbed. The disruption of equable conditions is often due not only to the direct disturbance of the microhabitat but also to the disturbance of the surrounding forest.

## THE ECOLOGICAL IMPORTANCE OF CROCODILIANS

Crocodilians are top predators in the food chains of their habitats. The food chain transfers energy, in the form of food from its source in plants to herbivores (organisms that eat plants), then to carnivores (animals that eat other animals), and finally to omnivores (animals that eat both plants and other animals).

The German scientist Ernst Josef Fittkau has studied the ecological importance of caimans as top predators in the food chain of central Amazonian habitats, where natives were surprised to notice a decrease, rather than the expected increase, in fish catches following the decline in caimans. According to Fittkau's hypothesis the tributaries of this central Amazon region contain scarcely enough essential life-supporting electrolytes (the substances such as acids, bases, and salts that, when dissolved in water, become ionic conductors) to sustain adequate primary production (production of organic compounds by green plants) to support higher life forms in the food chain.

Fittkau hypothesized that there were two other sources of nutrients that form the basis for the food chain — incoming organic matter entering the tributaries from surrounding forests and nutrient by-products of the metabolism of larger predators, including caimans. The larger predators form part of a natural cycling of nutrients that maintains the stability of the food chain. The food chain, and thus the community, is dependent upon the larger predators since they are a major source of nutrients for primary production in this electrolyte-poor habitat. Removing this source of nutrients naturally reduces the source of food for other components of the food chain, including fish, which thus eventually decline in number. In addition, the greater and more varied the animal life the more stable the community seems to be.

While there is some debate over whether Fittkau's theory can be applied to the Amazon basin, there is very good circumstantial evidence that a decrease in local crocodilian populations, either in lakes or river pools, has an adverse effect on local fisheries. In many areas local fisherman prefer to fish in areas with crocodilians. Whether

there is a direct causal relationship is unclear, it may be that nutrient recycling by the crocodilians is of benefit or their presence in fish-rich waters may be coincidence.

Some crocodilians are believed to make another important contribution to commercial fisheries since they may prey on fish that are considered commercially worthless but that, in turn, prey on those fish species prized by the natives. In some areas, crocodilians may thus eliminate the predator of an important human economic resource.

There are other ecological contributions to the habitat from crocodilians. They open up trails and aid in keeping waterways open through marshlands. They deepen waterholes during drought and provide microhabitats for smaller

▼ Despite its reputation as a predator, the American Alligator's role in its habitat is less confrontational and less destructive than that of the human population sharing the habitat throughout most of its range.

▶ Far from being protected from humans by inaccessible habitats, crocodilians are now vulnerable as human populations expand and what was once regarded as useless land becomes valuable for agriculture, industry, or forestry. Habitat destruction is a greater threat to crocodilians than hunting.

aquatic organisms. "Gator holes" in the Florida Everglades and other southern marshlands in the United States hold water even during the driest periods and provide refuges for fish and other aquatic animals. The vegetation surrounding these holes is relatively lush and even other plants may depend upon this microhabitat for their survival.

It is possible that crocodilians may qualify as keystone species although studies have not been made to prove this. A keystone species is one that determines the structure of a community. When a keystone species is removed from the environment, a drop in the species diversity of its habitat ensues. Sadly, the opportunity to demonstrate this ecological role for crocodiles in tropical Asia has been lost with the almost complete disappearance of the animals and their associated aquatic animals in forested habitats.

## THE DESTRUCTION OF CROCODILIAN HABITATS

Rainforests encompass a large part of crocodilian habitats. When forests disappear and their habitats are disturbed, crocodilians can disappear with them. The International Union for Conservation of Nature and Natural Resources stresses the link between habitat and wildlife:

> Wildlife, representing the faunal component of the ecosystem, is very closely associated with the vegetation in a tropical area. Any disturbance or destruction of the vegetation will be reflected in the disturbance or destruction of the wildlife. To the extent that the vegetation is conserved, the wildlife is correspondingly protected.

How exactly does the disappearance of forests lead to the disappearance of crocodilians? There are a few specific instances where forest destruction can aggravate more direct destruction of crocodilian microhabitats. Loss of forest cover, for example, results in increased siltation of nearby rivers and streams. As a result of siltation, the capacity of the rivers and streams to hold water decreases, they become shallower, and the width of the inhospitable flood plain is increased. This, in turn, results in a decreased quantity of fish, lower vertebrates, invertebrates, and insects — the primary food sources of crocodilians.

When forests are cleared soil erosion increases. The ability of the soil to hold nutrients decreases so that excess nitrates and phosphates get washed into streams and lakes. Nitrates and phosphates in lakes are nutrients upon which algae in the lakes thrive. An excess of these nutrients, however, can lead to algal blooms, which greatly lessen the oxygen levels of the lakes, thereby decreasing the chances of survival for other aquatic animals, including the fish upon which crocodilians feed.

Tropical rainforests can store large quantities of water. Rather than streaming unhindered into surrounding plains, the rainwater escapes slowly into streams and rivers. Without adequate forest cover to absorb rainwater, rivers can dry up during dry seasons and flood more often during wet seasons. Flooding is one of the main causes for the failure of crocodilian eggs to hatch since embryos die after being submerged for as short a period as 24–48 hours (embryos close to hatching will die even sooner since their oxygen demands are greater). Juveniles can get swept from the upper reaches of rivers into river mouths, as occurred in the Philippines in late 1971. The chances of survival for juveniles decreases when they enter the saline, estuarine environment of river mouths. With a greater body surface area to volume ratio than adults, juvenile crocodiles absorb a greater amount of salt through their skins, increasing the energy demands for pumping the salt back out.

Crocodilian microhabitats are directly interlinked with their surroundings. When the microhabitat is altered or polluted, the shelter and breeding grounds of its inhabitants are also altered. Unfortunately there are many ways in which habitats are destroyed.

All over the world, urban and industrial development, and high population growth rates have put heavy pressure on human beings to exploit the earth's natural resources to the maximum. In developing countries, especially, the race to industrialize and to feed growing numbers of people is taking a heavy toll on forested habitats. The situation in the Philippines is typical of the problems faced by rice-producing countries where, in addition, economic development is largely export-oriented, with more exports

▼ A small remnant population of Philippine Crocodiles has managed to survive in this portion of the upper Ilog River in southwestern Negros Island but the destruction of forests elsewhere in the Philippines has greatly reduced crocodilian habitat.

T. F. Luchavez

Lynn M. Stone/Animals Animals

▲ A canal through mangrove swamps in Key Largo, Florida, provides an ideal habitat for American Crocodiles. Elsewhere in the world, mangrove swamps are being cleared at an increasingly rapid rate for development. American Crocodiles have been the victims of such development and are in grave danger of extinction in some regions.

tending to be raw resources obtained from mining, fish farming, and timber logging.

In the Philippines, as in most Southeast Asian countries, the staple food is rice. To produce rice suitable lowland areas need to be converted into rice paddies. All these lowland areas have thus been farmed or turned into villages. In tropical Asian countries as a whole, 33 percent of the arable land is planted with rice. Marshes are now being looked at for possible conversion into rice fields. Were it not for the unsettled armed conflicts around the Liguasan marsh on Mindanao Island, which harbors Philippine Crocodiles, a government plan to drain parts of the marsh for agriculture and settlement would already be underway. (A similar situation probably exists in Kampuchea, Burma, and Thailand where armed conflict has restricted the development of some crocodilian habitats. Civil unrest in Nicaragua and Honduras may have assisted in postponing development in crocodilian habitats.)

Another important food staple in the Philippines is fish; consequently, there is heavy fishing in inland waters as well as in open seas. The few fish sanctuaries that exist in the country are often violated by fishermen. Lake Naujan Park on Mindoro Island could be a sanctuary for the Indopacific Crocodiles that are still found in the area but, since park rules cannot be enforced, it will only be a matter of time before this species becomes extinct in the lake. Its congener, the Philippine Crocodile, has already disappeared from habitats adjacent to the lake.

Pollution from mining companies destroys lake and river habitats. In 1976, 18 mining companies in the Philippines discharged more than 140,000 tonnes of tailings a day into nine river systems. In 1987 there were 19 mining companies

dumping their tailings and wastes into at least ten river systems. Silty copper-mine tailings in the Pagatban River and gold-mine tailings in a lake in Davao, Mindanao, have been the final factors that have led to the extinction of Philippine Crocodile populations at both sites.

Urbanization contributes heavily to the loss of crocodilian habitat. The largest lake in the Philippines, Laguna de Bay, is dotted with fish-culture pens and encircled by settlements, industrial complexes, and farms. Approximately ten million people live in Manila and the satellite cities surrounding the lake. Past populations of the Philippine Crocodile on the outskirts of this lake and the Indopacific Crocodile population that inhabited the lake undoubtedly succumbed to urbanization.

The drive for self-sufficiency and development has also had an impact on mangrove swamps. About 200,000 hectares (500,000 acres) or 40 percent of the mangrove swamps in the Philippines have been converted into fishponds. Salt beds, settlements, and, more recently, prawn farms for the export market account for a further 40 percent of the original 500,000 hectares (1.2 million acres) of mangrove swamps.

Timber logging also takes a heavy toll on mangroves. Mangrove trees have been felled for firewood, charcoal making, building construction, and for the manufacture of wood chips for export. After the trees are removed from an area, the elevated regions of the cleared areas are transformed into human settlements.

Due to the destruction of the mangrove forests of Isla Fuerte, on the Caribbean coast of Colombia, the American Crocodile population there is now extinct. Mangrove swamps all over Asia and South America are being converted into development projects at increasingly alarming rates, displacing or eliminating many of the estuarine crocodilian populations. In Indonesia 100,000 hectares (250,000 acres) of mangroves are to be converted into shrimp farms and 500,000 hectares (1.2 million acres) into agricultural plots. In Thailand, as well as in Indonesia, mangroves are also dredged in tin-mining operations. Will the Indopacific Crocodile in these countries face the same fate as the American Crocodile of Isla Fuerte? Although the extent of the decline is not known, based on their absence from many estuarine and mangrove areas in which they had previously been sighted their populations have decreased dramatically.

A similar impact on crocodilian populations comes from the destruction of lowland freshwater swamp forests. In 1934 the Philippines had 10.7 million hectares (26.4 million acres) of virgin lowland dipterocarp forest (composed mainly of mahogany trees), which encompassed swamp forest. An estimated 1.2–1.5 million hectares (3–3.7 million acres) of primary lowland forest remain today, and some islands of the archipelago have zero percent forest cover. The disappearance of forests, combined with other factors such as hunting, has led to the decline of Philippine Crocodile populations. Probably no more than 500 remain in the wild in the entire archipelago.

Habitat destruction has affected many other parts of the tropical world. Shifting cultivation, timber harvesting, and cattle ranching have pushed the only surviving forests of Mexico to the country's southern border. Cattle ranching has removed nearly two thirds of Central America's primary tropical forest. It is possible that the American Crocodile has been pushed to the peripheries of its habitat. Logging, shifting cultivation, timber harvesting, and a burgeoning population growth rate have ravaged the tropical

forests of West Africa and those of virtually all Southeast Asian countries. In some countries, illegal timber smuggling poses a decisive threat to the remaining patches of forest. Whether crocodilians once inhabited those regions of tropical forest that have now been cleared is difficult to establish.

There are some crocodilians that have adapted to a wide range of environments and have been better able to withstand habitat destruction. In India the Mugger, well adapted to both estuarine and freshwater conditions, appears to be holding its own although in reduced numbers, in spite of widespread mangrove swamp and forest conversion. Since they can also inhabit fresh waters ranging from rivers to small ponds, it would be possible to breed 5,000 –10,000 Mugger and to release them into suitable habitats in the wild.

For the Indian Gharial, however, habitat destruction could pose a big threat. The Gharial inhabits deep pools of fast-flowing rivers. Siltation of the rivers brought about by forest destruction could severely affect the food source of Gharials, which are primarily fish eaters. In 1983 the number of Gharial adults in the entire region of India, Bangladesh, Nepal, and Pakistan was 200 – 400. It is quite possible that this low number is the result of a combination of habitat destruction and hunting.

It is often difficult to determine whether the disappearance of crocodilian populations is due to direct exploitation or to habitat destruction. Depletion in crocodilian numbers cannot always be correlated with loss of habitat. In many instances, the habitat remains preserved; it is the crocodilians that are singled out for destruction. In other instances, it can be the destruction of the natural habitat that leads to the disappearance or facilitates the killing of crocodilians. A prime example of this was the construction of the

▼ The Panama Canal, of great benefit to humans, was less so for crocodilians — their habitat in the surrounding tropical forest was destroyed and survivors became only too accessible to hunters in boats.

Vincent Serventy and Associates

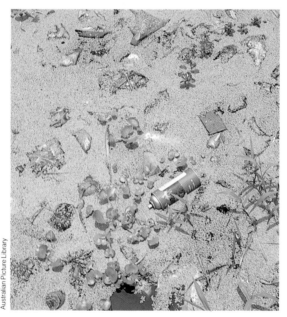

Australian Picture Library

▲▶ Habitats that provide ideal growing conditions for plants and their accompanying fauna (above) can become alien and deadly for crocodilians and other life forms when polluted with the flotsam and jetsam of the human world (right).

Panama Canal. Built in a humid tropical forest zone, it led to increased boat traffic and human settlement, displacing much of the wildlife and its habitat. Ultimately it also gave easy access to previously inaccessible habitats of crocodiles, and killing them became a popular sport.

Developments along many of the large river systems of the world have made it easier for hunters and explorers to penetrate remote habitats. The Nile and Yangtze rivers have been used since the beginning of civilization for transport, and their banks for agriculture and settlement. The Nile Crocodile (*Crocodylus niloticus*) practically disappeared from the Egyptian Nile at the end of the nineteenth century. It later reappeared during World War I. During the

1950s and 1960s, however, on the delta above Cairo, the Nile Crocodile started to disappear again probably because escalating boat traffic destroyed its breeding habitat.

Where sections of rivers were uninhabitable, crocodilian populations were able to flourish. The estuarial delta portion of the lower Yangtze River is inhospitable to human settlement because of perpetual flooding and it is in this region that the Chinese Alligator was known to thrive.

Although human settlement along the Amazon River has always been relatively sparse because of poor soil conditions, the flurry of international boat traffic on the river from 1850 to 1910, when the international rubber trade was booming, provided explorers in search of crocodilian skins and other resources greater access to crocodilian habitats. Early European explorers who set foot in the Amazon found it to be teeming with caimans; by the 1970s, however, due to extensive caiman hunts, certain caiman populations became almost extinct.

### THE ROLE OF HUMANS IN CROCODILIAN HABITATS

Unlike the fundamental ecological role that crocodilians play in their microhabitats, the human role in the crocodilian habitat has been a confrontational one. Human beings compete with crocodilians for usable space and resources, as well as hunting them for food, hides, and out of fear. By encroaching upon the forests and waters where crocodilians dwell, humans are now as dependent on the habitat as the crocodilians. However, in their dependency people can and do destroy the habitat.

When humans convert forests into farms, marshes into rice paddies, mangrove swamps into aquaculture projects, and river banks into human settlements, they displace the animals from their prime habitats, driving them to the marginal periphery of their range where they may, ultimately, never breed successfully. Rivers and inland waterways used for navigation and commerce disturb the crocodilians, possibly making them unable to maintain the optimum population sizes required for reproduction. Soil waste and mine tailings dumped into rivers render river pools shallow and pollute the water with silt and poisonous chemicals.

As a result of the direct and indirect assaults on habitats — from exploration, colonization, settlement, exploitation, and habitat conversion — crocodilians are steadily losing ground and some species may be headed for extinction. Prime crocodilian microhabitats have already undergone drastic changes due to human pressures. Some of these changes, if not irreversible, may require long periods of time to remedy through schemes that will minimize the confrontation between humans and crocodilians.

Protecting and rehabilitating crocodilian habitats are two major ways of reducing the confrontation between humans and crocodilians. A successful protection and rehabilitation program requires habitats of generous size, as space is the critical factor in attaining conservation goals, especially in countries with rapidly expanding human populations. Determining the habitat range large enough to maintain many species in equilibrium and to keep the rate of extinction down is of the utmost importance.

Parks and wildlife sanctuaries must be made to serve their real purpose. Education, effective legislation, and clear-cut government policies on wildlife are necessary to ensure that poachers do not encroach on these areas. While it may not be possible or practicable to restock crocodilian populations to their original numbers, it should be possible to ensure the survival of several thousand animals in the wild.

Reafforestation programs can be set up to encompass river systems or wetlands suitable for crocodilian sanctuaries. A good beginning in mangrove reafforestation is already underway in Thailand, the Philippines, and other Southeast Asian countries. The next step would be to reafforest river mouths with sanctuaries stocked with juveniles from captive breeding centers.

Countries most aware that devastating the world's forests has a severe effect on our environment and its capacity to produce food are more open to habitat protection and rehabilitation. If more countries were aware of the link between reafforestation and improved fisheries in inland and nearshore waters, protection and rehabilitation would stand a better chance of success.

There are other positive developments occurring today, including instances where habitat alteration benefits crocodilians. In southern Florida, for example, the Turkey Point Power Plant is providing sanctuary for American Crocodiles living in the reactor cooling-water canal system. In central Florida, the Kennedy Space Center in the Merritt Island National Wildlife Refuge provides sanctuary for American Alligators. The newly constructed Burdekin Dam in North Queensland, Australia, is expected to provide extensive new habitat for the Indopacific Crocodile.

Captive breeding of crocodilians, another positive development, is gaining hold in some countries. Captive breeding is conservation oriented; adult crocodilians are caught from the wild, bred, the eggs incubated, and the hatchlings raised to a certain size before being released into the wild or being used commercially. India, Thailand, China, the Philippines, Venezuela, South Africa, and Australia have all launched captive breeding programs. Other countries, such as Colombia, are planning to start their own captive breeding programs.

Crocodilians need not be doomed to extinction. In some parts of the world, there has been a marked change in attitude toward crocodilians as people come to realize that they are a valuable economic resource. There is a growing sense of awareness that we need to keep our environment unpolluted, and to protect and replenish our vanishing forests and wildlife. The necessary steps to save the crocodilian — captive breeding, habitat protection, and rehabilitation — have begun. It may be that our desire for economic profit, which in the beginning spelled doom for crocodilians, will provide the spark to help save them from extinction.

▼ Habitat protection and rehabilitation are vital to ensure the survival of living crocodilian species. Captive breeding also has a positive role to play — this female Philippine Crocodile is guarding her nest at Silliman University's Crocodile Project.

Angel Alcala

Indopacific Crocodiles at the Edward River Crocodile Farm in Queensland, Australia.

# CROCODILIANS

# AND HUMANS

# MYTHOLOGY, RELIGION, ART, AND LITERATURE

G.W. TROMPF

Crocodilians have made a contribution to many cultures through the ages. They have been revered and reviled, deified and vilified, protected and slaughtered. Societies have incorporated crocodiles and alligators into their beliefs, customs, and even laws, attributing to them the power for both good and evil. From these beliefs has sprung a wealth of fables and legends from ancient civilizations to primitive tribal peoples as far apart as South America and Australia. These beliefs have also been incorporated in a variety of visual art forms from Chinese calligraphy to crocodile-tooth necklaces and from ancient Aboriginal rock art to twentieth century movies.

▶ Australian Aboriginal artists were familiar with two species of crocodiles — the harmless, fish-eating Johnston's Crocodile and the predatory Indopacific Crocodile — which they portrayed as food items and as totemic creatures with spiritual powers. This rock painting is in Quinkan National Park on Cape York Peninsula.

Keith A.W. Williams/ Australasian Nature Transparencies

## THE CROCODILE-GOD OF ANCIENT EGYPT

The ancient Egyptians revered the crocodiles of the Nile and held them to be sacred. Since crocodiles appeared in great numbers during the annual September flooding of the Nile, the Egyptians associated them with the eternal sustenance of their lands. Sobek (or Souchos), the crocodile-god, was one of 438 ancient Egyptian deities and was thought to be the son of Neith, the oldest of the goddesses. In the ancient pyramid texts both Sobek and Neith were depicted as gods who would "endure forever," while the affairs of state and the fortunes of other great gods could fluctuate. Whether the crocodile was first made sacred out of terror or because the god of such fearful beasts was in need of placation is impossible to tell. But certainly by 2400 B.C. Sobek had emerged as one of the great gods.

Sobek was normally depicted with a human body and a crocodile's head. He carried a staff in his left hand and a symbol of eternity (the ankh) in his right. Incorporated in his headdress was the sun disc since, by the time of the New Kingdom (1400 B.C.), Sobek was being worshiped as a manifestation of Ra, the sun god, and was known as Sobek-Ra. (Ra was one of the supreme Egyptian gods in whose chariot the deceased god-king pharoahs rode across the sky during the day.)

Ronald Sheridan/Ancient Art & Architecture Collection

▲ Sobek (center), a crocodile-headed god of ancient Egypt, was gradually transformed from a minor protective deity into one of the most revered of the Egyptian gods.

Ronald Sheridan/Ancient Art & Architecture Collection

◀ The Nile Crocodile's status as a powerful predator was reflected in its religious status: this crocodile figure from the tomb of Seti I bears a human head and the feather of truth. Failure to speak the truth to such a divine creature would be punished with violent death.

# MUMMIFIED EGYPTIAN CROCODILES

LÉONARD GINSBURG

Animals always had an important place in the religion of ancient Egypt. From predynastic times, the tribal god in every town was incarnate in an animal protected by a taboo, whether it was a cow, sheep, dog, cat, baboon, lion, hippopotamus, snake, falcon, ibis, wasp, shrew, gazelle, or crocodile. These animals were associated with the cult of the god throughout the history of Egypt, despite the growing importance of major divinities (such as Ra the sun god, Isis, and Osiris) and the establishment of monotheism as the state religion under Amenophis IV (Akhnaton). During the Late Epoch (1085–30 B.C.), as a reaction against foreign occupation by the Persians, Greeks, and Romans, the Egyptians affirmed their national identity by reverting to their ancient forms of religion. The animal cult underwent an extraordinary revival and development, and most of the mummified animals seen today in museums date from this time.

Crocodiles were generally associated with the god Sobek to whom various temples were consecrated. The most important of these were at Kom-Ombo in Upper Egypt and Crocodilopolis in the Fayoum. In these temples sacred crocodiles were looked after in special pools. They were adorned with pendants of gold or precious stones and had bracelets on their front feet.

When the crocodiles died, they were embalmed. It is likely that the internal organs of the large crocodiles were removed without cutting open the carcass; the organs being removed *per anum*, as was the practice for the sacred bulls, all of which were traditionally named Apis. The internal organs of small animals were not removed. The carcasses were kept in a bath of natron salt for two months to dry out the flesh completely then covered by papyrus leaves and wrapped in aromatic cloth bandages to ensure their preservation. Finally, they were locked in special coffins.

Mummies of adult crocodiles over 5 meters (16 feet) long, newborn crocodiles, and even mummified crocodile eggs have been discovered. At Kom-Ombo, small mummified specimens 30 centimeters (1 foot) long were piled by their thousands in some tombs. At Maabdah Caves in central Egypt, crocodile mummies were packed to a height of 6–9 meters (20–30 feet). These included large adults and an incredible number of young specimens of 30–50 centimeters (1–2 feet), which were packed together in batches of 15–20 in the same linen bandage.

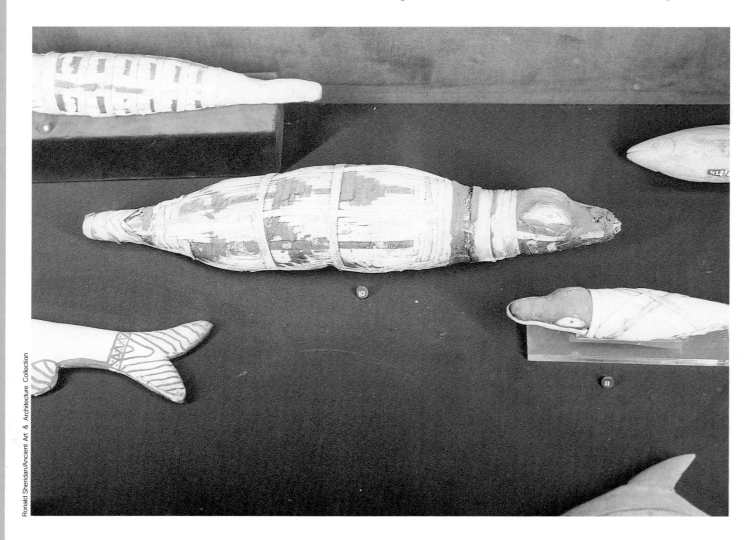

In the delta or near-delta areas of Fayoum, Thebes, and Lake Moeris, the cult of Sobek flourished and excavations at Tebtunis, in 1900, revealed a large temple dedicated to him. In a court more than 30 meters (100 feet) long, wall decorations show scenes of adoration, with offerings and processional rituals being made before the great Sobek. According to Herodotus, the ancient Greek historian, Egyptians in the Nile delta "treated crocodiles with every kindness," and young crocodiles were often adopted as pets and carefully mummified at death. Elsewhere, however, crocodiles were looked upon as enemies and were hunted for their meat. Hunters at Elephantine on the upper Nile would beat pigs to make them squeal and so lure crocodiles to a bait and hook. The ancient Egyptian story of the founding of Crocodilopolis, the major center for the worship of Sobek, may be the source of a later European folk tale — "The Gingerbread Man." King Menes, the first of the pharaohs, was set upon by his own dogs while out hunting. In his flight he came to Lake Moeris, where a large crocodile was basking in the sun. Apprising the situation quickly, the beast offered the desperate king a ferry service to the site of the city Menes then founded and which the Greeks named Crocodilopolis. The story symbolizes Egypt's flight from evil (the dogs) and chaos (the waters). Crocodilopolis became a favorite city for New Kingdom pharaohs and, under the Greek rulers of Egypt, it became a thriving metropolis.

Crocodilopolis, intriguingly, was also the name given to another city in the ancient Near East. South of the Carmel range in southern Phoenicia, it was first mentioned by the Greek geographer Strabo in the first century B.C. The city was situated in swampy country on the coast and "saltwater crocodiles" were being captured around the city up until the nineteenth century. There is no reference to any crocodile cult in this second city of Crocodilopolis, but its closeness to the Palestinian region raises questions about possible references to the crocodile in the Bible. Scholars are now more or less agreed that the creature referred to as "Leviathan" in chapter 41 of the Book of Job was the crocodile:

> Can you draw out Leviathan with a fish hook?
> Or press down his tongue with a rope? . . .
> Will he make many supplications to you?
> Or speak to you with soft words?
> Will he make a covenant with you?

These rhetorical questions mark the start of elaborate descriptions of the crocodile as a terrifying creature with "a mouth of burning torches" and "a breath of kindled coals." The questions were also apparently sardonic comments on the human belief that one could develop mystical relations with the crocodile. The Hebrews and those further inland were, in fact, fearful of the sea. For them it was a place of death,

chaos, and the monstrous. The crocodiles on its edges came to symbolize the sea's perils. In the prophetic poetry of Isaiah II it would seem that the crocodile as Leviathan is the archetypal cosmic dragon, symbolizing the disorder and evil that God would subdue.

**THE DRAGON OF ANCIENT CHINA**

If the crocodile was of such significance to ancient peoples, what of the alligator? Alligators are less widespread than crocodiles and China is the only country with an ancient literary tradition that refers to them. Both crocodiles and alligators were known (from rumors and verbal accounts) to the people of ancient China whose civilization arose in the northern region along the Yellow River around 2200 B.C. It is probable that the cosmic twin-tailed dragon (*lung*), "the Lord of all scaled reptiles," which was thought to ascend into the heavens at the spring equinox and plunge into the waters at the autumn equinox, derived much from reports of these great beasts at the far boundaries of the Celestial Empire.

Much later, especially during the Tang dynasty (A.D. 618–906), naturalists and the compilers of pharmacopoeia in southern China were able to distinguish between crocodiles and alligators, though they still associated both with mythical dragons. The southern "barbarians," who were incorporated into the Tang empire, were known to foretell rain by the alligator's call and to distribute its prized flesh at weddings. In addition, the alligator was seen as a harbinger of war because of its armored hide.

▼ Although regarded with affectionate respect by the ancient Egyptians, by the time that this picture was painted in the nineteenth century, Nile Crocodiles were being hunted for food and out of fear.

Su Gooders/Ardea London

# THE CHINESE DRAGON

ZHOU GUOXING

The dragon is a symbol of the Chinese people and those of Chinese descent proudly regard themselves as "descendants of the dragon." But just what the dragon is and where it comes from have puzzled generations of scholars and scientists.

According to ancient texts, a dragon was a creature "with horns like those of the deer, a head like a camel's, eyes like a hare's, and a neck like a snake's. Its belly resembles that of the *shen* [a mythical flood dragon that lives in water and resembles the crocodile]. Its claws resemble an eagle's, its paws are like a tiger's, and its ears like those of a buffalo." The dragon could transform itself almost instantly from thick to thin, from long to short. It could also soar into the heavens and descend into the depths of the sea. The dragon, it seems, was a supernatural creature that could take an infinite variety of forms.

A Chinese character representing the dragon appears among the inscriptions on bone and tortoiseshell that date from the Yin and Shang dynasties (from the sixteenth to the eleventh centuries B.C.), the time of China's earliest written records. The inscriptions depict a reptile with horns, teeth, scales, and with or without feet. The character is often surmounted by a symbol that seems to indicate that the dragon was considered a violent,

evil, unlucky creature. On the basis of this evidence, the original "dragon" was thought, by some Chinese scholars, to be an alligator.

Generations of scholars have suggested many explanations for dragons. There is no doubt that in its earliest form, or forms, the dragon was some kind of reptile, such as a snake, alligator, or lizard. In recent years, relics and archeological sites dating from the various periods between 5,000 and 6,000 years ago have provided evidence of the use of lizards, alligators, and dragons in totemic worship and rituals. By examining these simple pictograms, we can trace the early portrayal, evolution, and final emergence of the traditional dragon.

Although the earliest dragons had a single form, as the different peoples of ancient China established contact with each other, they began to depict their own totemic images more imaginatively. Over a long period, a hybrid image evolved, which combined features of the different totems or dragons.

The dragon, therefore, is a product of imagination; a mythical creature that has been worshiped and venerated by the Chinese for centuries. The dragon still takes myriad forms in modern Chinese art; ethnic and cultural minorities portray it in many shapes from fish or alligator to human.

D. & J. Heaton/Australian Picture Library

Service Historique de la Marine, Paris/Giraudon

## THE AMERICAS

Far across the Pacific to the east, where written literature began much later, there are fewer records of the place of crocodilians in the religion and myths of the great Meso-American civilizations. The Mayans in the tenth century and the Aztecs in the fourteenth century thought that the known world lay on the back of a gigantic reptile in a lily pond. This reptile was probably a crocodile or caiman, since alligators were confined to what is now the southeastern United States. Among the Mayans, the fearsome god of death, Ah Puch, seems to be represented with a crocodile's spine, while the Aztecs apparently inherited the veneration and iconic representation of a separate crocodile deity from the preceding Teotihuacan culture.

In more recent times we have been able to assess the significance of crocodiles and alligators to the American Indians. The earliest known drawing of an American Alligator (*Alligator mississippiensis*) was an etching by the French explorer Le Moyne in 1565, which shows Florida Indians thrusting poles down an alligator's throat to kill it. In the nineteenth century William Holmes, an anthropologist, went to live among the

Chiriqui Indians of the Panama region. He was able to plot the history of the importance of crocodilians to the tribe by tracing back from highly stylized, virtually unrecognizable saurian images that appeared on the tribe's pottery to ancient and non-extant ware bearing more conventional crocodilian designs.

## AFRICA

In Africa, especially along the upper Volta River to the west of the continent and in the great Lakes area above the headwaters of the Nile, crocodiles have been venerated in a way that is reminiscent of ancient Egypt. Near the villages of the Bobo or Bwa in Upper Volta, for example, there were many crocodile-infested pools. Food offerings were made to these crocodiles, which were thought to be the spirits of the departed protecting their former villages. Boys were sent to the banks to call each crocodile by name, and a crocodile only responded to the voice of the boy naming it.

During pre-colonial days in east Africa, the island of Damba on Lake Victoria (Uganda) was sacred to the crocodiles and sometimes the Baganda people threw parts of the bodies of their

▲ Theodore de Bryce Le Moyne's etching of a hunt in Florida shows two improbable alligators meekly awaiting butchery by top-knotted Indians.

enemies to the crocodiles. A temple dedicated to crocodiles sat on the island and a report from a missionary described how a medium gave oracular responses to visitors, wagging his head and opening his jaws as if possessed by a "crocodile spirit."

▶ Ofo, a bronze ritual casting by the Ibo of Nigeria, is a more subdued form of homage to the crocodile than the practice elsewhere in Africa of employing crocodiles as judges to decide on the guilt or innocence of those accused of crimes.

British Museum (Natural History)/C.M. Dixon

▼ A vignette from the Book of the Dead of Lady Cheritwebeshet shows a crocodile dozing or lurking among the reeds as farmers toil in their fields. The risk of attack was accepted with equanimity by those living on the Nile.

Cairo Museum/Werner Forman Archive

Among other black African groups crocodile worship was more subdued. The Nuer, who lived in the Nile valley, respected the crocodile if it was their totem and made a sacrifice to the crocodile spirit if the taboo on killing (and eating) it was broken. The Nuer believed that animals entered into reciprocal relations with humans and, when the great anthropologist Evans-Pritchard waded with a group of Nuer through streams that were frequented by crocodiles, he was assured that he would come to no harm because "people whose totem was the crocodile lived nearby."

In some regions of Africa crocodiles were also associated with notions of punishment and retribution. In Madagascar, for example, the principle of an "eye for an eye" was applied to crocodiles — only kill a crocodile if it has killed a human being; expect a human to be killed by a crocodile if another crocodile has been wantonly destroyed. Crocodiles were so intimately connected with ideas of reciprocity that the Malagasy would take suspected wrongdoers to a river and let the crocodiles make the judgment. After a ritual specialist addressed the creatures, the accused would be expected to cross the stream. If he was taken by a crocodile he was deemed guilty. The Baganda on Lake Victoria had a similar practice. Elsewhere the crocodile was considered a medium of revenge. The Akan and Twi-speakers of Ghana, for example, believed that witches could send snakes, tsetse flies, and crocodiles on terrible errands.

## SOUTHEAST ASIA

In parts of Southeast Asia, the crocodile was believed to be the reincarnation of a departed ruler and therefore the continuing imposer of fierce authority or punitive power. In the traditional societies of the Philippines (for example, among the Panay) the crocodile was considered to be almost god-like and could not be killed. Early this century, Major G.B. Bowers discovered among the coastal people on north Luzon, at the mouth of Cagayan River, a curious fear of one crocodile as the reincarnation of a savage mountain chief; it was therefore not to be molested. In 1884 in West Timor (now in Indonesia) it was reported that the princes of Kupang sacrificed perfumed and prettily dressed young girls to the crocodiles. The princes claimed that their chiefly line descended from the crocodile and they were sending these girls to be wives to the deceased "great ones."

On Borneo, the Kayan believed that the crocodile was actually a guardian angel who could become one's blood relation or who had the power, through his clay image, to drive away evil spirits. Most cultures of Borneo, including the Dyaks, generally refrained from killing crocodiles. However, the aggrieved family of a child who had fallen prey to a crocodile would entreat a magician to retrieve the child's body. The magician would stalk crocodile after crocodile, slicing open each stomach until he stumbled upon one containing human remains. The villagers would then sacrifice a cat to the remaining crocodiles to atone for the slaughter of the innocent crocodiles.

These beliefs were linked to a number of legends and folk stories about crocodiles that abound in small traditional societies. According to one story from central Borneo, the Dyak hero Batangnorang descended into a crocodile's lair under a river bank in pursuit of gold. Disguised in tiger skin and hornbill feathers, he posed as the crocodile's returning child, sent by his far-off mother. The great reptile, however, smelled him as a man. To test Batangnorang, he seized a human from the river bank, cut the body up, stewed it,

and offered it to his visitor. The hero had no trouble eating it (a reflection of cannibal practices) and so convinced the crocodile he was not human. Making as if to leave a little later, Batangnorang swiftly turned on his crocodile host and speared him in the belly. All the treasures of diamonds and gold now belonged to Batangnorang.

This story may stem from traditional versions but, in its present form, it has been influenced by imported ideas such as treasure and precious stones. The coming of Muslim merchants to Southeast Asia had its effects on the indigenous cultures. The strong influence of Islam is shown in the Malay legend of the origins of the crocodile:

> There was once upon a time a woman called Putri Padang Gerinsing, whose petitions found great favour and acceptance with the Almighty.
> She it was who had the care of Siti Fatima, the daughter of the Prophet [Mohammed]. One day she took some clay and fashioned it into the likeness of what is now the crocodile. The material on which she moulded the clay was a sheet of *upih* [the sheath of the betel-nut palm]. This became the covering of the crocodile's under-surface. When she attempted to make the mass breathe it broke to pieces. This

▼ The famous "Mugger Pit" near the Pakistani city of Karachi is today no more than a tourist attraction. In former times the crocodiles it contained were sacred and the pit was a center of animist ceremonies to placate the dangerous and ferocious inhabitants of the Indian subcontinent's great rivers.

Popperfoto

▶ Its jaws held shut in the coils of a python, a crocodile is immortalized in stone at Mukteswara Temple in the Indian Holy center of Bhubaneswar. The crocodile's central role as a predator is not, however, reflected in India's religions.

▶ Richly carved according to strict ritual prescriptions, this crocodile-headed ancestor figure from the East Sepik Province of Papua New Guinea represents the totemic female progenitor of humans — impregnated by a spirit, from her womb sprang not only humans but snakes, eels, and fish.

crocodiles whose heads and torsos are covered with tattoo-like designs and whose tails taper into snake heads. The villagers also produce wooden trumpets with a crocodile-head mouthpiece. The Sepik area is famous throughout the world for the richness of its masks, effigies, and carved instruments. Mindimbit carvings for mortuary rites sometimes have crocodiles and men reclining in the one entangled piece, with shells or beads inserted into the eyes and knots in the wood, and colorful bird feathers attached to the whole.

The Iatmul of the middle Sepik believe that the Indopacific Crocodile *(Crocodylus porosus)* was the creator of all things. In the beginning, there was water everywhere. The crocodile caused dry land to appear and a crack opened up in the earth. The crocodile (the first male) mated with the crack in the earth (the first female). Out of the crack came the first plants, animals, and humans. The lower jaw of the crocodile fell to earth and the upper jaw became the sky; then the first dawn broke.

The Iatmul also tell of the ancestral crocodiles that traveled from place to place, founding villages, and these legends may be based on historical migrations. The Indopacific Crocodile was undoubtedly common in the mangrove-lined Sepik basin and the swamps created as the coastline retreated to its present position. It is therefore little wonder that the crocodile figures so prominently in myth and legend and that its skull is kept in the men's cult houses and regularly provided with offerings of betel nuts. During the initiation of the young Iatmul men, it is believed

happened twice. Now it chanced that the Tuan Putri had just been eating sugar-cane, so she arranged a number of sugar-cane joints to serve as a backbone, and the peelings of the rind she utilised as ribs. On its head she placed a sharp stone, and she made eyes out of bits of saffron [*kuniet*]; the tail was made of the mid-rib and leaves of a betel-nut frond. She prayed to God Almighty that the creature might have life, and it at once commenced to breathe and move. For a long time it was a plaything of the Prophet's daughter, Siti Fatima; but at length [it] became treacherous and faithless to Tuan Putri Padang Gerinsing, who had grown old and feeble. Then Fatima cursed it saying, 'Thou shalt be the crocodile of the sea, no enjoyment shall be thine, and thou shalt not know lust or desire'. She then deprived it of its teeth and tongue, and drove nails into its jaws to close them. It is these nails [that] serve the crocodile as teeth to this day.

In this tale, unlike the various myths of primal peoples, the crocodile is not a subject of reverence or admiration. In fact, with the impact of religious and cultural traditions like Islam and Christianity the image of crocodilians as dangerous, hideous, and evil creatures was enhanced.

## MELANESIA
Among the primal societies, sculptures of crocodiles are most prevalent in Melanesia. Villagers along the Karawari River, a tributary of the great Sepik in New Guinea, are renowned for their long, thin, serrated wood carvings of legless

Oliver Strewe/Wildlight Photo Agency

that the primeval crocodile swallows them then regurgitates them as men. They are subjected to skin cutting of their torsos and shoulders, the scars being explained to the uninitiated as the teeth marks of the crocodile. The prows of canoes are frequently carved in the likeness of crocodile heads, thus making the canoe itself a crocodile, carrying its "children" on its back.

Crocodile totemism and the consequences of breaking totem relations feature in many Melanesian tales. The well-known Melanesian figure Yali of Sor, leader of the Madang cargo cult, was troubled when a Sepik comrade killed a crocodile in the jungle in order to survive. The crocodile

was his friend's totem and, without its protection, he was lost in the bush and never seen again.

Along the Gulf of Papua, the Elema believed that a sorcerer could enter into the crocodile itself and deviously move through the swamps and estuaries to seize its victim by surprise. (Other nearby inland peoples believe that sorcerers could travel great distances into enemy country as cassowaries.) Sometimes indigenous beliefs and introduced ideas can flow together, as in Papua New Guinea's first modern novel, *The Crocodile* by Vincent Eri, which tells how the wife of the hero Hoiri is dragged off by a sorcerer-crocodile into the swamps of the Papuan Gulf.

▲ Decorated in the style of the Gulf Province on Papua New Guinea's southern coast, this shield portrays a mythical figure awaiting birth from the womb of a crocodile — a potent symbol of the intimate relationship between humans and crocodilians in Melanesia.

R. Berthold/Australian Picture Library

◄ The people of the Sepik pay homage to the crocodile — which plays an important role in magic as well as being both a competitor for food and a food source itself — by preparing crocodile skulls, coating them with coloured clay, and decorating them with *tambu* shells.

## AUSTRALIA

Many crocodilian myths and stories are told among northern Aborigines in Australia's tropical zone. Some myths concern the beginnings of the known universe. According to a Gunwinggu narrative from Arnhem Land, what has now been named the Liverpool River derived from a great crocodile ancestor "who rose inland behind the mountain ranges [and] slowly made his way overland towards the sea, chewing the land as he went and making deep furrows, which filled with water to become the Liverpool River."

Other stories link the crocodile with both taboo and law; for example, the story told among the Murinbata people of the fight between two totemic ancestors — Johnston's Crocodile (*Crocodylus johnsoni*) and the heron. Two old men cheated one another while sharing food and began to fight. When they decided to cool off in the billabong (a waterhole in the wet season) they turned into Yagpa, old-man crocodile, and Walgutkut, old-man heron. The story ends with the moral that old-man Yagpa should never be killed or "old-man Yagpa will come and take [the killer] away." The legend is as much about the social rule to share food as it is about a taboo against killing a totemic creature.

Other Aboriginal stories are less obviously moralistic in their content. Australian newspapers still carry stories of tragedies in the north when tourists are caught unawares in unsafe rivers; the Aborigines have similar stories. According to one from Arnhem Land, huge waves at sea forced a hunter and his daughter to canoe to a small island.

▼ A traditional ochre painting on an Arnhem Land rock wall, Australia, perhaps showing an ancestral crocodile figure giving birth to humans in the Dreamtime when all things were created.

On the island the girl was taken by a large crocodile. Her father gave chase but his spears kept missing the great reptile and he too was eventually devoured.

The Aborigines are renowned for their rock art and perhaps the most ancient depiction of a crocodile is the Aboriginal engraving of a great scaly beast at Panaramittee, South Australia. This work could possibly date as far back as 30,000 years ago.

Among the most striking Aboriginal bark paintings of crocodiles are those by the Manggalili people of northeastern Arnhem Land, especially those by the artist Banapana. In these paintings the crocodile is represented as an ancestral being who tries to save humans from dying and is also sometimes depicted with star-like scales as the Milky Way. At Oenpelli, to the west of the same region, there are bark paintings of the death of a hunter in a crocodile attack and the consoling of the wife by the dead man's younger brother. Crocodiles have also been depicted in non-Aboriginal art in Australia, for example, in Thomas Baines's 1856 painting *Killing an Alligator on the Horseshoe Flats.*

Cinematography, of course, has often highlighted crocodiles and alligators. They were monsters in 1930s horror movies, they wrestled with Tarzan in the jungles of Africa, and became a central focus of interest in the recent Australian movies *Crocodile Dundee* and *Crocodile Dundee II,* starring Paul Hogan and Linda Kozlowski. The first movie in the series drew more money at the box office than any other movie in history. It played on media reports of crocodile tragedies in northern Australia, projected the Australian legend of "mateship," and used the apparently naive and unsophisticated ways of the "Aussie bushman" to expose the seaminess and pretentiousness of life in New York.

Kris Nobbs/South Australian Museum Anthropology Archives

◄ Resembling in its technique other rock engravings known to be more than 30,000 years old, this carving of a crocodile's head from Panaramittee in South Australia poses the question of whether crocodiles were once more widespread in Australia or whether their existence was known only from trading parties to the tropical north of the continent.

▼ A colorfully depicted crocodile pursues a garfish, a barramundi, and a bream in this Aboriginal bark painting. Australian Aborigines were familiar with the crocodile's role as a competitor for fish, as well as a source of food.

Leo Meier/Weldon Trannies

▶ Explorer and artist Thomas Baines pictured himself dispatching an improbably fanged "alligator" — actually a large Indopacific Crocodile — on an expedition to northern Australia in 1856. His fellow expeditioner Humphrey is rushing to his aid, despite Baines's formidable array of weapons.

## WESTERN ART AND LITERATURE

Crocodiles and alligators were almost unknown in Europe in historic times and therefore do not feature widely in Western art. Compared to other wild creatures such as the lion, the deer, the eagle, and even the humble armadillo, these great reptiles are artistically under-represented. They are even absent in Henri Rousseau's jungle scenes. In the 1830s, however, the French sculptor Antoine-Louis Barye did not exclude them and depicted the struggles between savage crocodiles and other fauna (such as a jaguar, an antelope, and a python) in his work.

In the history of Western literature, crocodilian allusions are also few and far between. In Shakespeare's *Anthony and Cleopatra* (act 2, scene 6) there still remains the touch of the mythical and the monstrous, which owe more to medieval bestiary than to direct observation. Shakespeare's contemporary Edmund Spenser was the first writer to use the poetic image of crocodile tears. In 1565 the famous sea captain Sir James Hawkins had reported "many Crocodils" in the New World. He observed that they "cry and sobbe" to provoke prey to come to them, giving Spenser the inspiration to write in his great poem *The Faerie Queene:*

> . . . a cruell craftie Crocodile,
> Which in false griefe hyding his harmful guile
> Doth weep full sore, and sheddeth tender teares.

Powerfully symbolizing the human stratagem of crying before striking back, this same image was to be exploited a generation later by Robert Burton (sometimes referred to as the first psychoanalyst) and Francis Bacon (jurist and philosopher). It is also used in a nineteenth century nursery rhyme — to the question "What are little boys made of?" comes the answer "Crocodile's tears."

The ancient Egyptian belief in the crocodile's wisdom was replaced by a later emphasis on the crocodile's cunning, treachery, and savagery. Even J. M. Barrie's well-loved story of Peter Pan does little to relieve the gloomy picture of the evil crocodile although at least the tick-tocking, clock-swallowing crocodile is meant to bring justice to a still more evil Captain Hook. In 1977 the crocodilian equivalent of *Jaws* — Shelley Katz's *Alligator,* a novel about a giant killer from the Everglades — was published. Our appetite for sensation and excitement has distorted our image of crocodilians, which now bears little resemblance to the revered crocodile-god of ancient Egypt.

◄ Romance and symbolism triumph over accuracy in Boucher's *Crocodile Hunt,* one of the few representations of crocodiles in Western art. An attenuated pyramid places the scene as outside Europe, although the huntsmen and their dogs are wholly European.

▼ A sixteenth century German etching shows hunters using pigs as crocodile bait in a slightly more modern interpretation of the technique described from Elephantine on the Upper Nile.

# ATTACKS ON HUMANS

A.C. (TONY) POOLEY, TOMMY HINES, and JOHN SHIELD

Early accounts of Chinese Alligators (*Alligator sinensis*) portray this species as formidable and dangerous to humans. Marco Polo who, in the thirteenth century, was the first European to report the presence in China of these "great serpents with feet," described their mouths as "large enough to swallow a man whole . . . with great [pointed] teeth. And in short they are so fierce-looking and so hideously ugly that every man and beast must stand in fear and trembling of them."

These early accounts either exaggerate or are the result of confusion with other crocodilians. Everything we now know of the Chinese Alligator, and most other crocodilian species, suggests that they are relatively timid and inoffensive, and of no real danger to humans.

Despite this, almost all species of crocodilians are loathed as potential predators on humans. There are some species, such as the American Alligator (*Alligator mississippiensis*), possibly the Black Caiman (*Melanosuchus niger*), the Mugger (*Crocodylus palustris*), the Orinoco Crocodile (*Crocodylus intermedius*), and the American Crocodile (*Crocodylus acutus*) that do occasionally prey on humans. But instances of this behavior in these species are very rare.

Two species of true crocodiles, the Nile Crocodile (*Crocodylus niloticus*) and the Indopacific Crocodile (*Crocodylus porosus*) are, however, justly accused of being notorious "man-eaters." Both species are widely distributed and grow to large size. Both have greatly influenced the way humans view or fear all crocodilians.

Most loss of life to crocodilians probably occurred in the past among tribal peoples in Africa and the Indopacific islands. Historical statistics on crocodile attacks in these areas are nonexistent. Our clue as to the prevalence of attacks rests on reports from early explorers and ethnologists. Certainly, from accounts throughout these regions, crocodiles had a great impact on primitive cultures and it is likely that the Nile and Indopacific crocodiles preyed on these people whenever circumstances made it possible.

Occasionally, circumstances occur that permit animals to display grossly atypical behavior. One such instance occurred in Southeast Asia during World War II — a widely known and horrific incident involving Indopacific Crocodiles and nearly one thousand Japanese soldiers trying to make their escape through the mangrove swamp separating Ramree Island from the coast of Burma, 30 kilometers (18 miles) away.

The naturalist Bruce Wright was a member of the British forces who had trapped the Japanese on Ramree. He was sitting on a marine launch grounded on the slimy mire of a channel running through the labyrinth of the swamp and his account of the night of the 19 February 1945 outlines the grisly scene:

"That night was the most horrible that any member of the M.L. [marine launch] crews ever experienced. The scattered rifle shots in the pitch black swamp punctured by the screams of wounded men crushed in the jaws of huge reptiles, and the blurred worrying sound of spinning crocodiles made a cacophony of hell that has rarely been duplicated on earth. At dawn the vultures arrived to clean up what the crocodiles had left . . . Of about one thousand Japanese soldiers that entered the swamps of Ramree, only about twenty were found alive."

Recently, accounts of crocodilian attacks on humans and the circumstances surrounding these attacks have been studied in three areas of the world — Africa, Florida, and Australia. These studies are incomplete and are very regional, encompassing only part of the range of each species. But they indicate that some similarities or patterns of attacks do exist.

▶ Perhaps because its size, speed, and formidable teeth fit our preconceptions of a "ferocious monster," the American Alligator has acquired a fallacious reputation for unprovoked aggression toward humans. Although it does occasionally attack humans (usually because they have invaded its habitat or disturbed nests or hatchlings) such events are rare. Nile Crocodile and Indopacific Crocodile attacks on humans are more common and their reputations as "man eaters" more justified.

Hans Reinhard/Bruce Coleman Ltd

▲ The Nile Crocodile is large, aggressive, and widely distributed in areas of Africa where encounters between crocodilians and humans occur daily. Most of these encounters do not result in an attack but those that do have earned for the Nile Crocodile — and unfortunately also for other more innocuous species — the reputation as a killer.

▶ The domain of the Nile Crocodile includes the very areas of water where Africans fish, bathe, clean food or clothes, and through which they wade or punt in small boats. This juxtaposition of crocodile and human populations has led to deaths . . . on both sides.

Jonathan Scott/Planet Earth Pictures

## NILE CROCODILE ATTACKS IN AFRICA

The Nile Crocodile has the reputation of being the biggest killer of beast and human on the African continent. In comparison with the other dangerous or predatory animals responsible for human fatalities — lions, leopards, buffaloes, hippopotamuses, hyenas, rhinoceroses, and elephants — the Nile Crocodile is far more widely distributed across the length and breadth of the continent, and is far more abundant than all of the other species combined. Crocodiles occur in rivers, streams, swamps, lagoons, estuaries, lakes, and along the floodplains of numerous rivers where millions of people across Africa live, work, and play daily. In these areas too, the only forms of transport are canoes, rafts, or small boats poled through narrow papyrus- or reed-lined channels, or by foot, wading across the wide, shallow rivers inhabited by these predators.

In the more developed countries of Africa, humans utilize the aquatic habitat for recreational pursuits and are increasingly invading the domain of the crocodile. Ignorance of the crocodile's habits, its methods of hunting, and some of the basic precautions that should be observed in areas where the crocodile occurs, have resulted in many needless human fatalities.

Adult Nile Crocodiles weighing as much as 1,000 kilograms (2,200 pounds) and up to 6.5 meters (21 feet) in length have been recorded. The Nile Crocodile has evolved on a continent where it has had to contend and compete with a far greater variety of competitors, as well as

S.C. Bisserot

potential prey species, than any other crocodilian in the world. Competitors in the aquatic habitat include predatory fish and sharks, monitor lizards, three other crocodile species, and hippopot-amuses. On land, it needs to defend territory, nest sites, and offspring against a range of predators and competitors ranging in size from small mongooses to elephants, and, of course, humans. Conse-quently, the Nile Crocodile is one of the most aggressive of the crocodiles. In order to survive in habitats populated by such a diverse fauna, it has become a versatile and opportunistic hunter, and master predator of the aquatic environment.

### HUNTING STRATEGIES
Like most crocodiles, when lying motionless in the water, the Nile Crocodile is cryptically colored and difficult to detect. It regularly enhances this natural concealment by lying next to a stand of reeds, under an overhanging tree, among water lilies, or drifting alongside a floating object.

It can breathe, smell, see, and hear while only the top of its nostrils and the top of its head are visible above the surface. From this sit-and-wait

position it will make the final lunge at unsuspecting humans or antelope that approach the water's edge.

Alternatively, the crocodile may detect a potential victim when it is drifting some distance offshore. It will submerge and approach closer and closer, swimming underwater and bringing its head to the surface perhaps once or twice to check the location of the prey. The final lunge may carry

T. Pooley

▲ Although readily visible against a background of green grass, in murky waters with the added natural concealment of overhanging trees or floating objects, the coloring of the Nile Crocodile makes it all but invisible to unsuspecting prey. Stealth, silence, and surprise are the crocodile's main assets in an attack.

◄ Although the Nile Crocodile takes most of its victims when they are at the water's edge, it is an extremely aggressive species and will launch itself onto land, often in a fearsome burst of speed, in pursuit of potential prey.

Peter Johnson/NHPA

▲ From a partially submerged position in the water, a Nile Crocodile makes a final, and in this case ultimately unsuccessful, lunge at a group of goats. Almost any other species of animal would elicit the same response and the slowest or smallest in the group is no match for a crocodile once it has established its grip on any part of the victim's body.

the attacking crocodile several times its own length up the beach. Acceleration imparted by the powerful tail is combined with a simultaneous forward swing of the hind legs as the crocodile beaches. The toes and feet dig into the bank and the powerful legs lever the body upward. If the bank is steep, the crocodile appears to vault straight out of the water. If the prey is still out of reach, the hind-leg stride may be repeated and the crocodile may lower its head and hook it over the top of the bank to support its body while its legs swing forward for another stride. Many an unsuspecting antelope or relaxed fisherman has been seized in this form of attack, even when 1.5 meters (5 feet) above the water.

An adult crocodile can also dash across land for several meters, moving swiftly in a running stance with its trunk held high above the ground, to seize its victim in powerful bone-crushing jaws.

In another attack technique, the crocodile may erupt from the water in a burst of speed and, using its heavy, bony head, may knock the victim over with sledge-hammer blows, before seizing and pulling it back into the water. It must also be remembered that the crocodile can snap sideways fast enough to capture fish or a bird alighting on the surface of the water. The elements of attack are always silence, speed, and surprise.

### DOCUMENTED ATTACKS
Nile Crocodile attacks may be categorized as defense of territory, defense of nests or hatchlings, self-defense (for example, when the crocodile has been threatened or accidently trodden on), and hunting for food. From an analysis of attacks recorded in the literature and from personal

investigations of 43 cases of crocodile attacks on humans in northern Zululand and in southern Mozambique, a number of pertinent facts emerge.

Of the 43 attacks, 39 occurred between November and early April — the period of territorial defense from rivals by large dominant males at the nesting grounds and nest guarding or defense of newly hatched young by both male and female crocodiles.

These attacks coincide with the period when cold-blooded (poikilothermic) creatures like crocodiles are more active because water temperatures are warm, the weather is hot, the rivers and pans are flooded and discolored (conditions that favor attack), and the crocodiles have resumed feeding after their inactive winter. At this time too, crocodiles not normally found in small feeder streams or pans and channels, which are a mere trickle over the dry winter months, swim up from larger bodies of water downstream making unexpected appearances, even in farms or effluent dams close to human habitation, in search of food. Crocodiles washed out to sea during peak flood periods may return to beaches then appear in quiet lagoons and estuarine pans many kilometers up or down the coastline from where they are normally found.

Contrary to popular belief, noise or safety in numbers does not deter a crocodile attack. Of the attacks investigated, only five of the victims were alone when seized. Several of the victims were snatched from amidst groups of men, women, and children who were either fording rivers, washing clothes or food, or bathing, and who were making a considerable amount of noise at the time. Field studies have shown that crocodiles are attracted from considerable distances to the sounds of a struggling animal in shallow water or to a shoal of leaping fish and that sound is often how prey is located.

Many witnesses and survivors of non-fatal attacks estimated that the crocodiles involved were in the range of 2.5 meters (8 feet) in length. These animals could be placed in the weight range of about 100 kilograms (220 pounds) and thus, weight for weight, the average human adult would stand a chance of escaping and surviving attack from a crocodile of this size. One could conjecture that these crocodiles were subadult or young adult animals. The injuries suffered by the survivors of these attacks also suggest that the crocodiles were small to medium-sized animals, for the wounds inflicted included the loss of hands, feet, and breasts, severe lacerations, and broken arms or legs.

However, the accounts of fatal attacks by large Nile Crocodiles — 23 of the 43 attacks investigated — indicate that these crocodiles were extremely aggressive and ferocious. There were several instances where crocodiles, having seized their victim, were either repeatedly stabbed with spears or knives, beaten with sticks, pelted with stones, or had sticks rammed down their gullets in order to prise the human victims from their jaws . . . but to no avail. In these attacks few bodies or remains were retrieved. Considering that a large adult Nile Crocodile may weight up to fourteen times that of an average human and can seize and drown Cape buffaloes as heavy as themselves, a human being, out of his or her element in the water, has little chance of surviving such an attack.

Several attacks on small boats, rafts, and canoes have been reported in the literature. One may surmise that, from its position in the water, the crocodile sees the silhouette or shape of the approaching boat or canoe but not necessarily the occupants of the craft. The crocodile might well attack the boat in the belief that it was defending territory or offspring against another crocodile. There are documented cases of boats being sunk in lakes and the human occupants swimming to safety while the attacking crocodile concerned itself with savaging the rubber boat or canoe, paying no attention to the escaping humans.

Crocodiles, like sharks, are rarely seen prior to an attack. The attack is swift, silent, and without warning. Notice boards or warning signs, indicating the presence and danger of crocodiles in areas where they occur, are seldom heeded by tourists because the danger is unseen. Unfortunately, when an attack on a human does occur, the resultant adverse publicity often leads to an extermination campaign to rid the area of crocodiles; the human victim is rarely blamed for his or her folly.

To the millions of tribal peoples who go about the daily routine of herding and watering livestock along river banks, washing clothes, bathing, poling canoes, and tending fishing gear, the crocodile is a

T. Pooley

fact of life — a natural hazard — and they tend to have a fatalistic attitude to the possibility of an attack. The crocodile has, after all, occupied the rivers and lakes for some 70 million years or more, long before humans appeared on the scene. Like sharks in the sea, crocodiles surely have a claim to their domain.

◄ Women of the Tembe-Thonga tribe in Maputaland on the Zululand-Mozambique border prepare to fish, well aware that crocodiles occur in the floodplain lakes and pans in this area. They mistakenly believe that there is safety in numbers and that their noise will frighten off crocodiles.

▼ Far outweighing a human being, an adult crocodile, such as this Indopacific Crocodile captured in Sumatra, Indonesia, is quite capable of taking a fully grown man or woman. The dismembered remains recovered from its stomach are evidence of the crocodile's skill in reducing its prey to manageable size, often by literally shaking its victim to pieces.

John Lever/Koorana Crocodile Farm

▲ News reports of alligator or crocodile attacks in the United States and Australia often result in a dramatic increase in complaints about nuisance animals and in demands for the removal of all crocodilians, regardless of size, from populated areas. As the attack reports become yesterday's news, the public furore temporarily abates.

▼ Without a hint of aggression, an American Alligator walks sedately past a group of people on the Anhinga Trail in the Florida Everglades. Out of the water, the element of surprise is lost and an attack unlikely.

Martin W. Grosnick/Ardea London

## ALLIGATOR ATTACKS IN FLORIDA

Early explorers in Florida regarded the American Alligator as a threat to life and property, and it is claimed that alligators were a constant threat to the Indians who kept guard against them night and day. William Bartram, an explorer, described an encounter with three large alligators that attacked his boat while he was exploring on the St. John's River in the early 1790s. In more recent times, R. L. Ditmars reported in 1953 that "from a wave of extermination [by the mid 1900s] the alligator has retreated into more secluded swamps and bayous . . . [and now] envinces great timidity toward man . . . so great is the reptile's fear of man that one can safely go bathing in waters inhabited by alligators." There are, however, no scientific reports documenting alligator attacks before 1977 although the Florida Game and Fresh Water Fish Commission has collected newspaper clippings on attacks as far back as 1948.

Even though earlier records are not as good as they are today, it is evident that alligator attacks in Florida increased from the late 1960s until the mid-1970s. There were as many as 14 attacks reported each year during the early 1970s and six known human fatalities have been documented since 1973. In addition, there have been several other cases where serious injuries were inflicted on the victim. In most cases, however, the injuries inflicted were relatively minor.

From the late 1960s (when alligator populations were lowest) until the early 1970s alligator numbers increased significantly in Florida. During this period the state also experienced phenomenal human population growth with much of the subsequent development occurring adjacent to wetland areas. The problem of conflicts between humans and alligators was well publicized during this time and almost any episode involving alligators and people was covered in the news media. Almost all alligator attacks within the state were also reported to the Florida Game and Fresh Water Fish Commission, which investigated each reported attack. Consequently, from the mid-1970s there are good records of alligator attacks in Florida. Concurrent with these events, an intensive alligator research program was initiated by the state, which included some effort to evaluate attack behavior.

The first documented fatality from an attack in Florida occurred in August 1973 when a 16-year-old girl was killed while swimming with her father in Sarasota County, Florida. It was during this period (1968–73) that complaints about alligators increased and, by 1976, the Florida Game and Fresh Water Fish Commission was receiving at least 5,000 complaints each year about nuisance alligators, which were perceived as a threat to life or property. In response to this, the Commission initiated a program allowing private trappers to harvest alligators that were reported as nuisance animals by the public. This program targeted many potential problem animals and resulted in the removal of approximately 2,000 alligators each year. The complaint rate and the number of animals harvested have now stabilized. The number of attacks also appeared to have stabilized until 1986 when a near record of 13 occurred. Recently there were two very dramatic fatal attacks. A scuba diver was killed in a popular tourist area in north Florida in 1987 and a small child was killed by an alligator close to a residential area in south Florida in 1988. When such incidents occur the complaint rate increases dramatically.

## WHY DO ALLIGATORS ATTACK HUMANS?

The alligator is a primitive and unpredictable predator, and any serious effort to answer the question of why alligators attack must contain much speculation. There is ample evidence that alligators are able and willing, under some circumstances, to utilize humans as a prey species and will attack their human victim for food. The facts surrounding every serious reported attack in Florida since 1973 suggest that, in every case where it was possible to ascertain, the victim was unaware of the alligator's presence until the last minute or, more usually, until the animal had actually attacked. In every case, the victim had been, at least partially, in the water with the alligator. It appears that in most serious attacks the victim was actually stalked, suggesting that the aggression was hunger motivated. Yet, when one considers the thousands of contacts between alligators and people that occur each day without incident, it would appear that such behavior is extremely rare.

Food-habit studies demonstrate that alligators are largely fish eaters but significant numbers of amphibians, birds, and small mammals also appear in their diet. There is little evidence that alligators take animals as large as humans on a regular basis. However, they are very opportunistic and will take whatever they are capable of catching if they find it in their habitat. They commonly take calves on Florida ranches and dogs of all sizes; they have also been observed taking large swine of up to 45 kilograms (100 pounds) in weight and large goats. Humans obviously fall into a prey-size class that very large alligators are capable of taking. Analysis of information suggests that younger and/or smaller humans are more likely to be a target.

It is commonly reported in the news media that possible reasons for alligator attacks are female nest defense or male territorial defense. Females do, on occasion, defend their nest from intruders and may behave defensively when their young are disturbed but only a small percentage of females appear to do so and the defense is generally short-lived, particularly if the aggressive female is struck across the snout with a stout stick. (On rare occasions I have seen females so defensive that I

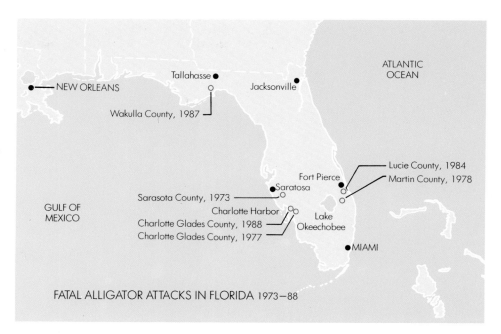

FATAL ALLIGATOR ATTACKS IN FLORIDA 1973–88

would leave the nest site and once I had a very aggressive female come into the airboat with me as I retreated from her nest.) Usually the female provides plenty of warning, with an obvious display of defensive behavior such as mouth gaping and hissing, giving the prudent person time to retreat.

Aggressive displays by males are less common and much harder to categorize. Large males have been seen to assume an apparently defensive posture against low-flying helicopters and sometimes inflate their bodies with tails arched out of the water in aggressive displays when small boats approach them. Even if the animal actually attacked, therefore, the obvious display would have provided plenty of time for retreat.

One of the common questions raised is whether large alligators in frequent contact with people become more dangerous. Alligators were persecuted in Florida from early settlement until the late 1960s. They were commercially hunted with little effective regulation on harvest until 1969 when a United States federal law (the Lacey Act)

▲▼ Warning notices are there for a purpose. Feeding alligators in the wild encourages them to associate humans with food — whether the "food" is willingly or unwillingly donated (above). The head of this American Alligator is probably a more effective deterrent to swimmers than the warning notice (below) but the notice is at least always visible; a submerged alligator is not.

▶ Unmolested alligators, very much at home in their own environment, show little fear of humans and an attack by such a self-confident alligator is probably more likely than attack by a wary alligator with previous experience of human molestation and harassment.

Jeff Simon/Bruce Coleman Ltd.

was amended. This was the first effective control of the illegal taking of alligators. In 1973 the Endangered Species Act was passed in the United States and, as a result of both laws, alligators were afforded greater protection than they had ever previously received. The population response was immediate but, in retrospect, it is clear that in addition to real population increases, some of the perceived increase was in fact due to the alligators becoming more visible as a result of less persecution.

Based on scientists' experience of capturing animals for research purposes and running managed hunts, it is apparent that alligators become very wary when harassed but, in those locations where large alligators live unmolested adjacent to humans, it is not common to see them attempt to escape at the mere presence of humans. Under these circumstances one must speculate that large unmolested animals may be more dangerous than those that show fear of humans. There are cases where large alligators are actually fed by people on a regular basis around fishing camps, public parks, and lakes. This is often put forward as a cause for attacks and, although no such cases have been documented, one must conclude that it has the potential to be a contributing factor.

# UNPROVOKED ALLIGATOR ATTACKS ON HUMANS IN FLORIDA

| Year | Attacks | Year | Attacks | Year | Attacks |
|---|---|---|---|---|---|
| 1948-59 | 4 | 1977* | 14 | 1983 | 6 |
| 1959-72 | 6 | 1978* | 5 | 1984* | 5 |
| 1973* | 3 | 1979 | 2 | 1985 | 3 |
| 1974 | 4 | 1980 | 4 | 1986 | 13 |
| 1975 | 5 | 1981 | 5 | 1987* | 8 |
| 1976 | 2 | 1982 | 6 | 1988* | 5 |

* includes fatalities

## ATTACKS IN SOUTHEAST ASIA AND AUSTRALIA

Southeast Asia and northern Australia are home to a number of crocodilians of impressive size. The area is also home to millions of people, many of whom live primitive lifestyles close to natural waterways. These conditions could be expected to result in widespread loss of human life and this is undoubtedly what has occurred throughout the area since the two groups first found themselves sharing the environment.

There are historical reports of hundreds of people being taken each year in India by Mugger and even by Gharials (*Gavialis gangeticus*), encouraged to eat human remains by the religious practice of disposing of the dead at riverside cremation ghats or floating the bodies downriver.

▲ This crocodile was apparently responsible for the deaths of two schoolgirls at Pindi Pindi in Queensland, Australia, in 1933. The girls disappeared while riding to school on a horse — one girl was later found drowned and the body of the second girl was found inside the crocodile pictured here with its captors.

▶▼ By taking advantage of food indirectly provided for them by human burial practices, Gharials earned a possibly undeserved reputation as human killers. There are few large Gharials left in the wild and most human contact is with captive Gharials (right). However, large Indopacific Crocodiles in the wild are still relatively widespread and these fishermen, standing at the site of previous attacks in Kakadu National Park, Australia, are unlikely to find the one swimming past them (below) quite so friendly as a captive Gharial.

If human lives were ever lost in large numbers in India, and there is considerable doubt, this is a thing of the past, with all crocodilians there now being drastically reduced in number. Large specimens in the wild are rare today.

Throughout the archipelagoes of Indonesia, the Philippines, and New Guinea, together with the adjacent land masses of Malaya and northern Australia, there is evidence that crocodiles have always exacted a terrible toll on villagers living close to the water. Only the problems of contact with isolated communities and poor communications have obscured the statistics on fatalities and when and how they occurred. Where reliable sources of information are available, they paint a picture of regular predation by crocodiles on villagers and even situations where entire communities have been terrorized.

A missionary at a village in northern Irian Jaya reported that no fewer than 62 of the villagers had been killed or maimed by a rogue crocodile in the 1960s. Six fatal attacks, and a great number of non-fatal attacks, occurred on Sarawak's Lupar River between 1975 and 1984. Tiny Siargao Island, off Mindanao in the Philippines, has reported the deaths of nine villagers in recent years, all possible victims of the same crocodile.

Of the several species of crocodilian in the region, the greatest offender against humans is the Indopacific Crocodile. It grows to 7 meters (23 feet) in length, is highly mobile, adaptable, and, once it has achieved maturity, fears nothing except its peers and humans.

As the Indopacific Crocodile grows, the mammalian component of its diet grows in proportion. An individual of 5 meters (16 feet) in length would generally be quite accustomed to killing pigs and, occasionally, cattle, buffaloes, and horses. There are reliable accounts of leopards being killed. Except where it has been hunted, there is no reason to believe that such an animal would recognize a human entering its territory as anything other than a potential meal.

The Indopacific Crocodile is quite competent on land and can walk considerable distances when necessary. It is also capable of short bursts of speed. The water, however, remains its essential element and it takes to the water as soon as it is alarmed or when preparing to kill. One can sometimes see this demonstrated in a zoo. When a potential meal approaches, in the form of a bird or perhaps a dog, a hungry crocodile, apparently asleep on the bank, may slip quickly and silently into the water. By the time the "meal" arrives on the scene there is no sign of danger but the crocodile is watching quietly from under the water. If the intruder approaches closely enough, the crocodile explodes into action and grabs it in a ferocious rush that has been compared to the eruption of a polaris missile from its underwater base. The crocodile seizes the prey animal with its jaws locked onto the head, muzzle, leg, or whatever part of the body is within reach. If the impact of this first contact is not sufficient to disable the prey animal, the crocodile tries to drag it into deeper water. The notorious "death roll" may be used at this stage to unbalance the unfortunate victim. Once the contest has moved into the water, the advantages are with the crocodile and the victim is drowned or killed by crushing bites. (There is no reliable evidence to support the long-held belief that the Indopacific Crocodile will deliberately use its tail to knock down a victim.)

When 32-year-old Peter Reimers was killed by a crocodile near Weipa, in far north Queensland,

Australian Picture Library

he appears to have been a victim of a "typical" encounter. Police who investigated Reimers's death found where he had walked to a shallow creek, stripped off, and waded in to cool himself in the water. They also found tracks indicating that a large crocodile had been lying on the bank nearby and had probably slipped into the water when it heard the man's approach. As Reimers waded into the water he was seized and killed. Had it been a pig or a wallaby approaching the creek, the outcome would surely have been no different.

◀ When food approaches, this Indopacific Crocodile in the Adelaide River, Australia, explodes out of the water exposing almost its entire body. Hand feeding any wild crocodilian is a foolish pursuit since no species — aggressive or otherwise — can be guaranteed to differentiate between the food being offered and the hand offering it.

▼ Ignoring a clear warning of the potential danger this group have entered an element where the Indopacific Crocodile is "master" and they, even with a gun at the ready, are not. Any crocodile that attacks them does so not because it prefers human prey but because the prey is there.

Mirror Australian Telegraph Publications

► Although its primary habitat is water, the Indopacific Crocodile is reasonably competent on land and capable of bursts of speed over short distances. Its aggressive nature, combined with large size and a wide distribution throughout the Pacific and Southeast Asia, make it the equal of the Nile Crocodile as a potential human killer.

E. R. Degginger/Animals Animals

When it has made a kill that cannot be consumed intact, the crocodile breaks the body into manageable pieces with a violent shaking action of its head and neck. During this process the body of the victim is held above the water and literally thrashed to pieces. Where the victim is large, arms, legs, and sometimes the head are thus removed from the torso. The crocodile then consumes its fill of the manageable pieces. People searching for a crocodile's human victim frequently find the horrifying aftermath of such a meal, with pieces of clothing and body strewn about the feeding area and sometimes hanging in overhead branches.

While a crocodile will eat carrion, as a general rule it eats its fill of fresh meat soon after a kill is made. There is little to support the theory that a crocodile will store a body in its "lair" until the flesh is putrefied.

Not all Indopacific Crocodile attacks on humans are motivated by hunger. Cases have been described, for example, of people who have accidentally encountered a crocodile and been injured by the reptile as it tried to escape. There are instances too where humans have been attacked in error, for example, by a crocodile pursuing a fish or a dog. One startled north Queensland fisherman recounted how a 3-meter (10-foot) crocodile snatched a fish from his hand while he was cleaning it at the edge of a creek. The crocodile could just as easily have taken a hand along with the fish.

The instinct to defend territory seems to have been the motivation behind a number of well-documented Indopacific Crocodile attacks. The female will frequently defend her nest, sometimes to the point of biting a human who ventures too close. There is no record, however, of a fatal attack by a nesting female.

Territory defense by the male may be much more significant, particularly during the breeding season when aggression is more marked. The male defends his territory vigorously against other males. It is possible that this aggression extends beyond reptilian competitors to include humans and, particularly, boats that intrude into his territory. It is easy to believe that the shape, particularly of a canoe, would elicit the same aggressive response from a male crocodile that he would show toward a competitor. There are certainly accounts of crocodiles attacking such craft without availing themselves of the meal provided by the occupants tipped into the water. Recent Australian reports provide some interesting examples of crocodiles' aggression toward boats. In the 1970s a large male crocodile, which came to be known as Sweetheart, attacked a number of boats in a stretch of the Finniss River near Darwin. Apparently stimulated by the noise of the motors, the animal damaged and upset dinghies but the occupants were uninjured, even when spilled into the water with the reptile. In 1985 Val Plumwood, a university lecturer, was paddling a canoe in a creek in the Kakadu National Park. A crocodile "challenged" the canoe by bumping it and then attacked Plumwood as she tried to get out of the canoe. She was able to escape, despite being severely injured.

The motivation behind any particular attack may not be simple. It seems possible, for example, that a crocodile might be stimulated to attack an intruder and then, having killed the victim, decide to make a meal of him or her.

A recent study in Australia looked at all reliable accounts of crocodile attacks on humans. Among the cases sufficiently well documented, most attacks occurred in the hottest months of the year and in the afternoon. While this seasonal distribution reflects increased feeding and sexual activity on the part of the crocodiles, it probably also reflects an increase in the number of residents using the waterways for recreation at those times.

To see if killer crocodiles were actually eating their human victims, the study looked at 27 cases of fatal crocodile attacks. It was found that in 16 cases there was evidence that all or part of the victim had been eaten; in eight cases the crocodile removed the body, which was never recovered and was possibly eaten; in three cases the victim's body was recovered intact.

Regrettably there is little recorded data on the individual crocodiles that have attacked humans. The Australian study found only 37 cases where there was reliable information about the crocodile itself. These 37 cases included 17 animals described as longer than 4 meters (13 feet), probably males since few females attain this length, while 15 crocodiles were less than 4 meters in length. Indopacific Crocodiles as small as 2 meters long have been implicated in apparently unprovoked attacks on humans in Australia.

▼ Adult Indopacific Crocodiles are territorial and will defend their territory against intrusion, even by boats. A local woman, only ankle-deep in the water beside this landing stage on the Daintree River, Australia, was taken by a large male crocodile in December 1985.

Hugh Edwards

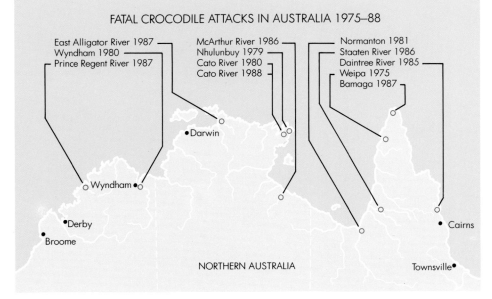

FATAL CROCODILE ATTACKS IN AUSTRALIA 1975–88

East Alligator River 1987
Wyndham 1980
Prince Regent River 1987

McArthur River 1986
Nhulunbuy 1979
Cato River 1980
Cato River 1988

Normanton 1981
Staaten River 1986
Daintree River 1985
Weipa 1975
Bamaga 1987

Darwin

Wyndham

Derby

Broome

NORTHERN AUSTRALIA

Cairns

Townsville

# SAFETY PRECAUTIONS FOR VISITORS TO CROCODILIAN AREAS

A. C. (TONY) POOLEY

1. Notices warning of the danger of crocodiles or alligators are there for a good reason. If you see one at a jetty, river bank, or lake shore . . . **take heed!** Remember too that small children cannot read notices; the responsibility is yours.

2. When visiting a holiday resort, caravan park, camping ground, boat jetty, or farmer friend, ask about the safety of paddling, swimming, fishing, or boating in that area.

3. Remember that crocodilians are rarely seen; they are silent, stealthy, and efficient hunters that attack very swiftly. When fishing, stand back a minimum of 3 meters (10 feet) from the water's edge, and even farther back at night. Your chances of being attacked will be greatly reduced by doing so. If a fishing line becomes entangled in the reeds, water lilies or whatever, do not allow anyone to wade out to disentangle it. A human life is surely worth more than a length of nylon and a fishhook.

4. Do not allow children to wade into or play around in the water if crocodiles or alligators are even suspected of being in the area.

5. Do not be misled into believing that noise frightens a crocodilian. Noise if anything alerts it to the fact that prey — animal or human — is available and it might not be too choosy about its prey.

6. Do not assume that a shallow pool, weed-covered pan, drainage canal, or even a ditch is safe for you or your pets. Even if it is situated some kilometers from the nearest lake or river, crocodilians do travel overland at times from one body of water to another. A large crocodilian can lie submerged in barely 30 centimeters (12 inches) of water, for well over an hour.

7. If your dog is feeling the heat and panting on a hot summer day do not encourage it to go into the water but take it to the nearest tap.

8. Never leave the carcasses of animals or fish you consider inedible anywhere near water where people swim, paddle, fish, or moor boats. The carcasses should be properly disposed of.

9. Do not gut fish from your boat or a jetty into the water. Depositing unwanted fish entrails or unused bait will quickly attract crocodilians to scavenge these scraps or perhaps to attack you.

10. Do not allow anyone on your boat to dangle their limbs in the water where crocodilians occur. Make sure that your passengers sit on the seats provided in the boat and not on the edge with their bottoms hanging over.

11. If you discover a hatchling crocodile or alligator drifting past your boat or lying basking on the bank, move away from the area and, above all, do not try to capture it; the adults might well be close by. (In any case it is illegal to capture or kill a crocodilian or to remove eggs without a permit.)

12. The discharging of a firearm into the water to frighten away crocodilians before crossing a river or stream is no guarantee of safety. The volume of sound produced does not travel very far under water.

13. The eyes of a crocodilian glow red in the beam of a light at night but the failure to see glowing eyes in a light scan does not mean that the area is free of them. One may be lying submerged and invisible beneath the jetty or your boat.

14. Do not walk around at night without a torch if you are fishing or camping close to the water's edge.

15. Investigations have shown that when a crocodilian has successfully attacked and killed a victim at a site to which people come daily, it will usually return again and again to repeat such attacks. The construction of a simple screen or barrier of logs and branches is often all that is necessary to provide protection and to prevent tragedies.

▶▲ Crocodile warning signs proliferate in crocodile areas of northern Australia (top left) but are not necessarily understood by children or by non-English speaking tourists. For this reason conservation organizations increasingly use simple symbols to pinpoint the danger (above). Their main aim is to save human lives while conserving the indigenous Indopacific Crocodile.

# CROCODILE-SKIN PRODUCTS

KARLHEINZ H.P. FUCHS, CHARLES A. ROSS, A.C. (TONY) POOLEY, and ROMULUS WHITAKER

Historically, utilization of crocodilians was modest and parts of the animal were used mainly for food, medicine, or religious purposes. American Indians in the southeastern United States, Aborigines in Australia, tribal peoples in India and New Guinea, and some ethnic groups in Southeast Asia ate alligators or crocodiles where they were available. In parts of China and Southeast Asia, crocodilian dorsal scales, internal organs, and musk were valued for their medicinal properties or were used in the manufacture of perfume. In the northern Philippines, Borneo, and Malaysia the teeth and claws of crocodilians were used as ingredients in magicians' potions. In New Guinea, crocodiles played an integral role in the lives of the inhabitants of the lowland marshlands and swamps; decorated crocodile skulls and other artifacts were used to adorn homes and communal houses. In many areas throughout the world's lowlands, crocodile-tooth necklaces were prized.

However, it was not until the Industrial Revolution in Europe, with the concurrent colonization and the expansion of Anglo-Saxon influence into the interior of previously remote areas, that utilization of crocodilians for their skins became "big business."

## COMMERCIAL UTILIZATION OF AMERICAN ALLIGATORS

There is little information on the actual take of crocodilians worldwide for skins in the 1800s and early 1900s and what information there is refers to American Alligator (*Alligator mississippiensis*) utilization. "Commercial" utilization of American Alligators started in the late 1700s and John James Audubon commented on the use of alligator skins for saddlebags, boots, and shoes. The small, local market was insignificant and alligators were killed wherever they were found, mostly as vermin or for sport rather than for their skins.

The systematic slaughter of American Alligators for their skins reached a peak during and immediately after the American Civil War (1861–65) when leather made from alligator skin was in great demand for footwear and, later, for traveling bags, saddlebags, belts, card cases, and other items. Trade statistics for this period are fragmentary and anecdotal but it is obvious that large numbers of alligators were being harvested. In 1888, ten hunters in the Cocoa area of Florida took 5,000 skins; understandably their take decreased by 50 percent the following season. One of these hunters had, a few years earlier, killed 800 alligators in a single season while another had taken 42 in a single night. In some other parts of Florida during the late 1880s takes of 200–400 alligators per hunter were commonplace and there were a number of skin buyers scattered throughout the state. These buyers sold their skins primarily in New York and some trading firms handled up to 60,000 skins a year. At the same time there was a lively trade in stuffed and live baby alligators and a smaller trade in teeth.

The American demand for skins quickly outpaced the available supply of domestic American Alligators and new sources of skins from Mexico and Central America were developed before 1900. These skins, from true crocodiles (genus *Crocodylus*), were easily distinguishable from American Alligator skins although all were marketed as alligator. In the early 1900s the annual output from United States tanneries was nearly a quarter of a million skins; there were also large tanneries in Europe. At this time Common Caimans (*Caiman crocodilus*) were not killed for their skins as these were of inferior quality and, interestingly, imitation crocodilian skin was already being marketed.

By the early 1900s fashion had again changed and most crocodilian skins in the United States market were being used for ladies' handbags and men's belts as well as footwear. In 1907 a newspaper reported that a firm in Louisiana handled up to half a million crocodilian skins a year and that skins were also being used for book covers and even upholstering chairs. In 1925 and 1926, 22,000 and 36,000 skins respectively were bought by dealers in Louisiana and, during the same period, approximately 10,000 skins a year were traded in the state of Georgia. The demand for hornback or dorsal skins of crocodilians also increased and, as supplies of alligators and Central American crocodiles dwindled, additional sources of skins were sought in Africa and Asia.

Trade records from Florida indicate that although 190,000 skins were traded in 1929 only 120,000 were traded in 1934. The trade in Florida

◄ Traditionally exploited for food and for ritual purposes, crocodilians only came under heavy hunting pressure in the nineteenth century when the quality of crocodile and alligator leather was recognized. Initially, commercial hunting was conducted primarily by native peoples, such as these American Indian hunters at work in the Florida marshlands.

continued to decrease until 1943 when only 6,800 skins were traded. In 1944, Florida introduced legislation protecting alligators during the breeding season and prohibiting the killing of alligators of less than 1.2 meters (4 feet) in length. By 1947, 25,000 skins were traded in the state.

## HUNTING AND HUNTERS

Following World War II, hunting of crocodilians for their skins was circumtropical. During the mid-1950s nearly 60,000 Nile Crocodile (*Crocodylus niloticus*) skins were exported from East Africa each year but the hunting of crocodiles in Africa goes back much further. Unfortunately data for most areas of Africa is non-existent or scanty. In the Transvaal and Natal only rough records of crocodiles and skins exported or sold locally were kept by hunters. Tanneries will not disclose or do not have records of the numbers of skins purchased in the old days but diaries and newspaper reports do provided some patchy, anecdotal information.

William Charles Baldwin described the hunting of crocodiles on the Black Umfolozi River, in the vicinity of Lake St. Lucia, Zululand, in 1852. At that time crocodile skins were apparently not used but the fat from the animals was used to make candles. Other hunters over the period 1850–1900, of whom there were many, shot crocodiles and bartered the fat and other parts to local medicine men. On 2 July 1869 a local newspaper, the *Natal Herald*, carried an article copied from an English newspaper. It was brief but of tremendous significance: "Crocodiles are in great demand, it having been recently discovered that the skin of the monsters is suitable for ladies' boots, being of a pliable and soft nature. Furthermore of a value that takes a bright varnish." To the hunters who were making their living off elephant ivory, rhinoceros,

hippopotamus and the antelope herds of Natal there was now an incentive to kill crocodiles for profit and not only because they were a nuisance.

Crocodiles were of course regarded as vermin and, in 1913, Government Notice No. 77 in the *Government Gazette* stated that in an effort to exterminate these creatures a reward of ten shillings was payable for each dead animal and a "tickey" (2.5 cents) for each egg, the rewards being payable at the nearest magistrate's office. Countless thousands of eggs were destroyed and adults shot, or baited then shot, over the following years.

In 1907 Cornish-Bowden wrote up the diaries of L. C. von Wissel, a German immigrant and pioneer trader who settled the Ndumu district in the late 1880s and the following is recorded:

> The pans bordering the Pongola River were full of crocodiles. As the Government paid out ten shillings a head I sent a good few of all sizes down to one foot [30 centimeters] in length to the Magistrate at Ingwavuma. I laid poison [strychnine] sufficient to cover a tickey piece in a lump of meat and tied around with string and placed these lumps along the shores or on sandbanks where there were signs of crocodiles and this method of killing them was successful. One month I received for this service a cheque for seventy-five pounds. Some twenty years later when I moved into Swaziland I went for crocodiles in the Usutu River where twenty shillings a head was paid. This did not last long owing to the administration had not organised for such wholesale destruction.

The *Natal Advertiser* of 11 October 1935 reported that a Scot nicknamed "Tshaywa-ingwenya" (he who kills crocodiles), operating in the Ndumu area, had shot 200–300 crocodiles for their belly hides in three years (1932–35). Professional and part-time hunters like him continued to operate throughout Zululand particularly over the period

► In 1869 the *Natal Herald* reported that Nile Crocodiles were in great demand, "the skin of the monsters" being suitable for making boots. A massive slaughter followed and, by the time protection was instituted almost a century later, there were few "monsters" as large as this 4.8-meter (16-foot) Nile Crocodile left in Lake Rudolf in modern Kenya.

Peter Beard

1950–68. One, Percy Jackson, estimated having shot 1,300 crocodiles in some 20 years of part-time hunting, mainly in the rivers flowing into Lake St. Lucia. Other hunters stated in interviews that they had each shot in the region of one hundred crocodiles a season; this included juveniles that were injected with formalin and sold as curios. All of these hunters sold their skins to a company, S.M. Lurie of Port Elizabeth, Cape Province, that tanned and also exported raw crocodile skins. This company also purchased some 40,000 skins from hunters in neighboring Botswana over the period 1956–77.

Because of the exploitation and steady decline in crocodile populations in Natal, the reptile was finally afforded protection under the Natal Reptiles Protection Ordinance of 1968, which came into effect on 24 April 1969. Also, because of the decline in numbers of crocodiles as an observable part of the fauna, the Natal Parks Board initiated an Experimental Crocodile Research and Restocking Station in the Ndumu Game Reserve in 1966, which operated until 1975 rearing crocodiles and releasing them back into local rivers.

In India, hunting crocodiles for sport has been documented in naturalists' accounts of experiences in India and in every old "shikari" (hunting) book there was a chapter on the art of hunting crocodiles. Two of the classic works on crocodile hunting were W.H. Shortt's "A Few Hints on Crocodile Shooting," published in 1921 in the *Journal of the Bombay Natural History Society* and Hornaday's *Two Years in the Jungle* (1885) in which he describes his collection of specimens of adult Gharial (*Gavialis gangeticus*) from the Yamuna River. Records of commercial hunting in India, however, are scarce.

Several hunter-gatherer tribes (most of whom still occasionally practice some form of hunting) were probably the main contributors to the skin

industry, usually being induced to hunt crocodiles by middlemen from skin-processing centers. The main centers for skin dealing and tanning in India were Kanpur and Calcutta in the north, and Hyderabad, Mysore, and Madras in the south. Groups of hunters from Uttar Pradesh used to roam to neighboring states and hunt crocodiles during the dry season. The standard methods used were baited hooks or trapping the crocodiles in their tunnels. In Bihar, fishermen on the Ghagra River were said to have caught Gharials by planting hooks, with long ropes attached, in the sand at the Gharials' basking sites. When the Gharials came to bask the fishermen, waiting at a point some distance away, pulled the hooks, snagging the Gharials in the bellies. Another method was to submerge nets in the water on the edges of the basking sites.

In the Sind State of what is now Pakistan, crocodile hunters used to dive into the salt lakes and attach ropes around Mugger (*Crocodylus palustris*) hiding at the bottom. The gang of hunters would then pull the Mugger up. With a similar kind of daring, crocodile hunters in Sri Lanka would enter crocodile burrows to tie a rope around the Mugger hiding inside.

Indopacific Crocodiles (*Crocodylus porosus*) lost habitat so fast that their demise in India has been attributed as much to the steady loss of habitat as to direct commercial hunting. In the Sunderbans (West Bengal), up to the time of crocodile protection, there were professional hunters using harpoons and guns on Indopacific Crocodiles but it was never a large-scale commercial enterprise. The Indopacific Crocodile population in the Andaman and Nicobar Islands (the small archipelago in the Bay of Bengal) was quickly decimated by just a handful of hunters between the end of World War II and the 1970s. The two best known hunters based themselves in

Diglipur in North Andaman, one was named Kesavan and the other Roy and between them they claimed to have killed about 2,000 adult crocodiles over the years. There are now very few crocodiles in North Andaman but this must be attributed to egg collection as well as hunting.

In the Philippines, roving bands of commercial hunters systematically harvested crocodiles from all accessible bodies of water and apparently exterminated many isolated populations of the Philippine Crocodile (*Crocodylus mindorensis*). In the mid-1950s systematic hunting of crocodiles in New Guinea began and reached its peak a few years later. In almost all areas the pattern of hunting was similar. Expatriate hunters would enter an area and "shoot out" the more desirable crocodilians in accessible waterways such as rivers, estuarine areas, and large lakes. As the number of animals in accessible areas decreased, indigenous hunters were often enlisted to search for and kill crocodilians in the more remote areas that motor-powered boats could not reach. The expatriate hunters then acted as traders, purchasing or bartering for the skins. As the resource was depleted, the number of traders also decreased and many moved on to more profitable regions. Eventually, even the least valuable crocodilian skins were sought after and traded.

Commercial hunting in South America began in the late 1950s and early 1960s. At first hunters concentrated on Black Caiman (*Melanosuchus niger*) in the Amazon basin – the only species with a near "classic" skin. When the Black Caiman was reduced to commercial extinction the industry switched to Common Caiman, mainly in Venezuela and the Amazon. Most hunting is now concentrated on Common Caiman in the pantanal of Brazil. Hunting is done from canoes with harpoons and lights; most hunters are poor peasants who earn little money from their hunting. The skins are collected by organized smugglers to be exported; in the pantanal, planes often bring in drugs and take out skins. Most South American countries now have legislation banning or regulating hunting but it has not been significantly reduced. Common Caiman skins now account for at least 60 percent of world trade but, because of their low quality, they do not represent anywhere near as much in monetary value. Smugglers generally do not like legalized hunting as it increases the price that they have to pay the peasant hunters.

Skins are still the major product from crocodilians; the stages and processes involved in converting the raw skins into today's high quality leather goods are, however, long and complex.

## THE STRUCTURE OF CROCODILIAN SKIN

The basis for successful crocodilian leather production is a knowledge of the fiber structure of the skins. All the chemical and mechanical procedures have to take the morphological differences into consideration.

The skin of crocodilians is composed of the epidermis (removed in the liming process), the corium (the actual leather), and the subcutis or flesh layer (removed by the mechanical treatments of fleshing and shaving). The epidermis, composed of the protein keratin, is made up of several layers of cells and is divided into the germinal layer and the outer horny layer. The horny layer, which consists of dead material of low plasticity, cannot grow and is shed at intervals — crocodilians do not shed skin like other reptiles, they merely lose isolated horny scutes from their armor. The corium, composed of the protein collagen, is characterized by the regularity of the fiber arrangement but the close two-dimensional interlacing of the corium fibers, which is particularly noticeable when the skin is cut in sections, makes the production of elastic, glove-like leather impossible.

In all crocodilians, the skin is protected by bony plates or osteoderms formed mainly by the deposition of calcium carbonate and calcium phosphate in the connective tissue of the corium. These osteoderms are interconnected, somewhat like joints, so that a certain mobility is retained. All crocodilians have more or less well-developed osteoderms in the dorsal skin. However, in the production process it is necessary to distinguish among skins with double, single, or no osteoderms in the belly, and among skins with small, medium, or large scales as chemical and

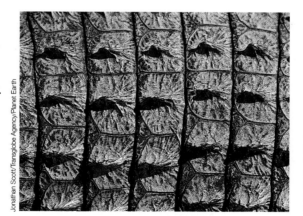

◄ The dorsal scales of a Nile Crocodile are formed of bony osteoderms overlaid with skin. This portion of the skin is difficult to process and is therefore rarely used in contrast to the supple leather derived from the skin of other areas of the body.

◄ Much in demand, the skins of "classic" species have no osteoderms in the belly scales, making them ideal for the manufacture of high-quality handbags. The tough, protective epidermis is removed during the liming process and the subcutis or flesh layer during shaving so that only the corium or leather layer remains.

191

▲ Common Caiman skins are often sold as part rather than whole skins with the flanks (bottom) and throat (top) fetching the highest prices. The value of a belly skin is determined by the number and extent of osteoderms.

▲ The belly skin from a Cuvier's Dwarf Caiman (left) has double osteoderms (visible as dark spots here) and is less profitable than the belly skin from a Johnston's Crocodile (right), which has only a single row of osteoderms.

Kartheinz Fuchs

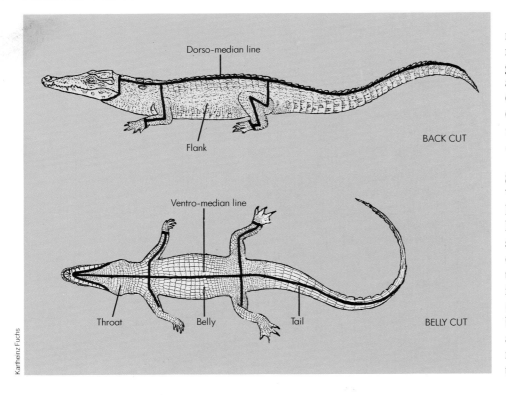

Dorso-median line

Flank

BACK CUT

Ventro-median line

Throat       Belly       Tail

BELLY CUT

Kartheinz Fuchs

mechanical treatments must be individually modified according to skin type. For the leather goods and shoe industry, the most valuable hides are those from Indopacific Crocodiles, Siamese Crocodiles (*Crocodylus siamensis*), and Nile Crocodiles from Tanzania and Madagascar since these are medium- or small-scaled and have no osteoderms in the belly and flanks.

## SKINNING AND PRESERVATION

When skinning (flaying) is done in the wild, the killed animal is laid on its belly with forelimbs and hindlimbs extended; the snout and anus are stuffed with dry grass to prevent blood, urine, and excrement from escaping. A straight ripping cut is then made either down the dorso-median line from the base of the skull to the tip of the tail (especially for small skins) or at the border between the lateral scales (of the sides and flanks) and the dorsal plates (back scutes). The leg skin is ripped at right angles to the dorso-median cut or the cuts on both sides of the lateral-dorsal border.

After the skin has been stripped off the limbs and the trunk (the dorsal section with the heavily ossified plates remains on the carcass) it is folded back and the carcass, with the skin still attached to the belly, the underside of the tail, and the lower jaw, is laid on its back. The skin is peeled off the skull along the two branches of the lower jaw and the flaying is completed at the head and the tail ends of the carcass. Any flesh adhering to the skin is scraped off (not cut off, as this might damage the skin) with a butcher's knife.

At farms or ranches the skinning technique is much the same but more clean and hygienic since the carcass is allowed to cease bleeding overnight.

The preservation or salting of crocodilian skins is a most important process that requires a great deal of expertise and care. Only a fine-grain grade of salt, free of dirt and other contaminants, can be used. Bad or indifferent salt curing of crocodilian skins and lack of knowledge concerning salt-grain size and the use of preserving agents can cause irreparable damage or scale slip (peeling of the scales off the skin) due to bacterial damage of the skin protein. The salt is rubbed thoroughly and evenly into the flesh side of the skin. A highly effective and environmentally safe non-tanning preserving agent, with bactericidal and fungicidal properties, is added.

An alternative and more effective salting system is to soak the skins in a liquid prepared with 1,000 liters (220 gallons) of water, 300 kilograms (660 pounds) of common salt, and 5 kilograms (11 pounds) of preserving agent for 48 hours. By leaving the brine to drain from the skins in a shady place, much of the skin moisture is removed. Draining takes one or two hours. The skins are then given a second salting.

Following these preliminary operations, the skins are taken to a storehouse for final treatment. For storage and transport the skins are folded in a special way then rolled up with scales inward and with a layer of salt separating the individual skins. The salt-preserved crocodilian skins are then kept in a cooling house to inhibit the action of bacteria that thrive on salt.

### BEAMHOUSE OPERATIONS
After skinning and preservation, the next stages in leather production are the so-called "beamhouse" operations. The term "beamhouse" dates back to the times when the epidermis was removed from the skin on a beam (a sloping, curved table or large log) using a two-handled knife. Now "beamhouse" operations refer to the soaking, liming, deliming, and bating processes in leather production.

The aim of soaking is to allow the skins to reabsorb all the water lost after flaying, either in preservation or during transport. The absorbed water rehydrates any dehydrated or dried interfibrillary protein. The collagen fibers of the

corium and the keratin cells of the epidermis also take up water and become more flexible. Soaking is generally accomplished by placing the crocodilian skins in water, containing additives (wetting, washing, degreasing agents) and preserving agents or disinfectants. The disinfectants are of major importance since the fresh or cured skins carry a large quantity of a wide range of bacteria that become active during soaking and damage the very sensitive crocodilian skin.

The aim of the next stage — liming or "descaling" — is to remove the epidermis and, to some extent, the interfibrillary proteins. The action of liming chemicals on proteins results in hydrolysis of the protein and a gradual breakdown of the protein structure. During the liming process the natural fats are saponified and partly removed. This is particularly important for skins harvested on farms since their fat content is 5–10 times

▲ The process of transforming a crocodilian into leather begins as soon as the animal has been killed. A series of cuts is made to divide the skin of the back; these usually leave the tough, bony midline scales on the carcass.

▶▲ On farms and ranches, such as this one (left) near Darwin, Australia, the skinning process is more streamlined and hygienic, with cuts being made so as to preserve the valuable flesh for human consumption. After thorough and careful salting (right) to inhibit bacterial action, skins are rolled and stored in a temperature-controlled cooling house to prevent further bacterial contamination before the "beamhouse" phase of preparation begins.

◀ For most species the skinning cuts are made on the back of the animal. However, for hornbacks the skin is cut down the belly to leave the dorsal scales undamaged as an attractive feature of the finished product.

higher than it is in wild catches. The liming process is also responsible for the softness, fullness, and dyeability of the leather. The process is carried out by immersing the skins completely in a lime, sodium sulfide, and water mixture.

The limed crocodilian skins or hides are a more or less three-dimensional network of protein fibers that have absorbed the liming chemicals. The hides are greenish-white, semi-translucent, swollen, and rubber-like. They contain undesirable chemicals, saponified fats, and protein-degradation products from the liming. The next stage is therefore deliming, the purpose of which is to remove alkaline, eliminate the swelling, and adjust the acid-alkaline pH value (to 8.0 – 8.5) for the bating process. Chemicals used in deliming crocodilian hides are products based on citric or lactic acid, sodium bisulfite, and ammonium salts.

Bating is the final step in purification of the hides before the pickling and tanning stages. The unwanted components consist of some of the protein-degradation products on the surface of crocodile hides and in the scale pores of caiman hides. Other proteins will also be removed. In the bating process enzymes (usually rennin from calf's stomach and trypsin from pig's pancreas) act on these unwanted components.

## WET-FINISHING OPERATIONS

Prior to tanning the hides are pickled in a salt, water, and acid solution to bring them to the desired pH (3.3–3.8) for tanning. A "deossification pickle" is applied to all hides with osteoderms in the belly region (extremely pronounced in caiman hides). The treatment time for the hides is 8–14 days, until at least 80 percent of the calcium phosphate and calcium carbonate are dissolved and removed.

The tanning process itself converts the putrefying proteins of the raw, pickled hide that dries out hard and horny, and putrefies on rewetting into a product — leather — that dries out soft and flexible, and does not putrefy on rewetting. Chrome tannage, carried out in drums of commercially available chrome salts has proved ideal for the manufacture of crocodilian leather. It has advantages over vegetable tannage in that uniform results can be achieved from one batch to the next, the tanning process is considerably shorter, the chrome-tanned skins have better physical properties (heat resistance, tear resistance, elongation at break, stitch-tear resistance), and excellent dyeing properties.

After the first tanning, the hides are shaved and neutralized. The purpose of shaving is to bring the tanned leather to a uniform thickness with an accuracy of one tenth of a millimeter. The cutting knives of the reptile-shaving machine are mounted on a rotating cylinder. When the foot treadle is depressed a feed roller feeds the reverse side of the

leather against the knife cylinder. The leather that is removed falls as shavings into the base of the machine. After shaving, the leather has to be neutralized by the application of weak alkaline products to remove all inorganic acids that would damage the leather and all hydrolyzable acid bound to the skin protein. The main purpose of neutralizing chrome-tanned leather is to suppress its excess positive charge sufficiently to prevent the negatively charged particles of the products used in the processes that follow — retanning, dyeing, and fatliquoring — from being unevenly distributed and fixed on the surface of the leather.

Retanning confers on the leather its fundamental properties and prepares it for dyeing and finishing. Crocodilian chrome-tanned leather is usually retanned with synthetic tannins in combination with vegetable tannins to improve the glazing and polishing properties. Vegetable tannins include the following:

Quebracho — occurs in the wood produced in Argentina, Brazil, and Paraguay; gives a full, firm leather of reddish color, which deepens markedly on exposure to light.

Wattle/mimosa — occurs in the bark of some species of acacia, indigenous in Australia but now grown commercially in South Africa, East Africa, and Brazil; gives a full, medium-soft leather of pale reddish yellow color, which deepens on exposure to light.

Chestnut — occurs in wood produced in France, Italy, the United States, and Yugoslavia; gives a firm, well-filled leather of brownish yellow color, with a much better light-fastness than either quebracho or wattle.

Sumach — occurs in the leaves and small twigs from several species of the genus *Rhus* produced in Sicily; gives a soft, mellow leather of greenish yellow color with a light-fastness superior to chestnut.

Tara — occurs in the pods of *Caesalpinia spinosa* commercially grown in some South American countries; gives a soft, mellow leather of very pale cream color. Tara has the highest light-fastness of all vegetable tanning agents.

The aim of dyeing is to give the retanned leather a certain color as a base for the finishing process. The absorption of various tanning materials in tanning and retanning affects the reactivity of leather toward colorants — chrome-tanned leather shows a higher affinity for anionic and sulfur dyes, while the vegetable and synthetic tannins used in retanning crocodilian leather preferentially link with kationic, that is, basic dyes.

Since all crocodilian leather is given a pure aniline finish (neither inorganic nor organic pigments are used in the finishing process) the quality of the dyes must be selected carefully. The finishing process depends on the evenness, saturation, and extent of the dyeing. Evenness cannot always be achieved with anionic dyes alone. A preliminary, intermediate, or subsequent application of basic dyes not only improves the hiding power but also the brilliance of the finish.

At the completion of the tannage, crocodilian leather does not contain sufficient fatty substances to prevent it from drying into a hard mass. It has to be fatliquored to give it the required properties of softness, pliability, stretch, feel, resistance to abrasion and chemical attack, and good dirt-proofing. Crocodilian leather is fatliquored with light-fast synthetic or semi-synthetic fatliquors that contain no harmful fatty acids, bond firmly to the leather fiber, and do not migrate. A combination of deeply penetrating fatliquors that leave the surface of the leather dry and products that penetrate only superficially and impart a slightly greasy touch is most suitable for crocodilian leather.

## DRY-FINISHING OPERATIONS

Finishing is almost the last step in leather manufacturing and is probably the most complicated one. The composition and the application of the finishing chemicals or natural products should lead to a "ready-to-manufacture" leather that suits the requirements of the customer not only in terms of color, feel, gloss, and resistance to water, solvents, and rubbing but also in terms of uniformity of the visual effect and the aesthetic appearance of the surface. The classic finishing agents for such valuable and prestigious material as crocodilian leather are natural albuminous products — casein, egg albumen, milk, ox blood, or gelatine — which are still the most widely used in the processing of reptile leather and are unlikely ever to be replaced entirely by synthetic products.

After the application of the stained or clear-glazed finish by padding, brushing, or spraying, the leather is dried and glazed. The glazing of crocodilian skins is done on a special reptile-glazing machine or "alligator jack." The dried leather is placed with the reverse side on a small wooden table covered with a vegetable-tanned leather belt. A polished glass or agate cylinder of about 6 centimeters (2–3 inches) with a reciprocating arm is fast-stroked, under high pressure, over the finished surface of the leather; a mirror-like gloss is the end result.

To enhance and set the "bombé" effect (the convex deformation of each individual scale or shield of the crocodile skin) on "classic" crocodile leather, the glazed leather must be given a special flesh-side finish. After the bombé-effect finish has been applied, the leather is laid out on a perforated, galvanized platen, below which steam pipes are installed at 10–15 centimeter (4–6 inch) intervals. The temperature above the perforated platen must be 100°–120° C (212°–248° F) since only at this temperature can the bombé effect be achieved and fixed. A "softy crocodile" finish is applied only on heavily ossified caiman leather. It is not a finish in the true sense of the word for the drum-dyed leather is merely polished without any prior application of binders. The polishing is carried out by hand or on the reptile-glazing machine, using a medium-hard felt cylinder rather than a glass or agate cylinder.

The numerous labor-intensive processes involved in crocodilian leather production go some way toward explaining the high prices paid for crocodile handbags and shoes. But the production of the actual leather is only the first stage in a complex trade that involves importers, exporters, designers, manufacturers, and marketing people who transform the leather into products for sale to the ultimate consumer.

◀ ▲ ▼ After being dyed in a stainless steel drum using carefully selected dyes (left), the leather is glazed under pressure on a mechanical "alligator jack" (below left). The leather is then ready to be turned into exclusive leathergoods such as the handbag (below), which used a contrasting band of hornback from crocodilian dorsal skin.

# THE TRADE IN CROCODILIANS

PETER BRAZAITIS

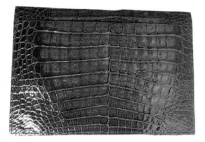

▲ Many of the world's crocodilian species have been and still are exploited for commercial gain. The high quality of crocodile and alligator leather has placed many of the "classic" species in danger of extinction.

Exotique/Winfried Kralle Exclusive Leatherware

Crocodilians have long been a source of highly durable leather from which a wide variety of products may be crafted or manufactured. While native crafts range from simple decorations on ceremonial accessories to products and trade goods for local sale or limited export, commercial utilization is geared to the manufacture of the highest quality products destined for the luxury, exotic leather markets of the high-fashion world.

Of the 22 traditionally recognized species of crocodilians found throughout the tropical and subtropical regions of the world, 15 or more types have been commercially exploited for their skins and other products. Unlike the limited utilization by native people, commercial utilization is generally on a large scale, involving large numbers of people and employing modern hunting methods and equipment. Combined with increasingly adverse environmental pressures and burgeoning human populations that have seriously encroached upon crocodilian habitats, the overutilization of crocodilians for the commercial exotic leather trade has, in past years, brought many species of crocodilian to the brink of extinction and has seriously threatened the continued existence of others.

With the increase in international conservation legislation from 1973 the destiny of crocodilian species and the future course of the worldwide industry in exotic leathers (as well as the thousands of people it employs) have become inextricably interrelated. Wildlife law-enforcement agencies, biologists, conservationists, farmers and ranchers, importers and exporters, fashion designers, and tanners all find themselves in a new and complex relationship.

## THE SCOPE AND NATURE OF THE TRADE

Although the principal trade in crocodilian products today continues to center around the utilization of skins for the manufacture of exotic leather goods, the commercial crocodilian industry has begun to develop markets for other products — meat and meat products (for human and animal consumption); skeletal bones and osteoderms used as nutritional supplements in agriculture and animal feeds; teeth and claws sold primarily to tourists as curios; and gonads (sex organs), musk, and urine now being used in the manufacture of perfume.

▶ At least two million caimans, alligators, and crocodiles are killed each year to supply the international skin trade, which converts hides into expensive footwear, handbags, and wallets.

Exotique/Winfried Kralle Exclusive Leatherware

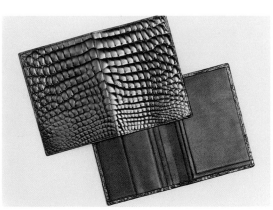

It has not been an easy task for monitoring agencies to determine the annual worldwide volume of crocodilian hides and manufactured products in commercial trade. Raw skins may be tanned within the originating country then cut into pieces, making it impossible to estimate the number of animals involved. The skins may be exported to other tanneries and manufacturers as whole skins or pieces. Several pieces, representing a number of animals of different species from several origins, may be used in a single manufactured product and exported, imported, and reexported through several countries before reaching a final destination. The resulting trail of documentation may, at best, be confusing and, at worst, can serve to conceal the true (perhaps illegal) origin of the skins.

As far as can be determined, current world trade in crocodilian skins of all species is estimated at around two million skins annually. The vast majority of these skins — probably 1–1.5 million — are caiman from Bolivia, Brazil, Paraguay, and Venezuela. (While many of these skins emanate from legally sanctioned sources, more than half are estimated to be taken from wild populations in violation of national wildlife regulations.) The remaining 500,000 skins are made up of other species, including true crocodile, taken from wild populations under a quota system, or from farming or ranching enterprises around the world.

While the raw materials most often originate in developing countries, the markets for finished products are largely in the more affluent industrial nations. The trade in crocodilian hides and products is far-reaching and encompasses a number of diversified industries.

The raw materials of the trade are the skins from the living animals. At its most basic level the trade therefore includes those hunters, often in remote regions, who stalk the animals in a small boat by moonlight perhaps armed only with a flashlight, a harpoon, a knife, and an axe, and who live by harvesting forest crops and wildlife. Hunters may, however, be commercially funded and well-equipped hired men in well-organized camps. Skins are taken, salted in the field, and stored until the time comes to sell them to regional buyers. Other sources of skins are ranching operations (where the endemic population serves as a reservoir of eggs or young that are then reared until they are of a suitable size for harvesting) or farming operations (where breeding groups of animals are kept to produce eggs and young that are then reared for harvest).

At the next level of the trade is the army of dealers, brokers, and buyers who collect the skins from the field and move them to the next level — the tanneries.

The tanneries are the centers of the crocodilian hide and product industry. Historically, tanneries in France, Italy, and to a lesser extent Spain and the United States enjoyed the reputation for manufacturing the highest quality crocodilian leather. Now Japan and the Far East have entered the tanning industry and are developing technologically advanced tanning techniques and a new generation of tanning machinery.

Tanneries, particularly in France and Italy, are family operations handed down from generation to generation. Each tannery zealously protects the secret formulas it uses to process different types of skins and to produce its own unique finishes. A tannery may buy skins from many different sources around the world and may specialize in certain species of crocodilian or types of skins. A tannery may have its own agents in the most remote regions of the world and in the capitals of fashion and technology. It is at this level that much of the price structure for hides and, ultimately, for the finished product is determined. It is at this level too that both the legal and illegal trade in skins are supported.

Above the level of the tanneries the trade diversifies into a number of interrelated industries or segments that specialize in exotic leathers. Included at this level are importers, exporters, buyers, and brokers as well as designers of leather fashions and the entire high-fashion industry.

L. C. Marigo/Bruce Coleman Ltd.

Since the crocodilian leather industry is directed at producing a luxury product that has no practical or necessary purpose, merchandisers and marketing specialists must identify and promote the consumption of these exotic products. At the final level are the wholesale and retail department stores, shops, and boutiques that will bring the product to the customer. All are part of the trade, and at every level that the skin, hide, or finished product changes hands — from the hunter to the manufacturer and ultimately to the consumer — the cost of the skin or product may double.

**HOW THE TRADE WORKS**

The core of the market for crocodilian leather is represented by a few very affluent consumers who regard the finest quality crocodilian products as the desirable height of fashion and luxury. Annual sales to these consumers are relatively stable. However, the vast majority of average, middle-class consumers, even in highly industrialized countries, appear to have left the market, or are unwilling to pay $1,500–3,000 (at 1988 prices) for a crocodilian handbag, $600–800 for a pair of shoes, or $300 for a belt. Marketing efforts are therefore

▲▼ Although the bulk of international trade and demand is for crocodilian leather, markets also exist for other products, such as keyrings made from crocodile feet (above). Attempts to reduce the illegal trade in skins include the impounding of poached crocodilian skins (below), when or if these are located.

Christian Zuber/Bruce Coleman Ltd.

Romulus Whitaker

C. B. Frith/Bruce Coleman Ltd

▲ Commercial ranching and farming are making inroads into the traditional techniques of hunting for the skin trade, and are significantly more efficient than nocturnal hunts with harpoon and flashlight. In areas such as Irian Jaya where traditional hunting by local villagers still continue, hunters often have only sporadic success.

▼ CITES regulations and other internationally recognized legislation are beginning to affect the trade in crocodilian skins and, fortunately, in the bizarre and questionable use of hatchlings for curios.

directed at the middle- and lower-income consumers who might be stimulated by fashion promotions and advertising to increase their purchase levels. Timing is crucial as it would be fruitless for the industry to increase consumer interest in crocodilian products if those products were not available in shops at affordable prices.

The cycle begins when tanners and skin buyers find that there will be an abundance of raw skins available for the immediate future as, for example, when the United States lifted restrictions on American Alligators (*Alligator mississippiensis*) and put skins into international trade in 1979, and when Venezuela introduced *Caiman crocodilus crocodilus* skins into trade around 1982. With the guaranteed availability of raw materials in sufficient quantities to sustain anticipated increased sales levels, tanners and manufacturers collaborate with fashion designers to produce products that can be available for the retail market the following year. As products become available at the high-fashion level, advertisers and fashion promotions bombard the consumer with the message that "the

fashion for the year" is crocodile. (Such promotions followed the introduction of alligator and caiman skins into trade in 1979 and 1982 respectively.) The consumer is primed to buy at the precise time that the products are available for sale. Thus, much of the buying interest is created by the trade once the trade is confident it will have products to sell.

Once sales increase, the stimulated demand begins to manifest itself in increased prices for the raw materials. As the raw materials become increasingly more costly, production wanes, sales drop, and fashion moves on to something else. There are other factors operating as well. In a buoyant market, cheap simulations and poor-quality handcrafts begin to flood the market to take advantage of the new consumer mood. Strong currencies in importing countries may make the importation of these cheaper manufactured products more attractive, while a weak currency may make the importation of raw materials for domestic manufacture more attractive. All of these factors affect the price of the product.

Consumers are not well informed about the product they are buying; in many instances, neither is the importer or merchandiser. In the manufacture of high-quality designer products, caiman skins, which may be purchased from the hunter for little more than some sugar or, at most, $2–5 in cash, are frequently substituted for crocodile and alligator "classic" skins, which may cost several hundred dollars per skin in the raw state. Classic skins are the skins of those species that either lack bony plates on the belly or where the plates are greatly reduced. However, products of bony species such as caiman may still be labeled as the more expensive species and the retailer or consumer is unaware of the differences, which should be reflected in a much lower price. Little has been done by the trade to educate consumers or merchandisers in intelligent buying.

The problem of substitution is compounded by the fact that tanners buy skins from many regions, representing several races or species of the same commercial category. Tanned skins are graded by size, number of defects, cut, and type of skin so that skins from several origins may be tanned together. Protected as well as legally taken commercialized species may be acquired and then processed together (this is particularly true in the case of South American caiman). The processed hides are then exported indiscriminately. The effect on importers and manufacturers who purchase raw or finished hides can be a lack of confidence in their suppliers and a reluctance to deal in crocodilian products. The following hypothetical example illustrates the problem. A United States–based importer of tanned South American caiman skins, imported to Singapore perhaps from Colombia and then reexported to the United States with appropriate documents indicating the species contained in the shipment to be *Caiman crocodilus crocodilus,* may find that the shipment has been seized on entry by United States wildlife authorities for containing *Caiman crocodilus yacare* (a protected endangered species under the US Endangered Species Act and a prohibited import). Although *Caiman crocodilus yacare* is not found in Colombia and although the importer specified the legal species on his purchase order, he is still the importer of record and subject to legal action. The minimum consequences for the importer would be the forfeiture of the skins, loss of orders and clients, loss of shipping costs and other payments already made, substantial legal fees, and a penalty payment for the violation of United States law. The skins involved may have been illegally taken in south-central South America where *Caiman crocodilus yacare* are endemic, shipped to Colombia and exported as the legal *Caiman crocodilus crocodilus* to Singapore, where they were then given reexport documents and sold indiscriminately with other caiman skins. The

Peter Brazaitis

importer has no assurances that his order will be accurately filled and that he is not going to be inadvertently importing a protected species.

As caiman skins are generally not marked or tagged it is difficult or impossible for wildlife authorities to trace their origins. Market stimulation and an increased demand for raw materials promote the increased taking of protected species to meet these increased demands. Difficulties in differentiating between the skins from protected and non-protected species once they are tanned, cut into pieces, and manufactured into products often mean that large numbers of illegally taken crocodilians enter the commercial trade to fill the market's needs.

**THE FUTURE OF THE TRADE**
While farms and ranches as sources of crocodilian skins are increasing in numbers around the world, there continues to be a strong incentive to harvest wild populations. Ideally, such harvesting is accomplished under a system of monitoring, controls, and export quotas. As monitoring systems become more sophisticated, it will become increasingly difficult for illegal skins to circulate freely in commercial trade.

There is a trend in many developing countries with endemic crocodilian species of commercial value toward the creation of their own complete industries, including managing and harvesting their crocodilian populations, establishing farms and ranches, tanning the skins, manufacturing products, and exporting finished goods. Higher profits and increased national benefits, such as the employment of workers, are realized in contrast to the situation previously when the natural resources were sold off with little immediate gain and no long-term benefits. Such enterprises initially produce products of relatively low quality because of the lack of technology. However, as the technology is developed, products in the future will become more competitive in quality. Other countries, such as Japan, have developed a keen interest in assisting Third World countries in the development of farming and tanning technologies as well as the development of support industries

◄ Before the introduction of tags, export approval documents, and other forms of protection, agencies attempting to quash the illegal trade in crocodilian skins had few tools. However, the processing of skin pieces, such as these caiman flanks, from a number of sources still makes it difficult to distinguish legally exported skins from skins of protected species.

C. B. Frith/Bruce Coleman Ltd.

▲ The cost of tanning crocodilian skins puts high quality leather goods out of the reach of most consumers, but "souvenirs" are less expensive and are a source of revenue from material that would otherwise be discarded.

# MARKETING OF CROCODILE SKINS
# IN PAPUA NEW GUINEA

GREG MITCHELL

There are four "classic" crocodilian hides in legal world trade today — American Alligator, Nile Crocodile (*Crocodylus niloticus*), Indopacific Crocodile (*Crocodylus porosus*), and New Guinea Crocodile (*Crocodylus novaeguineae*). In Papua New Guinea, two of these species — Indopacific Crocodile and New Guinea Crocodile — are native. Papua New Guinean populations of these species are not on CITES Appendix I (prohibited commercial trade) as the country pioneered a conservation-through-utilization program. Papua New Guinea has approved CITES endorsement, with both species being on Appendix II of the Convention. This allows for the export of skins under CITES-approved export documentation and all countries that are signatories to CITES, with the exception of Australia, allow trade. Papua New Guinea now produces about 40 percent of the world's legal "classic" hides.

During the years of overexploitation, conservationists successfully made the public aware of the plight of the "classic" crocodilians. The Washington Convention in 1973 had the effect of banning trade in skins where wild populations were threatened. These bans affected Australia and the United States, whose Indopacific Crocodile and American Alligator populations respectively were considered threatened, while Papua New Guinea's crocodiles were exempt since their wild populations were not considered endangered. The effect of these bans has seen major recoveries in both the American Alligator and the Australian Indopacific Crocodile. Producers of "classic" hides must now make the consumer aware that numbers have returned to acceptable levels and controlled production is not depleting the wild stock.

Most of the wetland peoples of Papua New Guinea have an intense cultural and economic relationship with crocodiles. Because of this traditional association, legal limits were set to protect crocodiles of breeding size by restricting the harvest to crocodiles with a belly width of 18–51 centimeters (7–20 inches). For many years the majority of skins being exported were therefore from juvenile crocodiles. Low foreign earnings led to the licensing of several commercial ranches to purchase live crocodiles from village smallholder farms and hunters; in many areas income from the purchase of these crocodiles was the only cash available to the hunters.

As the commercial ranches increased their crocodilian numbers, wild-skin exports decreased over a four-year period. Skin exports are now fluctuating at around 29,000 –32,000 a year; the fluctuation being due to the marketing strategies of the commercial ranches. These numbers are similar to the average level of exports over the past 20 years but foreign earnings have increased dramatically. The aim of a current monitoring program is to boost earnings by growing small crocodiles through to a larger size with a greater per centimeter value, thereby maximizing the utilization of the resource without increasing hunting pressure.

Stocktakes at commercial ranches are carried out in conjunction with the annual cull. This is the only satisfactory means of gaining a hands-on feel for the condition of the animals, and statistics are kept to maintain accurate growth records. Culling is determined by cash-flow requirements, and the sizes of the animals culled depends on market requirements, which alter from year to year as fashions change.

Papua New Guinea's traditional markets of France and Japan have now expanded to include Germany, Italy, Korea, Taiwan, and North America. Although new markets are opening, many more commercial farms are starting so skin production is also increasing. Because of this balance between demand and supply, prices remain stable.

Bill Green

▲ Conservation through utilization is helping to provide Papua New Guinea with export earnings, industry training for its citizens, and an efficient means of crocodilian population monitoring for the country's wildlife biologists.

Jack Green/Australian Nature Photographs

for the manufacture of processing chemicals (currently manufactured primarily in West Germany) and tanning machinery.

Countries in the Far East have begun to import large numbers of common non-endemic species from around the world for rearing in ranches for the production of skins and meat. Large numbers of juvenile *Caiman crocodilus fuscus* have been exported from Colombia to ranches in Taiwan in recent years. Exports of caiman products from Thailand, labeled true crocodile, have recently appeared in the international market. Such a shift in the trade might threaten international control of the illegal trade as the flow of skins and hides is no longer subject to the well-established customs and wildlife scrutinies that have been implemented throughout the European Common Market where most of the tanneries are. The crocodilian leather industry is now going through a period of evolution. To what extent wild populations of crocodilian species will benefit from this evolution remains to be seen.

In recent years, the crocodilian leather industry has come to recognize that wildlife, including crocodilians, is not an unlimited commodity. Commercial trade names for species

have given way to the adoption of standard scientific terminology, enabling law enforcement agencies and the scientific community to monitor the species accurately. The various segments of the industry have begun to support research by national and international scientists into the demographics of crocodilian populations, reproductive biology, and captive husbandry. The financial resources of the trade should be directed toward broadening our scientific knowledge of critically endangered species as a resource for the future, as well as toward developing data of immediate interest for purposes of utilization. An emphasis on developing farming and ranching strategies should not take precedence over the protection and management of wild populations as a continuing natural resource and a national heritage. Most of the species of crocodilians that have recovered from depletion and the effects of overutilization have done so because their potential as a commercially useful revenue-producing commodity has made them sufficiently valuable to save. Perhaps we should ask ourselves whether this is the most important criterion upon which we should be judging the future survival of the world's crocodilians.

▲ Artificial "crocodile leather" may satisfy the small middle and lower income portions of the market, and it is becoming increasingly difficult to distinguish the artificial product (rear) from the genuine product (front) as quality improves.

# FARMING AND RANCHING

CHARLES A. ROSS, DAVID K. BLAKE, and J.T. VICTOR ONIONS

Crocodile and alligator "farms" have been in existence since the early twentieth century. However, these early "farms" were similar to zoological parks that specialized in exhibiting crocodilians. There was no emphasis on breeding crocodilian stock and the primary source of income was tourism. These operations had little effect on utilization, conservation, or knowledge of crocodilians.

In the early 1960s, the wild crocodilian resource necessary for the skin trade had dwindled and the first conservation laws were enacted, resulting in a simultaneous rise in prices and in the demand for skins. It was at this time that farsighted conservationists and skin producers started to investigate the feasibility of farming and ranching crocodilians on a sustained, commercial basis.

▼ Crocodile "farms and ranches" in the early days were merely displays of "fierce predators" for public titillation. However, the decline in world crocodilian populations through loss of habitat and predation by humans led to the realization that crocodile farms could also play a vital conservation role.

UPI/Bettmann Newsphotos

◄ As well as breeding alligators for their skins, the St. Augustine, Florida, "gator" farm provided thrill-seekers with the experience of surviving — or perhaps not — a walk through pens crowded with potentially dangerous animals.

## PURPOSE OF FARMS AND RANCHES

The term "crocodile farm" is often used to describe any facility — ranch or farm — raising crocodiles for commercial purposes. However, "farm" is the term more correctly used for a closed crocodile-farming system where all the stock marketed must be bred on the farm or from captive-bred sources. Once established, the only (occasional) outside input is breeding stock to maintain genetic viability.

Conservation and educational farms (often called banks or rehabilitation projects) aim at breeding endangered species of crocodilians in captivity for possible release back into protected areas in the wild. Primary income comes from tourism and/or grants from local government and conservationists, not from the sale of skins. Unlike the earlier tourist-trap "farms," these operations can supply the public with up-to-date information on conservation and natural history. Many zoological parks now fall into this category as there is an emphasis on accumulating breeding groups of crocodilians rather than "postage-stamp collections" of individuals from a number of species for exhibit. Other farms, which received original stock from a variety of sources but which, through captive breeding, have a closed, sustained system for supplying skins to the trade, derive their primary income from skin sales although they may also derive some income from tourism.

The term "ranch" is used where crocodilian stock — eggs, hatchlings, or adults — are taken from the wild on an annual basis and raised for market. There are two major categories of ranch. Rearing stations, where eggs or juvenile crocodilians are collected from the wild and reared to skinning size, derive their income from the sale of skins and possibly tourism. Other ranches are dependent on taking crocodilians of marketable size from the wild as well as juveniles and eggs for rearing. Their emphasis is on management of habitat for sustained-yield harvesting. (Management of habitat may serve multiple purposes—cropping of fur-bearing animals, birds, and other marsh or swamp dwellers as well as harvesting of building materials, and food from plants.) Tourism is not a source of income.

Commercial development and international trade in endangered species such as crocodiles must satisfy the criteria of the Convention on International Trade in Endangered Species of Fauna and Flora (CITES). Commercial farms must be able to demonstrate a viable second generation progeny for the species. Ranching programs must operate under an Approved Management Plan that must demonstrate, for a defined geographic area, that the impact of harvesting is not detrimental to the survival of the species.

## ALLIGATOR FARMING IN THE UNITED STATES

The bequest of coastal Louisiana marshlands to government land and wildlife management agencies by E. A. McIlhenny (author of *The Alligator's Life History* and founder of the McIlhenney Tabasco Sauce Company) earlier this

▼ While crocodile and alligator farms breed their own stock, ranches rely on establishing a sustainable population through the capture of adult and hatchling crocodilians from the wild or through the collection of eggs. Here, Gharial eggs are being collected from a nest beside the Narayani River in Nepal.

Mike Price/Bruce Coleman Ltd

century had a major impact on the conservation, management, and ultimately the development of crocodilian farming technology.

McIlhenny required that all revenue generated from the bequeathed lands must be reinvested in them, and to satisfy this proviso the Wild Life and Fisheries Commission of the State of Louisiana assumed management control of the bequeathed lands. On part of these lands, Rockefeller Wildlife Refuge was created. The Refuge is rich in oil and, under careful management, this resource was tapped and has provided a steady source of revenue for the Refuge and ancillary projects. Using these funds, the Commission initiated a pioneer program of alligator management in the early 1960s.

The primary aim of the Commission was to conserve the wetlands habitat of Louisiana. One method of doing this was to crop, on a sustained-yield basis, fur-bearing mammals, waterfowl, and alligators. It was hoped that this revenue, coupled with tax incentives and other government grants, would make income from managed marshlands competitive with agricultural development. In effect, the entire coastal marsh habitat of Louisiana was to become a giant alligator ranch.

Under the United States Endangered Species Act of 1969, the American Alligator (*Alligator mississippiensis*) became a federal responsibility. Management of the species was under the control of the United States Fish and Wildlife Service. Although the State of Louisiana and the Fish and Wildlife Service may have had the same ultimate goal — preservation of the alligator — their methods differed and a historic "state's rights" battle ensued. During this time, cropping of wild,

▼ American Alligators have been farmed for many years but the conditions under which they were maintained in the past, were subject to few imposed standards. Alligator farms today use modern technology to raise commercially valuable animals in sanitary conditions.

Jeff Foott/Bruce Coleman Ltd

ranched alligators was not possible and research at Rockefeller Refuge turned more toward rearing and farming of alligators in captivity.

Early research at Rockefeller Wildlife Refuge included penning wild-taken alligators in native marsh habitat to determine the optimum pen size, feeding routine and the effect of diet on fertility of eggs, water-land relationship, and sex-stocking ratios required for maximum production of eggs. Subsequently the staff developed methods for the collection and incubation of eggs, hatching, and rearing hatchlings to optimum skinning size. This required research into optimum diet for hatchlings, temperature-dependent sex ratios, the causes of malformations, and bacteriological and disease prophylaxis. The results of this Rockefeller Refuge–based research, modified for local conditions, have been used by farms worldwide.

Current farming research in Louisiana includes rearing alligators in controlled environments for maximum commercial advantage. In effect, alligators are reared in hothouses with heated water and a steady source of food. Music, preferably Cajun, is piped into the chambers and this evidently decreases the trauma to the alligators from external disturbances such as the cleaning of pens. Under these conditions, a commercially useful alligator of more than 1 meter (3.3 feet) in length can be produced in one year.

It was found that maintenance and nesting of "domestic" alligators (those reared in captivity) was more economical than using wild-taken or nuisance alligators. In addition, domestic alligators reared in environmental chambers nested at a young age — 6 years as opposed to 10 years for wild Louisiana alligators — and, if fed properly and stocked at the right density, eventually produced more nests than wild alligators. Clutch size increased with the age of the nesting female. The incubation temperature of eggs was found to influence post-hatching growth, with an incubation temperature of 31.7° C (89° F) producing the lowest number of runts and the overall best growth rates.

Alligator farms in Louisiana have to be licensed by the Commission. There are a variety of factors that influence licensing but a prerequisite is the use of environmental-control chambers. Research at Rockefeller Refuge has shown that commercially valuable skins can be produced economically by farms using current knowledge and there are now 13 established farms holding some 21,000 captive alligators in the State. The economic feasibility of rearing alligators in hothouses for maximum growth has been established only for animals up to the minimum sizes required by the skin trade. For larger alligators cropping of the wild, ranched population is still necessary.

Both Louisiana and Florida have a controlled, limited season for taking alligators and are attempting to manage their wild populations. The Louisiana strategy of managing and conserving alligator habitat by making it economical to ranch marshlands may, in the end, not only support the crocodilian skin trade by providing size classes of alligators not available from farms but also provide refuge and living space for all the native and migrant wildlife that utilizes these lands.

## NILE CROCODILE FARMING AND RANCHING IN AFRICA

As a result of the increasing demand for crocodile skins worldwide during the 1950s and 1960s Nile Crocodiles (*Crocodylus niloticus*) were hunted extensively throughout Africa. This hunting decimated crocodile populations and only the remoteness of some areas afforded crocodiles a measure of protection.

With the ever-increasing demand for crocodile skins and the reduced numbers available from the wild, other sources of skins were examined. In the early 1960s in Zimbabwe (formerly Rhodesia) proposals were put to the government to start crocodile ranching and the first two crocodile ranches were established on the shores of Lake Kariba in 1965.

It soon became apparent that the collection of wild hatchlings was uneconomical and the Zimbabwe ranches switched to the rearing of hatchlings from eggs collected in the wild. It was not until the late 1970s that the ranches looked toward farming. Up to that time, adults were held for exhibition purposes only, with eggs being a spin-off. The realization that the industry was dependent on eggs from the wild with no guarantee for future collections caused a swing toward keeping females for farming purposes. It had also been demonstrated by 1978 that the keeping of egg-laying females was just as economical as collecting eggs from the wild.

While the crocodile industry was expanding in Zimbabwe (from two farms in 1965 to ten in 1988) crocodile farms were also started in other parts of Africa such as Kenya, Tanzania, Zambia, South Africa, Mozambique, and Madagascar. The development of the industry, as in all new industries, has not been without its teething problems. Those involved in the industry had to learn all aspects of ranching and farming of crocodiles, from the collection and incubation of eggs, rearing, and breeding to the final stage of skin processing. In Zimbabwe the industry was given the go-ahead but was, initially, left to sort out its problems and to develop its own techniques. It was only in 1970 that an officer of the Department of National Parks and Wildlife Management was appointed to oversee the development of the industry and to prove the viability of farming crocodiles in captivity. In Natal, South Africa, a crocodile research station was established in 1965

in the Ndumu Game Reserve by the Natal Parks Board. Part of its brief was to research the rearing of crocodiles in captivity.

◄ Although the commercial farming and ranching of Nile Crocodiles in Zimbabwe had little biological or practical information on which to draw in 1965, the industry is now well established and profitable.

## EGG COLLECTION

Collections are made under permit from the appropriate authority. This permit usually demarcates areas of collection and the number of eggs to be collected. In some countries, for example, Zimbabwe, the permit made provision for the return to the wild of a number of immature Nile Crocodiles based on a percentage of the eggs collected.

The method of collection in the wild is to visit known breeding grounds some two months after laying, when the eggs still have about 30 days to hatching. This timing is important as eggs at this stage are less likely to be damaged than eggs in the early stages of incubation. The general area of a nest is located by observing tracks left by the female guarding the eggs. The actual nest is located by probing with a sharp steel spike until an egg is probed. Once located, the nests are opened and the eggs removed. Except under farming conditions, there is no danger from the females during collection since they have an inherent fear of humans. Each egg is marked as it is removed from the nest to ensure that it is packed in virtually the same position as it was in the nest. The eggs are packed into styrofoam transport boxes with vermiculite or other material as packing. Once packed the eggs are transported back to the ranch for incubation.

Egg collection on farms is similar except for two factors. With ready access to an incubator, eggs are collected as soon after laying as possible.

Eggs can be collected from under the female during the laying process with a certain amount of impunity. However, once having laid, captive females guard their nests against all comers including humans. In order to collect these eggs, the female has to be driven away from the nest and some form of barrier erected to keep her away while the eggs are collected.

## INCUBATION

Over the years, many methods of incubating eggs have been tried with varying degrees of success. Initially, nest simulation was carried out by reburying the eggs in sand in open enclosures. This method proved unsatisfactory as temperatures could not be controlled and hatching percentages were highly variable. The close proximity of clutches to each other also caused premature hatching probably due to the vocalizations from clutches ready to hatch stimulating the other clutches to hatch prematurely.

The next method tried was to pack the eggs in sand in individual boxes and incubate them in hothouses. This method evolved into the use of styrofoam boxes with vermiculite as an incubation medium. While various other methods such as open-tray incubation have been tried, the styrofoam vermiculite system has proved to be the best method, yielding the highest hatching percentages (up to 96 percent of the live eggs collected are incubated successfully). The temperature at which the eggs are incubated determines the sex of the hatchlings but, for a number of reasons, temperature-dependent sex determination is not practiced on crocodile farms or ranches in Africa. However, it has been found that varying the temperature during incubation will produce more robust hatchlings.

## HATCHLINGS AND REARING STOCK

The rearing of hatchlings in large numbers proved to be one of the major stumbling blocks in

establishing the African industry. Mortality was high among hatchlings due to outbreaks of endemic diseases. It was later found that these diseases were, in fact, secondary; the main problem was stress to the hatchlings due to highly fluctuating temperatures between day and night in the holding ponds. Once the hatchlings were placed in hothouses with a constant temperature of 32° C (89° F) mortality decreased rapidly and growth rates escalated.

Diet also proved to be a problem. In the wild, hatchlings live mainly on insects and small fish. It was found that the diet of chopped meat provided on the farms and ranches lacked both vitamins and minerals, and these had to be added. The farms along the shores of Lake Kariba had access to the freshwater sardine (*Limnothrissa* species), which proved an ideal feed for hatchlings.

After the first year, depending on local climatic conditions, the one-year-old crocodiles are either moved to outside ponds or continue to be reared in hothouses. At this stage, losses are minimal and the crocodiles can be reared to skin size by the age of two years or less. The rapidly growing crocodiles consume large quantities of meat. In Zimbabwe, meat from game culls forms the main feed. In South Africa most farms and ranches are situated near chicken farms from which large quantities of chicken can be obtained at low cost.

## SKIN PRODUCTION

Once the young crocodiles reach skin-production size — about 32 centimeters (12–13 inches) across the belly — they are culled. Culling is done quickly and efficiently, either by shooting in the head or severing the spinal cord.

The skins are removed as soon as possible after culling by trained skinners. The skin is removed in two pieces — the back skin and the belly skin. The belly skins are treated with salt and other preservatives before being placed in coldrooms awaiting shipment as wet-salted skins. Most of these skins are shipped to Europe, the traditional market where the expertise and equipment exists for the tanning of skins. The international demand for back skins is low and these are usually used locally for the manufacture of belts and other artifacts.

Most of the meat from the culled crocodiles is fed back to the rearing stock, with a small percentage being put on the market for human consumption, Heads (either mounted or as skulls) and feet are sold as curios to the public.

## BREEDING STOCK

Breeding stock is obtained from farm-reared crocodiles or from crocodiles captured in the wild. The rearing of crocodiles for breeding purposes is a long-term process as crocodiles, under natural conditions, only mature at 10 –12 years. Under

▼ At African farms and ranches vermiculite is used to incubate eggs at controlled temperature and humidity. In Australia, open racks are often used as these reduce infections due to fungi and make eggs easily accessible.

Jack Green/Australian Nature Photographs

Jack Green/Australian Nature Photographs

hothouse conditions, females can be brought up to egg laying in six years but it still has to be proved that such females are truly sexually mature. Breeding crocodiles from the wild are usually caught under permit or are caught because they are a threat to humans and livestock. Such crocodiles adapt well to captivity and, held under ideal conditions, will breed annually. The crocodiles are held in pens with ponds large enough and deep enough to allow for mating.

Two systems for the holding of adult crocodiles for breeding purposes are in use in Africa. The first is a multiple male-female system. This system has the disadvantage that males are territorial during the breeding season and can inflict severe, even fatal, injuries on each other. Another problem is that the dominant males are so busy chasing each other that the females are not served properly and a lower fertility in eggs is experienced. The other system used, more along the lines of other types of farming, involves holding one male to a number of females. Not only does this system give a higher fertility rate for

Bill Green

▲ American Alligator hatchlings reared in captivity grow twice as fast as wild hatchlings, which has increased the profitability of alligator farming in the United States.

◄ In Papua New Guinea villagers keep live juvenile crocodiles in pens made from native materials until buyers from large ranches come to purchase them. Some villages earn their entire cash income from such sales.

207

eggs but it also allows for the monitoring of the breeding performance of individual animals.

In either system, mating starts in the middle of winter, some three to four months prior to laying. The male repeatedly covers each female during this time. As the laying time approaches the females select nesting sites but, as this can lead to conflict between females, some farms install stalls in which the females can nest. These stalls separate the females from one another and can also be closed off to facilitate the collection of eggs.

Clutch sizes vary, depending on the size and age of the female — from 20 eggs for a first lay to 70 or more for a large mature female. Farms can expect some 40 eggs on average per female. For a farm to be viable it must produce 2,000 skins a year. To achieve this figure, the farm needs the input of 60 nests or 2,500 eggs a year.

## CAPTURE, HANDLING, AND DRUGGING

In 1971, as a result of close liaison between Zimbabwe's National Parks Department and the University of Zimbabwe, the drug Flaxedil (gallamine triethiodide) was tested and found suitable for the immobilization of crocodiles. This drug, while not an anesthetic, has proved to be of great benefit in the capture, handling, and transporting of crocodiles. Prior to the use of the drug as an immobilizing tool, crocodiles had to be roped during capture and handling. In the process, injury to the crocodiles and handlers was not uncommon.

With the increasing popularity of crocodile farming and ranching, the demand for adult crocodiles has increased, and in most African countries there is a trend toward the capture rather than the destruction of problem crocodiles. In some countries, permits have also been issued for the capture of crocodiles in areas considered to be overstocked. Large numbers of crocodiles in these two categories have been captured and moved to crocodile farms or ranches all over Africa. The crocodiles are captured either in a box trap or in a Pitman trap. The box trap consists of an oblong box or tube covered with wire mesh. One end is closed off while the other has a drop door that is triggered by the crocodile entering the trap and pulling on a bait. The disadvantage of this trap is that the crocodiles tend to injure their jaws trying to force their way out. The "Pitman" trap consists of three automobile leaf springs bolted together. These are mounted on a stand set into the ground at the head of a trench dug into the river bank. The springs are pulled down and fastened to a trigger from which a bait is suspended into the trench. At the mouth of the trench a wire (cable) running noose is set and fastened to the springs. The crocodile swims through the noose and sets off the trigger. The springs straighten upward, pulling the noose around the crocodile's middle. The running noose attached to the springs allows the crocodile

Michael Cermak

▲ The tendency of laying females to compete for access to favored nesting sites is alleviated on many farms by the construction of stalls, which, in addition to precluding conflict, can be blocked off to make egg collection easier.

▶ A variety of methods are used to catch crocodiles for measurement, tagging, research, or relocation. For large Indopacific crocodiles, rope traps are commonly used since these minimize possible injuries.

Bill Green

to swim around, as far as the noose will allow, without causing injury to itself.

The immobilization of captured crocodiles was done, initially, using a hand-held syringe. This was not satisfactory and various types of dartguns were used. These also had their problems because, while the dartguns put space between the

Jonathan Scott/Seaphot Limited Planet Earth Pictures/Transglobe Agency

▲▶ The box trap (above) is easy to set up, adapts to changing water levels in tidal areas, and may reduce the risk of damage to animals or handlers during capture but can be ineffective with extremely large animals. More efficient designs for trapping large animals are the rope trap or the "Pitman" trap (right), which permit a captured animal some degree of movement.

PITMAN TRAP

Automobile leaf springs

Wire running noose

Trigger

Bait

crocodile and the handler, there was a danger from ricocheting darts — crocodiles are covered on the side and back with bony plates, and darts striking these were inclined to ricochet off. The most effective method was found to be a pole syringe. The pole syringe consists of a modified syringe fastened to an aluminium pole, which acts as both an extended handle and a plunger. The usual site of injection is the tail, just behind the back leg.

Once injected the crocodile takes 20–30 minutes to become immobilized, depending on its temperature and the amount of the drug administered. Once the drug takes effect the crocodile is paralyzed but can still see, hear, smell, and feel pain. For this reason, the jaws are taped closed and the eyes covered during handling and transportation, and in this state the crocodiles remain dormant even when the drug wears off.

Using this technique, immobilized crocodiles have been moved thousands of kilometers by road and air all over Africa without ill-effects. Immobilization has also meant that injured or sick crocodiles can be treated easily. As the crocodiles can still feel pain, a local anesthetic is also used if surgery has to be carried out.

## BENEFITS OF FARMING AND RANCHING IN AFRICA

In Africa, farming and/or ranching of crocodiles has been confined to the Nile Crocodile. The ever-increasing number of good quality Nile Crocodile skins from the industry is increasingly supplementing the demand for skins from the wild, both legal and illegal, which has led to a reduction in poaching. Skins from farms and ranches should, in the future, replace the taking of skins from the wild completely.

There has also been a scientific spin-off from the industry. With the need to know more about their crocodile populations, most African countries have put funding and staff into projects on crocodilians. This was especially true in South Africa and Zimbabwe, where officers were appointed to monitor crocodile populations and to develop new techniques that would overcome problems in crocodile farming. Zimbabwe was a leader in the field of crocodile farming and, in 1982 at Victoria Falls, hosted the first international conference on crocodile farming, CROC '82, which was attended by 81 delegates from 18 countries worldwide. Research into crocodiles has given a better understanding of crocodile populations in the wild, their requirements for survival, and their position ecologically.

Crocodile ranching and farming has brought about a new perception of the crocodile, which has afforded it much more protection in the wild. Without this change in approach most crocodile populations outside game reserves would become extinct in Africa.

## FARMING AND RANCHING IN AUSTRALIA

Crocodile farming is a new area of animal husbandry in Australia. In 1969 the Applied Ecology unit of the Australian National University (later Applied Ecology Pty. Ltd. and now Edward River Crocodile Farm Pty. Ltd.) established the first small Indopacific Crocodile (*Crocodylus porosus*) farm at the Edward River Aboriginal Community, Cape York, Queensland. The original aim of the farm was to divert small Indopacific Crocodiles, not then protected in Queensland, from being taken for the "stuffer trade" by paying hunters to deliver them live to the farm. Some 600 crocodiles in all were supplied. Many, however, were in poor condition with little chance of survival and were released locally. The farm was thereafter largely inactive until 1976 when it was decided to develop an on-site breeding facility and a commercial crocodile farm. A permit for 50 adult crocodiles was given in 1979 and 49 crocodiles longer than 2.8 meters (9 feet) were taken. The farm was the first farm in Australia to meet all state, federal, and international requirements for trade.

There are now seven crocodile farms or ranches in Australia. The four in Queensland are farms, while the three in the Northern Territory are in fact ranches as they are supplied with Indopacific Crocodile eggs and Johnston's Crocodile (*Crocodylus johnsoni*) hatchlings from the wild each year under an Approved Management Plan. The Northern Territory Crocodile Management Plan allows the taking of 4,000 Indopacific Crocodile eggs each year from the Adelaide River, and the Finniss-Reynolds river system. Up to 2,000 Johnston's Crocodile hatchlings per ranch are also allowed under the Plan. Research in the Northern Territory over three seasons has recorded no negative impact; in fact, in the Adelaide River the adult population of Indopacific Crocodiles has been increasing significantly.

The Northern Territory ranches also hold captive-breeding populations of Indopacific Crocodiles, which, when combined with those from the Queensland farms produced more than 200 nests in 1988. Hatchling yields from captive-breeding populations are still increasing as most farms have had to settle wild-taken problem crocodiles (large crocodiles that encroach on urban or recreational areas and need to be removed for the safety of the public) and, especially in the case of Edward River, a high proportion of females have passed their initial low-yield breeding seasons.

As there is no accepted national or international standard in crocodile-farm design or in the husbandry involved in raising and breeding crocodilians, Australian efforts with both Indopacific and Johnston's crocodiles drew heavily on concepts and experience from Africa and the United States and, to a lesser extent, on

Romulus Whitaker

◄ Funded by the Commonwealth Department of Aboriginal Affairs and providing employment for the local Aboriginal community, the Edward River Crocodile Farm in Queensland grew in size from 600 crocodiles in 1969 to around 7,800 in 1988 and was the first crocodile farm in Australia.

Asian and Papua New Guinean farming methods, which were subsequently adapted to suit Australian conditions. These seven existing Australian crocodile farms/ranches plus an eighth planned farm are described in the following paragraphs.

1. Edward River Crocodile Farm is situated 500 kilometers (310 miles) northwest of Cairns, on the west coast of Cape York, Queensland, at Pormpuraaw (formerly Edward River) Aboriginal Community. The farm commenced in 1969 with the dual purpose of conserving juvenile Indopacific Crocodiles that would otherwise have been taken by hunters, and providing employment for the Aboriginal community. The farm is a research and development project funded by the Commonwealth Department of Aboriginal Affairs. The farm is a closed system and is registered with CITES as a captive-breeding facility for Indopacific Crocodiles. As of May 1988 the farm held 7,840 crocodiles of which more than 7,500 were captive bred. Some 134 nests were made on the farm in the 1987–88 season and the farm has exported skins since 1984 and marketed crocodile meat domestically since 1986. The major problems faced by the farm are remoteness and food supplies, particularly during the wet season when roads are closed for several months. The farm has plans to move the crocodile-raising component of the farm to the Cairns area where food supplies are more readily available and tourist numbers are greater.

2. Koorana Crocodile Farm, 30 kilometers (18 miles) east of Rockhampton, Queensland,

Bill Green

▲ Papua New Guinea now has two major crocodile farms producing high-quality skins. Australia drew to some extent on the experience of farmers in Papua New Guinea when setting up its own crocodile-farming industry.

commenced in 1981 with the aim of producing skins, meat, and a facility for tourism and public education. The farm is in part underwritten by a novel "lease-a-crocodile" investment scheme. Stock at May 1988 was 850 animals, made up of 100 Johnston's Crocodiles and 750 Indopacific Crocodiles. Twenty-four Indopacific Crocodile nests were made on the farm in 1988. Food sources are poultry, fish, and beef. Projected production is 1,000 skins a year. The major problem has been sources of stock, which were limited to problem Indopacific Crocodiles from the wild in the Rockhampton area, supplemented by small numbers from the Edward River Crocodile Farm.

3. Hartleys Creek Crocodile Farm, 60 kilometers (37 miles) north of Cairns, is the home of "Charlie the Crocodile" and has been a popular tourist park for many years. The farm has 500 Indopacific and 200 Johnston's crocodiles and is in the process of being stocked as a farm with allocated problem crocodiles, under the Queensland National Parks and Wildlife Management Plan for the East Coast. The Plan allows for the removal of all crocodiles more than 1.2 meters (4 feet) in length from populated and tourist areas.

4. Johnstone River Crocodile Farm, 4 kilometers (2–3 miles) southeast of Innisfail, Queensland, is a family operation, which commenced in 1986 and now has 26 Indopacific Crocodiles, all problem crocodiles taken in the local area. One nest was produced in the 1987–88 season, yielding 34 hatchlings. The farm has plans to

open soon for visitors on a restricted basis.

5. Crocodile Farms (N.T.), 40 kilometers (25 miles) south of Darwin, is a farm/ranch, which was opened in 1980, primarily as a tourist facility by a number of investors in association with a poultry farm. There were 40,000 visitors in 1984 rising to more than 100,000 in 1987. Total stock was 6,520 crocodiles in May 1988 consisting of 3,200 Indopacific and 3,320 Johnston's crocodiles. Breeding stock was originally collected from the wild as problem Indopacific Crocodiles from the Darwin area. The major difficulties have been settling problem animals and the mismatching of animals, that is, penning wild crocodiles unsuited in terms of size and sex, which reduces the efficiency of establishing a captive-breeding population. Thirty-seven Indopacific Crocodile nests were made on the farm in the 1987–88 season. The farm is concentrating on Indopacific Crocodiles because of their higher skin value and meat yields. The food source is mostly chicken, with a mixture of meat and fish for hatchlings. Projected turnover is 2,000 skins annually. The farm commenced exporting skins and marketing meat domestically in 1987.

6. Janamba Croc Farm at Fogg Dam, 70 kilometers (43 miles) southeast of Darwin, was started in 1982 in association with a poultry farm in Darwin. It does not cater for tourists. The farm changed hands in 1985 and has been extensively redeveloped with new pens and breeding enclosures. In May 1988 the farm had 2,100 Indopacific and 6,200 Johnston's crocodiles. Crocodile skin and meat sales commenced in 1987.

7. Letaba Crocodile Ranch, 95 kilometers (59 miles) southwest of Darwin, is a ranch started in 1982 in association with a large cattle station. The concept was to take Indopacific Crocodile eggs from wild crocodile habitats on the station, rather than maintaining a captive-breeding population. The farm is owner-operated and does not cater for tourists. It was relocated and rebuilt in 1987, and is now concentrating on raising Indopacific Crocodiles. Stock numbers in May 1988 were 2,200 Indopacific and 120 Johnston's crocodiles. Skins and meat were first marketed in 1987.

8. Broome Crocodile Farm is officially a fauna park but should be included in this section as it keeps and raises crocodiles, and is planning to become a farm or ranch. At present the park has only 134 crocodiles, including hatchlings, and four American Alligators from a variety of sources. The park successfully hatched 52 Indopacific Crocodile hatchlings in 1988. What makes the Broome Crocodile Farm different is its small size and the fact that it is being successfully developed on a tourist-income base, with more than 30,000 visitors in 1987.

The crocodile farms and ranches have developed different means of funding and generating income. Crocodile Farms (N.T.), Koorana, Hartleys Creek, and Broome are tourist oriented whereas Edward River, Johnston River, Janamba, and Letaba are solely producers of crocodile products. Edward River, Crocodile Farms (N.T.), and Hartleys Creek are corporate operations, while Koorana, Johnstone River, Janamba, Letaba, and Broome are owner operated. Crocodile farming and ranching are essentially long-term ventures. Raising hatchlings for market takes 3–4 years, while breeding and raising takes 8–10 years before returns are realized. To generate income, using crocodiles as a draw-card, integration of the venture to include tourist entry fees and sales of souvenirs, food and so on is, in many cases, the solution in the early years; in this case visitors rather than crocodile skins or meat are the main products of the venture.

Both species of Australian crocodiles are accorded legislative protection at state, federal, and international levels, particularly if taking, keeping, and trading in either species is contemplated. The penalties for non-compliance can result in loss of stock and licenses, severe fines and/or jail terms. All farms or ranches must have a state or territory permit to take from the wild, to hold or remove crocodiles, to deal in crocodiles or crocodile products, and must submit the necessary returns required by the respective permits.

The federal government, through the Australian National Parks and Wildlife Service, is the designated Scientific and Management Authority for CITES in Australia and, as such, must be satisfied that any farming or ranching of a CITES-listed species such as crocodiles meet CITES requirements for captive breeding (in the case of farms) or an approved management plan (in the case of ranching). The Australian populations of Indopacific and Johnston's crocodiles are on Appendix II of CITES, according both species a high level of protection.

The international crocodile skin trade has changed dramatically over the past three decades. Peaking in the late 1950s and early 1960s, when an estimated 5–10 million skins a year were traded, world trade today probably amounts to no more than 1.5 million skins annually. The major markets for Indopacific Crocodile skins are France and Japan, with Italy and Singapore expressing keen interest. There are good market prospects for these skins with a premium offered for smaller skins — 30–40 centimeters (12–16 inches) belly width. Johnston's Crocodile skins are worth about half the price of Indopacific Crocodile skins of the same size due to the presence of osteoderms, which make the skins more difficult to tan, and the larger relative size of the scutes, which make the skins unsuitable for high quality leather.

Crocodile meat has rapidly become a valuable

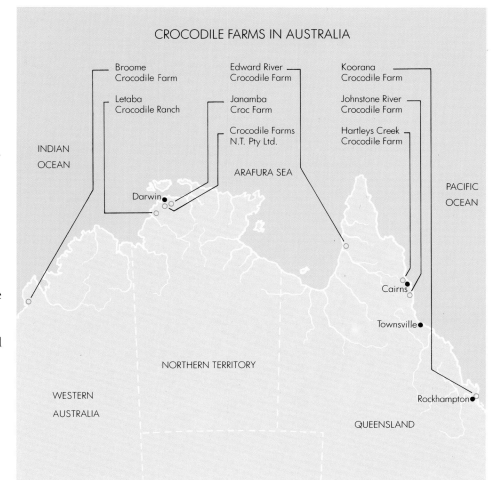

CROCODILE FARMS IN AUSTRALIA

product with restaurant and media interest Australia-wide. Even without promotion, demand far exceeds supply and crocodile meat has good domestic market prospects for the foreseeable future. There are a number of by-products — back-ridge skin for leather; skulls and feet for taxidermy; dried galls, spleen, and penises for Asian medicines — known to have some value or potential. These have remained largely unutilized by the industry in Australia.

Attitudes to crocodile conservation and management within Australia have been steadily changing from one of preservation to one of sustained-yield harvesting. Even so, there are organizations that remain opposed to any commercial development of wildlife on principle. However, the number of crocodiles maintained on Australian farms and ranches, particularly the 16,000 Indopacific Crocodiles, make a positive contribution to conservation as the number represents a significant percentage of the estimated wild population throughout Australia. This is clearly conservation "insurance" for the future. The farms and ranches have also housed large numbers of problem Indopacific Crocodiles, which would otherwise have been shot. Through media attention and tourism (at some farms), the industry plays a very significant role in public education and crocodile conservation.

# COMPARISON OF FARMS

ROMULUS WHITAKER and GREG MITCHELL

## MADRAS CROCODILE BANK

In 1971, at the first meeting of the International Union for the Conservation of Nature and Natural Resources (IUCN) Crocodile Specialist Group, it was proposed that a crocodile bank be established as a gene pool for the world's crocodilians. In 1975 a step toward this goal was made with the founding of the Madras Crocodile Bank. Starting with 14 Mugger (*Crocodylus palustris*) and finance from such diverse sources as the World Wildlife Fund and the West German Reptile Leather Association, the Crocodile Bank now has nearly 3,500 crocodilians of ten species. More than 400 of the offspring from captive breeding have been supplied to state restocking programs throughout India.

As a purely conservation-oriented crocodile "farm," the Madras Crocodile Bank concentrates on field as well as laboratory research on crocodiles including the status of wild populations, behavior, biology, and breeding technology. Covering 3.5 hectares (8.5 acres) of coastal land 40 kilometers (25 miles) south of the city of Madras, the Bank's major feature is a network of carefully landscaped enclosures and ponds, many dug into the naturally high aquifer. An air-conditioned laboratory and computer-equipped office operate in collaboration with Indian and foreign scientists and, currently, research is supported by grants from the Smithsonian Institution, the United States National Science Foundation, and the National Geographic Society.

Public education is an important activity and a number of publications and several films have emanated from the Madras Crocodile Bank. More than half a million annual visitors pay 15 cents each to see and learn about crocodiles, making the Bank a self-supporting institution. Operated by a board of trustees, future plans include the acquisition of breeding groups of all the

S.C. Bisserot

world's crocodilians. An eventual aim is the sponsorship of a tribal cooperative society that will make commercial use of surplus crocodiles bred at the Bank.

### CROCODILIANS AT THE MADRAS CROCODILE BANK

| | | |
|---|---|---|
| Mugger | *Crocodylus palustris* | 2,900 |
| Common Caiman | *Caiman crocodilus* | 300 |
| Indopacific Crocodile | *Crocodylus porosus* | 170 |
| Gharial | *Gavialis gangeticus* | 15 |
| American Alligator | *Alligator mississippiensis* | 12 |
| Morelet's Crocodile | *Crocodylus moreletii* | 10 |
| False Gharial | *Tomistoma schlegelii* | 5 |
| Siamese Crocodile | *Crocodylus siamensis* | 5 |
| Dwarf Crocodile | *Osteolaemis tetraspis* | 4 |
| Nile Crocodile | *Crocodylus niloticus* | 4 |

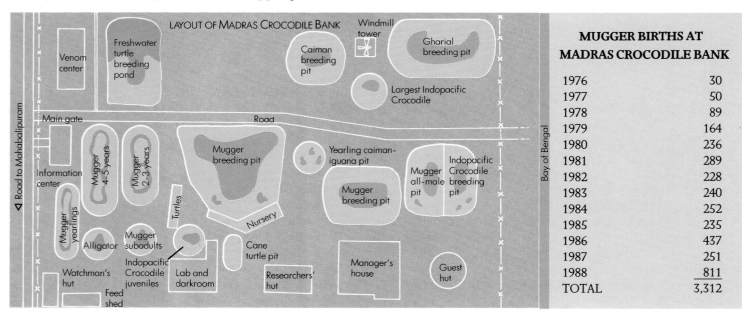

LAYOUT OF MADRAS CROCODILE BANK

### MUGGER BIRTHS AT MADRAS CROCODILE BANK

| | |
|---|---|
| 1976 | 30 |
| 1977 | 50 |
| 1978 | 89 |
| 1979 | 164 |
| 1980 | 236 |
| 1981 | 289 |
| 1982 | 228 |
| 1983 | 240 |
| 1984 | 252 |
| 1985 | 235 |
| 1986 | 437 |
| 1987 | 251 |
| 1988 | 811 |
| TOTAL | 3,312 |

## MAINLAND HOLDINGS CROCODILE FARM AND RANCH, PAPUA NEW GUINEA

Crocodile ranching was first established in Papua New Guinea in the late 1960s. For the next decade ranching was restricted to village smallholder projects, and government research and demonstration farms. Mainland Holdings was licensed to operate a crocodile ranch at Lae in 1979 and in 1982 the company was given approval to operate a breeding farm. The farm represents a capital investment in excess of US $3.5 million. The company is 100 percent nationally owned and has a permanent staff of eighteen.

In cooperation with the Department of Natural Resources, Mainland Holdings participates in the national monitoring program. The aim of the program is to boost earnings by growing small crocodiles through to a larger size with a greater skin value, thereby maximizing the utilization of crocodilian resources without increasing hunting pressures. Wild eggs have been harvested on a trial basis for the past three years as part of the monitoring program. Payment for these eggs is a direct revenue earner to the landowner.

Mainland Holdings has established a nationwide purchasing system for live crocodiles from the wild in cooperation with about one hundred smallholder farmers and around two hundred hunters who together supplied the farm with approximately 10,000 animals in 1988. As prices are significantly higher for live crocodiles than for skins from these animals, the hunters and smallholders are enthusiastic about the project. All stock purchased in the field is transported to Lae by charter aircraft.

The farm has a walk-in incubator with a capacity of 6,000 eggs. The incubator is designed to maintain close to 100 percent humidity with temperature control to ±0.5° C of the present optimum temperature, which allows for controlled sex determination of hatchlings. Current rearing stock on the farm is 28,500 crocodiles. These range in size from hatchlings of 60 grams (2 ounces) to 3-year-olds of 20 kilograms (44 pounds). In addition, 140 Indopacific Crocodiles are kept for research into breeding techniques, and the offspring supplement farm-ranched stock.

It is illegal to possess animals whose skin size would exceed 51 centimeters (20 inches) across the chest between the lateral dorsal scales if the animal was culled. All breeding stock is therefore the property of the Conservator of Fauna and held under license. The Conservator can, if necessary, direct that offspring from breeding stock be released back into the wild.

The success of the Mainland Holdings Crocodile Farm is directly related to access to a ready supply of feed from the farm's own poultry operation. Daily feed consumption is 2.5 tonnes of poultry by-products. The company has sufficient feed to support 40,000 crocodiles but this could be supplemented by the inclusion of dry feed.

The farm is divided into three areas — hatchery/infirmary, rearing farm, and breeder farm. New recruits arriving on the farm are checked for general condition, spear wounds, skin markings and so on. Should a new recruit have health problems, it is placed in the infirmary until healthy. Any sick crocodiles from the rearing farm are treated in the same manner. Healthy recruits are placed directly into the rearing farm with similar-sized animals.

Bill Green

The rearing pens measure 18 × 90 meters (60 × 300 feet) and can hold as many as 4,000 crocodiles, depending on size. In 1989 a new environmentally controlled rearing complex for young hatchlings will be constructed. Hatchlings will be raised in small pens, with control over temperature, light, and diet. An abattoir for skinning and export-meat processing will also be built. This will include a blast- and storage-freezer capacity and a refrigerated skin store. The complex will conform to USDA health requirements.

Crocodile farming and ranching can be described as farming the unusual. Much of the work involves trial and error, with mistakes made daily as new methods are pioneered. It is no more dangerous than cattle or other livestock ranching.

▼ Samut Prakan Crocodile Farm, south of Bangkok in Thailand, is one of the largest in the world with 30,000 crocodiles kept in vast open-air pools. The large majority of the crocodiles, which are raised for their skins and related products, are Indopacific or Siamese crocodiles — both species being native to Thailand — and the establishment of the farm has been instrumental in saving Thailand's population of Siamese Crocodiles from extinction. The farm is also a major tourist attraction and "crocodile-wrestling" shows are staged daily.

Romulus Whitaker

# CONSERVATION AND MANAGEMENT

F. WAYNE KING

The 1980s have been an important transition period in crocodilian conservation — the decade when conservation efforts returned several endangered species of crocodilians to former abundance, when many producer nations began to manage their crocodilians as a resource to earn valuable foreign exchange rather than as vermin to be eliminated, and possibly (although it is still too early to be sure) the period when the balance of international trade in crocodilian hides tipped from illegal to legal.

Much still needs to be done. A number of crocodilians remain perilously close to extinction. Some nations are doing little more than paying lip service to managing their wild populations and illegal trade still exists. Even those countries that rigorously control hunting of their crocodilian populations seldom adequately conserve the genetic diversity of the species by establishing the necessary network of national parks and wildlife sanctuaries to protect populations throughout their range. Nevertheless, a real opportunity now exists for saving the remaining threatened species; for putting the whole international reptile-hide industry on a legal, sustained-yield, rational-utilization basis; for bringing the last of the major markets for illegal hides under control; and, ultimately, for significantly increasing the income of hide producers in tropical nations around the world.

None of this success could have been realized without the efforts of dozens of individual biologists and government officials in producer nations all over the world. At the same time, few if any of these national programs could have succeeded were it not for the work of the Convention on International Trade in Endangered Species of Wild Fauna and Flora.

Twenty years ago, however, the situation was not so encouraging.

▶ Unlike many large predators, crocodilians do not need extensive areas set aside for their conservation. However, they do need adequate areas of wetland and it is the protection of tropical swamps and rivers in national parks that will achieve most for the conservation of wild crocodilian populations.

F. Prenzel/Australian Picture Library

Haroldo Palo, Jr./NHPA

◄ Most of the skin on a Common Caiman is too heavily ossified to make fine leather, but under the throat and along the flanks the scales are small and the skin soft and pliable. Although little is utilized from each carcass, so many caiman skins are taken that they make up three quarters of the international trade in crocodilian hides.

## HIDE TRADING 1950s–1970s

During the 1950s the international world trade in crocodilian hides of all species was estimated to be 5–10 million hides a year. Caimans accounted for approximately 6–8 million of the yearly estimate. Most of the trade was legal because there were relatively few laws regulating the hunting of crocodilians.

The international crocodilian hide trade focused initially on the true crocodiles (genus *Crocodylus*) and on the American Alligator (*Alligator mississippiensis*) — large species that are the source of the "classic" belly hides used in the manufacture of expensive leather goods. These hides either lack bony osteoderm buttons or have buttons that easily can be decalcified and removed during tanning so that the scales of the hides can be burnished to the high glaze required for haute-couture leather accessories. When the numbers of these crocodiles and alligators began to dwindle, the international trade turned to the bony, but still usable, Black Caiman (*Melanosuchus niger*) and Broad-snouted Caiman (*Caiman latirostris*). When they in turn were depleted, the trade shifted to the much more bony and less desirable Common Caiman (*Caiman crocodilus*). In the 1960s, caiman belly hides could not be glazed satisfactorily because of the surface pitting caused by the osteoderms. The hunters overcame this by throwing away the bony bellies and saving only the *chalecos* (the soft throat and strips extending down each side between the bony back and belly scales). When the *chaleco* is split in two at the

throat, it yields two flanks, one from each side. Since the 1960s, flanks of the Common Caiman (called *jacaretinga, tinga, baba, babilla,* and *lagarto* in Latin America and in the hide trade) have accounted for three-quarters of the world trade in crocodilian hides. With the trade concentrating more and more on the Common Caiman, considerable effort was devoted to improving the technology of tanning caiman hides.

▼ Even before there was a market for crocodile skins from northern Australia, Indopacific Crocodiles were shot on sight as potential molesters of people, cattle, and horses or for sport. Such sporadic shooting, however, had little effect on the crocodile population compared with the systematic hunting that occurred in the 1950s and 1960s.

Australian News and Information Bureau/National Library of Australia

DISTRIBUTION OF PHILIPPINE CROCODILE

LUZON

Manila
MINDORO
MASBATE
Calamian
Group
SAMAR

NEGROS

SULU
SEA
MINDANAO

Joto Island
CELEBES
SEA

■ Historical distribution
▲ Current distribution

▲ Formerly widespread throughout the archipelago, the Philippine Crocodile (*Crocodylus mindorensis*) is now severely restricted in distribution due to hunting pressure and habitat destruction. As its preferred habitat is converted to rice paddy, cleared for farming, or deforested, nesting sites and food supplies also disappear.

▶ Although Black Caimans are legally protected in Brazil, they are taken, along with the unprotected Common Caiman, whenever the opportunity arises. Unfortunately laws are useless unless enforced — the hunters who shot these caimans had no qualms about showing their catch to researchers.

Most producer nations did not manage their crocodilian resource on any rational biological or trade basis. Crocodilians were considered troublesome vermin and if anyone could make money while exploiting them so much the better. As a consequence, many species were overexploited, declined in numbers, and became endangered.

As wild populations shrank, the supply of hides dwindled. When they no longer could obtain sufficient hides to maintain their former levels of business, hide buyers began to shut down. By the late 1960s, even before protective legislation began to control the trade, the number of tanners, cutters, and brokers operating in the consumer nations — the United States and Europe — had declined significantly. The larger operators, however, stayed in business though many did so by dealing in illegal hides. Illegal traders therefore expanded their operations in an attempt to keep the former volume of hides flowing to international markets.

Producer nations, meanwhile, began to pass protective legislation as their wild populations waned. Some countries prohibited all hunting of crocodilians. Others protected crocodilians in those parts of the country where crocodilians had become scarce, while allowing trade to continue in areas where populations were still abundant. Between 1959 and 1970, for example, a majority of African nations implemented protective legislation for the Nile Crocodile (*Crocodylus niloticus*), African Slender-snouted Crocodile (*Crocodylus cataphractus*), and Dwarf Crocodile (*Osteolaemus tetraspis*). In 1969, the United States first provided federal protection for the American Alligator under the Endangered Species Conservation Act. In 1968, Colombia prohibited the hunting and sale of the American Crocodile (*Crocodylus acutus*), Orinoco Crocodile (*Crocodylus intermedius*),

William E. Magnusson

Black Caiman, and three subspecies of Common Caiman (*Caiman crocodilus apaporiensis, Caiman c. chiapasius,* and *Caiman c. fuscus*) but allowed trade in *Caiman crocodilus crocodilus* to continue.

Illegal traders thwarted these national and local efforts by smuggling hides to neighboring countries where the species were not protected and from where hides could be shipped openly to international markets. Others continued operations by declaring the hides to be from unprotected species or from parts of the country that still remained open to hunting. Some bribed government officials to obtain export permits that were otherwise unavailable. In an attempt to increase foreign trade, Colombia established Leticia as a free-trade zone. The illegal traders took advantage of this loophole by shipping illegal hides through Leticia and by declaring them to be Common Caiman regardless of the actual species. Brazil prohibited commercial hunting of all wildlife, including caimans, in 1967 but the trade continued unabated as illegal traders smuggled hides into neighboring Bolivia and Paraguay. In 1960, Bolivia itself had prohibited the export of raw hides of Black Caiman, Broad-snouted Caiman, and *Caiman crocodilus yacare,* allowing only the export of finished tanned hides. The following year, Bolivia set minimum size limits for these species. Nevertheless, the trade continued as corrupt officials issued export permits for raw and undersized hides, and as protected species were smuggled into Paraguay. In 1975 Paraguay prohibited the hunting, sale, import, and export of native wildlife, including crocodilian hides, but has studiously avoided enforcing the law.

**REGULATION OF THE TRADE**

International trade in illegal crocodilian hides continued because the majority of first world nations, where the international tanners and manufacturers were located, did not have laws prohibiting the importation of hides taken or exported illegally from their country of origin. These consumer nations contended that it was the responsibility of each producer nation, rather than the importing nation, to protect its own wildlife. The fact remains, however, that as long as a well-paying market exists for illegal crocodilian hides, disreputable dealers will strive to satisfy that market. In some producer nations, illegal hunters make more money in a single night of poaching than they can earn in six months of other labor. The fines for getting caught are often less than the profit from one night's poaching.

In 1900 United States Congressman John Lacey had first explained that to control commercial trade in wildlife it is necessary to control the market. When you take away the commercial hunter's market you destroy the trade.

The Lacey Act, which he authored, prohibited interstate commerce in wild birds and mammals taken or exported illegally from a state of origin within the United States. It has been amazingly effective and, when it was amended to include reptiles, amphibians, and fish, it became the basis of the United States Endangered Species Conservation Act of 1969. The Act also mandated that the United States host a plenipotentiary conference to draft an international endangered species treaty. In 1973 this conference was convened in Washington, D.C., and the 81 nations present drafted the Convention on International Trade in Endangered Species of Wild Fauna and Flora (CITES).

The principle of the Lacey Act — controlling commerce in wildlife by controlling the market — is the very essence of CITES. The Convention requires party nations to prohibit imports of wildlife taken or exported illegally from its country of origin. It also requires all party nations to report annually on all imports and exports of wildlife listed on the CITES appendices.

Appendix I lists endangered species that may not be traded internationally "for primarily commercial purposes." Appendix II lists species not at present endangered but which might become so if trade is not regulated. For the first time, under CITES, consumer nations agreed to share responsibility with producer nations by denying entry to illegal wildlife and products. In recognition of the decline that many crocodilian populations had suffered and the economic incentives for continuing the overexploitation, all crocodilians were placed on one of the two CITES appendices in 1973.

Although CITES came into force in 1975, many party nations simply continued to operate as usual, issuing export and import permits for wildlife without regard to the species involved or where they originated. However, two of the major CITES Articles require party nations to determine that trade in Appendix II species is not detrimental to survival of that species in the wild and to limit the number of export permits so that Appendix II species do not become candidates for Appendix I. These requirements forced a surprising number of nations to develop programs for monitoring their wildlife for the first time.

Species were listed on the appendices on the basis of varied data, some comprehensive and some less so. An attempt to make those decisions more scientific and less political was made when standards for listing and delisting taxa were adopted at the CITES conference in Berne, Switzerland, in 1976. These standards became known as the "Berne criteria."

According to the Berne criteria, addition of a species to Appendix I requires data on the actual or potential negative impact from international trade in the species in question. It also requires

biological data on the status of the species. Acceptable data on status would come, ideally, from detailed scientific studies that demonstrate trends in population size and geographic range over a number of years. Should long-term data not be available, data from a single survey of population size and range or, failing that, reports from knowledgeable, non-scientific observers or reports on habitat destruction, excessive trade, or other potential causes of extinction would be acceptable. Deletion of species from Appendix I (or transfer from Appendix I to Appendix II) requires stronger supporting evidence than that required for addition of species. Data supporting a deletion should include a population survey, evidence of an encouraging population trend, and a report on the potential for commercial trade in the species or population.

As a result of deletions, additions, and transfers between the two appendices, the present listing of crocodilians on the CITES appendices is as shown in the table on the following page.

Hans and Judy Beste/Auscape International

▲ The remnants of one night's catch of Johnston's Crocodiles, by poachers with spotlights and rifles on Australia's Cape York Peninsula, are left to rot. The skins from these animals would have to be smuggled to markets in Southeast Asia.

Bill Green

◄ A policeman examines a large skin from an Indopacific Crocodile poached in northern Australia. However, in comparison with South America where poaching is still rife, very little poaching now occurs in Australia.